LIVE & WORK in...

AMERICA

Visit our How To website at www.howto.co.uk

At www.howto.co.uk you can engage in conversation with our authors – all of whom have 'been there and done that' in their specialist fields. You can get access to special offers and additional content but most importantly you will be able to engage with, and become a part of, a wide and growing community of people just like yourself.

At www.howto.co.uk you'll be able to talk and share tips with people who have similar interests and are facing similar challenges in their lives. People who, just like you, have the desire to change their lives for the better – be it through moving to a new country, starting a new business, growing their own vegetables, or writing a novel.

At www.howto.co.uk you'll find the support and encouragement you need to help make your aspirations a reality.

You can go direct to www.live-and-work-in-america.co.uk which is part of the main How To site.

How To Books strives to present authentic, inspiring, practical information in their books. Now, when you buy a title from **How To Books,** you get even more than just words on a page.

LIVE & WORK in...

AMERICA

Comprehensive,
up-to-date,
practical
information about
everyday life

STEVE MILLS

howtobooks

Published by How To Books Ltd,
Spring Hill House, Spring Hill Road,
Begbroke, Oxford OX5 1RX
Tel: (01865) 375794. Fax: (01865) 379162.
info@howtobooks.co.uk
www.howtobooks.co.uk

How To Books greatly reduce the carbon footprint of their books by sourcing their typesetting and
printing in the UK.

First published in 1988
Second edition 1992
Third edition 1995
Fourth edition 1997
Reprinted 1997
Fifth edition 1998
Fifth edition revised and updated 2000
Reprinted 2001
Sixth edition 2004
Reprinted 2004
Reprinted 2005
Seventh edition 2009

British Library Cataloguing in Publication Data
A catalogue record for this book is available from the British Library

ISBN 978 1 84528 359 9

Cover design by Baseline Arts Ltd, Oxford
Produced for How To Books by Deer Park Productions, Tavistock, Devon
Typeset by PDQ Typesetting, Newcastle-under-Lyme, Staffs.
Printed and bound by Cromwell Press Group, Trowbridge, Wiltshire

NOTE: The material contained in this book is set out in good faith for general guidance and no liability
can be accepted for loss or expense incurred as a result of relying in particular circumstances on
statements made in the book. Laws and regulations are complex and liable to change, and readers should
check the current position with the relevant authorities before making personal arrangements.

Contents

Preface
to the seventh edition

Welcome

This book, like its companion volumes dealing with US jobs and visas, is for anyone who has ever thought about spending some time in the United States. Millions of Europeans have settled in the United States, but today modern communications make it possible for millions more to cross the Atlantic for business or merely for pleasure. The choice is no longer between emigration and the trip of a lifetime. Millions now visit the USA for a period longer than their annual holiday but without ever settling down there. This book is therefore for anyone who has ever thought of living or working in the USA for anything from a few weeks to many years. It is particularly geared to those who would like to experience the USA for more than just a few days' holiday, though even weekend visitors will find much here to inform them about what is available in the USA.

What follows results from living and working backwards and forwards across the Atlantic for the last 30 years, travelling from coast to coast by plane, hitching, driving a van, by hired car, and even at times on foot. It's the result of visiting some 30 different states and living for years in and around the federal capital as much as of teaching American history, cultural geography and landscape studies to Britons and Americans at Keele University and the University of Maryland, not forgetting advising those applying to study abroad. I've entered the USA by plane, by car, and on foot, on three totally different kinds of visa, crossing sometimes alone, sometimes with family, on holiday and on business. So this book is a little bit of what has become American within me, even while I live and write in the UK.

I hope you will find the lessons of my own experience enable you, the reader, to enjoy your own visits to the USA with just a little more emphasis on the fun and a little less on the hassle for having been that little more prepared than I ever was. Friends and colleagues have often said that I should pass on my experiences: so here they are. With the incredible bits cut out so that you don't think this is another Tom Sharpe novel, here is a guide to living and working in the USA. May you enjoy your own experience as much as I've enjoyed mine.

So what does this book do?

It's a guide to the USA, providing hints and suggestions that may help you gain just that much more from your decision to visit or even to live in the USA. Many aspects of being in the USA come as a shock even for those who think they are well prepared. When I first arrived with a newly minted American Studies degree in my pocket I thought I'd arrived in the wrong country, so little did I recognise or understand in my first few weeks. So bad was the *experience* I could have cheerfully hijacked a plane out and away (in any direction!) if only I'd known how. Nothing *bad* happened at all: no muggings, no illness, nothing specifically traumatic. But the experience overwhelmed me as I tried to cope with the reality of a new job, looking for somewhere to live, no car, no pay yet, though my savings were fast ebbing away, and the fact that I'd arrived in one of the hottest and most humid Augusts for years. The only guides had been my textbooks and guidebooks for those visiting the sights. I didn't even know that all the paper money was the same colour and size, that I'd have to pay a month's rent in advance plus a month's rent as deposit, that my pay wouldn't be paid directly into my account but that I'd have to do that myself every other Friday. Traffic on the right-hand side of the road was the least of my problems. That I'd expected!

So this guide will start by asking you to consider what you expect from the USA, for what you want will be the most significant factor in how the USA measures up to your expectations. Anyone expecting a Big Mac in a vegetarian restaurant is going to get a nasty surprise! Be honest with yourself as to what you want to do, and, just as importantly, what you don't want from a holiday, a family reunion, an American extended stay, or a new start in life, and you'll be able to explore precisely what opportunities the USA does indeed hold for you.

Once you've decided you're off to the USA there's the whole question of the paperwork. The US is not an easy country to deal with even once you've been let in. Many people expect US bureaucracy to be more efficient, or at least less convoluted than in Britain. They often find that the truth is far from pleasant. Don't forget that everything governmental is duplicated: a State income tax may well be payable as well as the Federal one. Income tax liability is by self-assessment, but it's usually so complex, and the penalties threatened so dire, that most people pay a tax specialist to fill out the annual forms for them. Just thinking of your local tax inspector in Britain may bring a warm glow to your heart (but only while you're in the USA!).

But what opportunities exist? These are discussed in terms of the various groups – such as students, business people, entrepreneurs, professionals and artists. Read widely here, for though all face different problems all share similar hassles as outsiders trying to get along on the inside.

Throughout the book there is a wealth of information, outlining where best to go for further advice, with addresses and phone numbers and websites for contacts both in Britain and in the USA. A careful use of the telephone and increasingly the Internet can be a great time saver, especially in such a complex and potentially overwhelming matter as going to the USA.

Caveat

I have tried to update all phone numbers and Web addresses listed here, but some old ones are sure to have lain low and escaped detection. Web addresses are notoriously volatile so please be patient if sites have disappeared into the electronic ether. You can probably use a defunct address in a search engine (such as *www.askjeeves.com*) to find something similar. And to phone abroad remember the international access code is 00, so to call the USA dial 001 before the US seven digit number.

Whilst every attempt has been made by the author to ensure that the information presented in this book is accurate at the time of going to press neither the author nor the publishers can accept any responsibility for any errors or omissions.

Steve Mills

1

Considering the USA

The country is so large and varied that a lifetime of visits would hardly exhaust its potentials; the USA is more a continent than the kind of country found in Europe.

WHY CONSIDER GOING TO THE USA?

The appeal of the United States is as varied as the country is vast. Millions have traditionally gone there to settle down. Nowadays more and more people visit the USA whether on holiday, to visit family or friends, on business or to study, as the jumbo jets ply backwards and forwards across the Atlantic. For many people a particular visit has been greatly enhanced by combining a business trip with a holiday, a family reunion with travelling around, or using an initial holiday as the way to sample American life before making a commitment to stay longer. The country is so large and varied that a lifetime of visits would hardly exhaust its potentials; the USA is more a continent than the kind of country found in Europe.

British associations

The British have a long association with the United States. The eastern (Atlantic) coast states were once British colonies, though they broke away from the empire in the late eighteenth century.

American or English?

In Illinois the state language is deemed 'American', but more usually 'English' will do.

English is still the main language, long since adopted as America's own. The initial settlers of the north-eastern States were English Puritans (and the states they founded are still together called New England). English and Welsh Quakers founded Pennsylvania further down the coast. Inland the mountains were first settled by

Ulster folk tired of defending Ireland for the Crown. In the south the English landowners and Scots soldiers, pioneers and convicts laid the foundation of a distinctively Anglo-Saxon, almost pro-British society, but one quite unlike that back in Europe, for here a plantation economy was directly based upon the labour of African slaves.

European immigrants

The Founding Fathers of the American Republic were essentially English gentlemen in rebellion, paradoxically, to protect their English rights against a despotic government far away in Britain. To the west their descendants carved out an empire dedicated to individual freedom, corporate growth and the Protestant work ethic, sweeping aside the native societies (and most other European settlers). When millions of Europeans then arrived at the end of the nineteenth century, not at first speaking English, a nation based firmly upon American experience was already in place, echoing only faintly its British origins. These immigrants created an urban and industrial society almost obliterating the rural British landscape and so recasting the language and the political system that the links with Britain became even more obscured. Even as immigrants learned in school that their new country spoke English and used the common law, their numbers and the needs of their new surroundings brought about a continual reworking of vocabulary and syntax, whilst their strident demands for action and protection recast both the legal and government systems. The British link became ever more submerged: the United States becomes ever more foreign.

A shared language

The British and the Irish, alone amongst Europeans, are uniquely able to ignore the foreignness of America if they choose to do so. Though America remains a very distant foreign country whose ethnic variety is today more firmly rooted in Africa or eastern Europe than in Britain or Ireland, the shared language opens up the USA to English-speaking Europeans as for no others from the Old World. Add the considerable number of such people with friends and family already in America and the British and Irish can retain their links with the USA even while the USA at large looks elsewhere, particularly today across the Pacific.

A familiar place

Even as the USA nowadays looks far beyond Britain and Ireland the British and Irish look ever more avidly at the USA. Hollywood movies first brought the rich variety of US life across the Atlantic. Today television and the web continue that tradition. The very quantity of TV movies, documentaries and situation comedies brings both fantasy and daily life into everyone's homes. The USA is a country we visit passively every day, year in, year out. No wonder it often seems more familiar than even unvisited parts of our country, and beckons with the promise of exotic parts where the locals reassuringly speak English. The educated and skilled middle classes already speaking English can consider settling down in the USA, melting into the background as quickly or as slowly as they want, like East German refugees did in West Germany; no language barriers to put off all but the most stout-hearted as happens when the French and German middle classes look across the Atlantic. No wonder it is to the USA that so many British people turn for holidays, business, or to start a new life.

THERE'S SOMETHING FOR EVERYONE IN AMERICA

This may sound like little more than an ad man's copy, like a Texan boast, or just a piece of wishful thinking. The size, the physical contrast, the ethnic variety, the particular rural-urban mix, the wealth and poverty and 400 years of European history (resting upon thousands of years of earlier people's!) means that whatever your interest, from landscape painting to railway trains, from ornithology to folk music, there is indeed something for everyone. And millions of British people have families over there, sisters and aunts who went over as GI brides in the 1940s, brain drain scientists from the days of the space race, software designers from the dot.com boom.

It's amazing how many people have never visited their families in the USA but have always thought they'd like to, always able to find a 'reason' for not going.

HAVE YOU EVER THOUGHT...?

■ **I haven't the time**
Well, save up your annual leave. Most of us now get two weeks, and three can usually be arranged if planned far enough ahead.

■ **I couldn't afford the money**
It's not all the QE2, caviare and dressing for dinner now. Wide-bodied jets fly across in eight hours for only a couple of hundred pounds if you can book a month or so in advance.

■ **They've never asked me over**
They probably did years ago, or thought they did. Why not ask if they'd like to come visit you? That would get the ball rolling!

■ **I don't like all that violence we see on TV**

Though Washington DC is more violent than Belfast ever was, most visitors never see anything more violent than a repeat episode of *Morse* on American TV. If you are sensible and are staying with family or friends, visiting the USA is less dangerous than staying at home. And US sports crowds are almost universally very well behaved!

■ **I couldn't stand all the junk food**

Fast food isn't the only food the US is famous for. Every kind under the sun is available (even fish and chips, from equipment made in Britain!). This is hardly surprising given all the different people (from Albanians to Vietnamese) who have settled there over the years.

■ **I wouldn't like the heat**

The US has taken central heating in winter and air conditioning in summer to its heart. You need only be hot (or cold) if you want to.

■ **I hate motorway travel**

Well fly, or take the train (yes, long-distance trains still connect the main cities with some degree of civilisation). Also, believe it or not, driving an air-conditioned mid-size hired car can be almost relaxing at a continuous 60 mph over the gently graded freeways of the south and west, with a comfortable motel at the day's end (including a swim in the pool followed by a steak supper and a film on the TV movie channel in your room).

NO RELATIVES IN THE USA?

■ **Well find some!**

Didn't a cousin go over, marry and stay? Now's the chance to visit that aunt you've not seen since Christmas 1993 to ask her about her daughter in Seattle. Doesn't someone have a US penfriend from days in the Scouts?

■ **Old school friends?**

Check out *Friends Reunited* and find who's gone abroad. An old school friend now in Alberta would give you somewhere to aim for as you drive westwards from Chicago. A trip just across the border would be quite interesting, and a worthwhile detour en route for Seattle!

■ **Ask around...**

for people at school, college, work or sports club who have been to the USA. They may have US friends who keep open house to visiting stamp collectors, squash players, local historians, bird watchers and so on. How would you respond if an American couple who shared your passion for bees or real ale wrote saying they were passing through your area on their next holiday? Wouldn't you get the spare room ready and take the risk of inviting in strangers on the basis of a mutual friend and a shared hobby?

■ **Ask at your school, college, rotary or town twinning meeting...**
about people who have gone on sponsored visits, scholarships and exchanges. Track them down and ask them how they arranged to go over, what it cost, who they stayed with. They'll probably be only too pleased to share their experiences with you. And many towns are twinned with their US namesakes.

Most of us can get to visit the USA one way or another if we are employed (or students with job prospects). It may take a year or so of overtime saving up the money or a couple of long vacations pulling pints in a holiday resort, and if you want to give up smoking or drinking a trip to the USA would be a worthwhile target to save for, and something to get you through the cravings. Some people have even taken to entering competitions as a hobby, and once into the swing of things, they start to recognise what's required of entries and tie-breaking slogans, winning prizes that can include holiday trips abroad. It's a long shot, but someone's going to win that trip for two to Disneyland. It could just be you!

LISTING YOUR INTERESTS IN THE USA

Make your own list, for example:

■ touring the sights;
■ going on a resort-based family holiday;
■ visiting friends or relatives;
■ going on a speciality trip (battlefields, bird watching, old cars);
■ making a business trip;
■ having a look around prior to emigrating.

All are excellent reasons for going to the USA. But if you can make it clear in your own mind why you are interested in the USA then it'll be easier to answer the essential question:

What do I/we want from our trip to the USA?

You may well be able to combine several concerns:

- visiting family then touring;
- family holiday after a business visit;
- family resort plus personal speciality;
- touring between business visits.

Beware!

Mixing your trips together could ruin the whole thing:

- What would happen if the children got sick while you are all hurrying to the next business appointment?

- Will the children be able to enjoy anything on a rapid, long distance chase between business appointments?

- What will you do if friends not seen for years now chain-smoke, wife swap, play bridge all the time, are workaholics or can't stand children?

However, some considerations can work out just fine:

- If you are geared up to tour you can make your excuses and leave any disastrous reunion.

- If militant chain-smoking friends have now mellowed with children and exercise you can always stay a night longer than planned, or even visit again on your way back to the airport.

WHAT KIND OF VISIT DO YOU WANT?

For some people holidays are action-packed, for others relaxed and gentle. Where you go depends upon how you feel about holidays:

	like	so-so	don't like
Big cities like New York			
Resorts such as Disneyworld			
Famous sights or battlefields			
Spectacular landscapes			
Lakes and forests			

Using a different coloured pen, go over and make the choices again, this time thinking how your children might respond. Then ask your children to fill in *their* choices: did you get their choices right? Did they like the choices you'd already made for them?

Would you gain relaxation from visiting the following:

	like	*so-so*	*don't like*
Manhattan's shops			
Niagara Falls			
Washington's museums			
Virginia's battlefields			
Casinos of Las Vegas			
Disneyworld			

If you've built up a column of no answers, then for a relaxing holiday you may need to go elsewhere, or perhaps concentrate upon some US version of what you've done successfully before:

■ If you like walking in the Lake District...
   try walking in the Rocky Mountain National Park.

■ If you like the Costa del Sol...
   try the Florida coast around Miami.

■ If you like Blackpool and Alton Towers...
   try Disneyworld or Busch Gardens.

■ If you like the British Museum...
   try Washington DC's Smithsonian Institute.

■ If you like the Normandy battlefields...
   try the Civil War battlefields of Virginia, Maryland and Pennsylvania.

■ If you like European Spa towns...
   try Saratoga in New York, White Sulphur West Virginia or Hot Springs Arkansas.

■ If you like salmon jumping in Scotland...
   try Minke Whales in a New England summer.

To know what kind of visit you want you must sort out your priorities in your own mind. Remember, people who like the Lake District often like Blackpool too. But such a person might find one day at a resort quite enough, a week in the hills not enough. If you want mountains with a day off in a resort then don't go to Florida, for unlike Britain the drive from resort to mountains isn't an hour up the motorway, but two whole days! If you make a mistake in the USA you may well be stuck with it, through no more perhaps than if you'd flown off to the Mediterranean.

GETTING MARRIED

The USA has long cornered the market in speedy weddings (and six-week divorces). In Nevada a wedding licence is easier to acquire than a rented car. If you are on the web try typing 'Weddings in Las Vegas' (without the speech marks) into your favourite search engine and you'll find a page of websites to choose from.

Start with general city guides (*www.las-vegas.cc*).

The Las Vegas Wedding Association sponsors a site (*www.nevadawedding.org*) providing an index of chapels, lodgings, services, travel and accessories. Type 'Las Vegas wedding chapels' into Google and a list plus maps of the main central city wedding chapels will appear. For specific details of how to get hitched try the Clark County Recorder's Office.

The Elvis Experience in Las Vegas is open 24 hours a day for the ceremony. In Florida ceremonies can be arranged at Disneyworld (licences $93.50 require passport and birth certificate).

Nuptial packages exist for a wide range of resorts, ranging from Hawaii to Key Largo. There are British websites that can arrange everything for you (such as *www.marryabroad.co.uk*).

FURTHER THOUGHTS ON STAYING WITH FRIENDS OR RELATIVES

It's worth thinking how well you relax with friends and relatives *back home* before you visit overseas.

- Do you dread visiting your wife/husband's school friends?
- Do you now find your old college friends boring?
- Do you leave Aunty Flo's as soon as possible?
- Do you leave your in-laws vowing never to return?

If family visits are fraught with suppressed anger at home perhaps you ought to reconsider such an option overseas?

You also need to consider:

- **How well** do you know your old friends and relatives?
- Have your **holiday demands** changed since you all last met?
- What **options** do you have if their welcome sours?
- Can you afford to **risk** your family holiday or business trip?

A leisurely week on a canal boat on North Staffordshire's Cauldon Canal with a couple of days at the Alton Towers leisure park plus canalside real ale and cream teas would be a more relaxing way to spend your hard-earned holiday if family and one-time friends simply get you het up rather than help you relax. Epcot with relatives you cannot stand is a nightmare to be avoided at all costs.

But you can always keep your options open. If there's any doubt about staying with family or friends in the USA make them just one part of a tour abroad. Knowing that you'll be off and away in a couple of days can help you relax and may make all the difference between a successful and a disastrous trip.

FAMILY REUNIONS

Family reunions can be short or long, good or bad. A short stay with friends or relatives in Britain can turn out to be brilliant, or little short of disaster. Imagine how awful it would be to leave Britain to spend the rest of your days with your family already long settled in the USA only to find out after a few weeks that you can't stand each other. If you intend to live with, or even nearby, a younger family it's essential that:

- it's been thought through carefully by all concerned;

- you've visited and seen what accommodation is available;

- everyone knows what the financial implications will be (will grandparents' pensions from Britain be sufficient to keep them, or will a family subsidy be necessary?);

- you have talked over and experienced each other's lifestyles in case the clash is too loud;

- each side should know and understand their responsibilities (from paying rent to babysitting).

Initially the most crucial thing is for the Europeans to visit and stay with the Americans. And stay beyond the holiday couple of weeks. Anyone can put up with almost anyone for a few weeks. But how about after three months? What is it like in the middle of a midwestern winter? – a Florida summer? Parents do go overseas to be with their grown-up children, and it can be the start of a very successful new life. But it can also be a recipe for disaster. But then staying at home never seeing children and grandchildren isn't much fun either.

A word of warning

A family holiday in, say, Florida can be quite expensive, even though you may get value for money and a holiday to remember. But if you dwell too much on how much it's costing you may be driven to cram in too many people and places to get your money's worth.

- Just think of a generation of US visitors that have done precisely that. ('If it's Tuesday it must be Belgium.')

- Trying to see everything, even in one State, will mean an awful lot of time will be spent on the motorway (whether on the bus or in a hired car). Would you advise Americans to see as much of Britain as possible by way of keeping to the M4, M5, M6, M74, A1(M) and M1 circuit? And yet Britain is smaller than most US States!

- If you visit a Florida relative it doesn't mean you will be able to drive to visit others in New Orleans, Chicago and New York City, even though on a map that looks like a reasonable drive around. Would you spend a continental holiday driving from home to Moscow and back again by way of Athens? If this visit to the USA is indeed the trip of a lifetime and you really must see everyone then consider flying instead. **Multiple destination tickets** can be arranged before leaving home, often in conjunction with your original online booking, at very advantageous rates. If you must drive either take as long as possible so that you can leave the motorways, visiting as you go along, or better still, plan to come back again to visit the rest of the family.

TRIP OF A LIFETIME?

It is a great temptation to try to do too much on an initial visit to the USA. If for reasons of health you know this is a one-off visit *focus* your trip.

■ What is the primary object of your visit:
  – to get away from it all?
  – to visit relatives?
  – to visit a specific site or resort?

■ Maybe your relatives should visit you where you want to stay (such as Disneyworld or the Grand Canyon) rather than you rush around central Florida and then dash on to Chicago?

■ Be firm in your own mind as to why you are in the USA.

■ Be explicit with your relatives as to where and what you want to do.

■ Be up front about who is paying:
  – if you are paying, relatives visit you;
  – if relatives are offering hospitality, careful negotiations may be necessary so you aren't at their beck and call and they don't feel you are taking advantage of their hospitality.

But remember: most visitors can return if they want to, even if not the following year.

■ Focus on your main interest during an initial visit.
■ Dare to leave other areas or people for next time.

During my first visit I planned to tour nationwide with a Greyhound Bus Pass I'd bought in Britain. Instead I cashed it in for a focused trip around the North East. I have never regretted that. I'm still returning to complete my original travel plans.

BEING IN THE USA FOR NEW YEAR

Though most Europeans probably prefer to celebrate Hogmanay at home or in a local hostelry, some will seek out warmer destinations such as the islands of the Caribbean. But many who have already visited the USA may well look across the Atlantic for first footing, even though by being away from home US visitors will be postponing the big moment for at least five hours.

New York's **Times Square** is New Year's Eve for most Americans, even if they would usually rather die than actually visit downtown New York in the middle of the night. Times Square is not actually a square. Rather it is a strange intersection of 5th Avenue, part of that great North-South grid pattern of streets and avenues, with Broadway, the far older track that once crossed the island from Manhattan's southern tip to Harlem. The modern tradition began as recently as 1904 when *The New York Times* at One Times Square started sponsoring rooftop parties. In 1907 someone had the bright idea of lowering a reflective ball down the flagpole atop the building as a visible countdown to midnight. The rest, as they say, is history. With the coming of television, millions across the USA and even overseas now time their festivities with the goings on in Times Square just as people in Britain do with the party in Trafalgar Square.

Each year New York City likes to believe that its Times Square celebrations are bigger than before and better than its rivals. Times Square is increasingly promoted as being the Crossroads of the World, though of course most of those present will be Americans. Giant video screens broadcast footage of celebrations from around the world. Given that it will probably be below freezing in New York City at the time, Miami is trying to become the focus of American celebrations with its more lazy climes. Where would you rather be: in frigid Manhattan or on a warm Florida beach? Of course, that may not be the choice: fans of *Get Shorty* will no doubt recall the less than tropical winter with which the film opens. Christmas card snow in Manhattan can be much more fun than an unexpected Florida cold spell. Nevertheless Californian desert resorts such as Palm Springs are trying to capture the interest of those who insist upon warm weather.

For **Miami ideas** contact the Greater Miami Convention & Visitors Bureau: (*www.miamiandbeaches.com*). For **Miami travel** details try:

- American Airlines: *www.americanairlines.co.uk*
- Virgin Atlantic: *www.virgin-atlantic.com*

For **Miami hotels there's:**

- Island Outpost with six trendy hotels: *www.islandoutpost.com*
- Leading Hotels of the World: *www.lhw.com*
- Sheraton: *www.sheraton.com*

For **New York City** start with the Visitors Bureau: *www.nycvisit.com*

- Four Seasons Hotels: *www.fourseasons.com*
- Sheraton: *www.sheraton.com*
- Westin Hotels: *www.starwoodhotels.com*
- Ritz-Carlton: *www.ritzcarlton.com*

ALTERNATIVE DESTINATIONS

If you want to experience life in another part of the English-speaking world, the United States is not the only country you might like to consider, whether for a visit or to live. Consider perhaps Australia, New Zealand, even South Africa. But the best and most appropriate comparison is probably with Canada just north of the border.

Just considering an alternative to the USA may help sort out precisely what you're looking for in going abroad. You may end up knowing that the USA *is* for you after all!

CANADA

Larger than the USA, but with only about half Britain's population, Canada is a bilingual country where English and French are equal in the eyes of the law. The British-settled Maritime provinces on the Atlantic coast are today far from economically buoyant particularly as fishing declines, and they now rely upon federal aid and tourism. The dynamic areas of English-speaking Canada are further inland, from Toronto on the Great Lakes westwards to Vancouver on the Pacific Coast, especially the rich farmlands and oil of the prairies around Calgary. French-speaking Canada, once restricted mainly to the farmland along the St Lawrence River, is now both urban and industrial, based upon Montreal and its massive iron ore fields and electrical generating stations to the north.

After a prolonged visit to the USA, English-speaking Canada may appear very British, though if arriving directly from Europe it'll probably appear very American with its sprawling cities, freeways, high summer humidity and deep winter chills. Increasingly cosmopolitan Canada retains for many visitors and residents alike the benefits of the old world in the new. Does it really have all the benefits of the USA but with few of the problems?

Getting there

- Similar air packages and fares exist as for the USA.

- A full British Passport is needed (and a valid US visa or Visa Waiver application is necessary for cross border trips to the USA).

- No visas are required for tourists up to 90 days.

- For long stays first contact the Canadian authorities *before* leaving home.

■ Air Canada (*www.aircanada.ca*) and British Airways (*www.britishairways.com*) both fly to all parts of Canada.

Staying there

■ As the recession tightened in the late 1970s immigration restriction became more stringent. Permission to live in Canada, 'landed immigrant status', became available only to certain people with specific skills needed but not locally available. This principle is rigorously applied.

■ Temporary work for foreign visitors is generally not allowed. Students are, however, permitted to apply for a permit to work on tobacco farms in southern Ontario. (Contact **British Universities North America Club** *www.bunac.org* for details. Early application is essential.) Casual jobs for cash are likely to be in fruit-picking in the Okanagan Valley of British Columbia, or in the bars of the Rocky Mountain resorts.

■ Immigration and visa enquiries should be made initially at the **High Commission**, 38 Grosvenor Street, London W1X 0AA.

■ Tourism enquiries to Canadian Tourism Commission (*www.canada.travel/ splash.en-gb.html*).

Considering Canada?

	yes	no
I don't mind no sub-tropical or desert areas		
Speaking in French would be fun		
I quite like the British heritage		
I like cities that aren't dangerous		
I'd enjoy harsh winters 'with all mod cons'		

If you've answered *yes* to three or more then further consideration of Canada seems a good idea. But you could be based in Canada and drive to sub-tropical or desert areas. You could ignore, depending upon where you are, either the French or the British heritage, or even both! You could also enjoy Canada-like conditions (social, economic and climatic!) across large parts of the USA, for instance in the harsh but anticipated winters of Minnesota.

Reconsidering the USA

- Don't think the USA is all New York City, Miami and Los Angeles. Small town America has been making a come back these last few years, with some very high growth rates. It isn't all *Law and Order* or *The Sopranos*.

- If you settle in the USA, Canada is there as a great place to visit.

- The US economy is generally more vibrant, and for the real go-getter the USA remains the place to be in certain fields such as the movies or rock music.

> **Beware:**
>
> *If your US stopover is in Los Angeles don't expect relatives from Canada to come to visit you. Would you go to greet a visiting American relative on their arrival in Rome, never mind Istanbul!*

Perhaps the phrase should be 'There's something for everybody in North America'?

OTHER OVERSEAS OPPORTUNITIES

In order to place the US in a wider context you might also consider the following:

Teaching English as a Foreign Language (TEFL)

If you want to use your native grasp of English, taking this qualification could well be a worthwhile investment in time and money. These courses are not grant-aided. If you already have a teaching certificate and a degree in English this added qualification could be profitable. The broadsheet newspapers, such as the *Guardian's* Tuesday education section, have adverts for colleges offering TEFL (postgraduate) courses. Any of the good colleges attempt placements for their successful students.

For those with a degree or teaching qualification plus a recognised TEFL qualification plus at least one year's TEFL experience, details of overseas posts can be obtained from The British Council (*www.british.council.org*).

Voluntary Services Overseas (VSO)

Despite the old gap year image, for the most part VSO prefers graduates with practical skills like home economics, animal husbandry or intermediate technology. Contracts can be for several years so that worthwhile projects can be undertaken. Contact **VSO** at *www.vso.org*.

Voluntary work

There are endless possibilities:

- *Kibbutz Adventure Centre (www.kibbutz.com.au)*. Expect to pay your airfare and stay for at least a couple of months.

- *The Project Trust (www.projecttrust.org.uk)* places volunteers aged 17½–19 on application in developing countries such as Cuba. Expect to have to raise sponsorship for your airfare, food and accommodation beforehand.

- *Lattitude Global Volunteering* (previously known as GAP Activity Projects) (*www.lattitude.org.uk*) charges a substantial arrangement fee, plus airfare and insurance (board and lodgings provided) for six months overseas.

For other possibilities see *International Directory of Volunteer Work.*

Paid employment

At your next job interview ask what opportunities exist for overseas work. At least it'll give you something to say when the interviewer asks 'Any questions?'.

Some useful books

- Roger Jones, *Getting a Job Abroad,* (2003).
- G. Golzen, *Working Abroad,* (1980) (still useful for general ideas).
- Guy Hobbs, *The Directory of Jobs & Careers Abroad* (2006).

There's always working your way around from country to country:

- Susan Griffith, *Work Your Way Around the World* (2003).
- The Central Bureau for Educational Visits & Exchanges (*www.centralbureau.org.uk*) an online working holidays directory with gap year projects, placements and work experience.

2

What's It Like in the USA?

The vastness of the American continent is beyond our island imaginings. Crossing from New York to Los Angeles means crossing time zones and a score of state lines each with their own police, drinking laws and parliaments. Some states are hot and wet as a steam room, others dry as the Sahara. Snow falls while flowers bloom. And beyond Los Angeles lies the Pacific Ocean where Hawaii lies as far to the west as Ireland does to the East of New England.

GETTING RID OF MISCONCEPTIONS

Americans know an awful lot about Britain and Ireland. They have seen Princess Di's funeral on breakfast television and London buses on the nightly news. Avidly they watch the Dickensian horrors of *Bleak House*, delight in the decadent affluence of *Brideshead Revisited* or *The Buccaneers* and thrill to the period pieces of Agatha Christie's rural detective mysteries. The Sherlock Holmes stories forewarn a further generation about London fog while reruns of *Poirot* confirm stereotypes of a perverted, class-conscious old world. No wonder they loved *Four Weddings and a Funeral* and *Love Actually*! It's hardly surprising the real Britain often comes as a great surprise to American visitors.

Stereotype		Reality
■ All US television is endless soap operas, commercials and cop shows.	*But*	■ Many stations are free of commercials within specific programmes – especially cable channels and publicly financed stations.
■ America is just too violent to visit let alone live in.	*But*	■ In a five-year stay I never once saw a single person even draw a gun from its holster and spectator violence is almost unheard of.
■ The New York City subway system is dangerous and very dicult for visitors to understand.	*But*	■ The Washington DC metro system is one of the world's safest and cleanest, and it's easy to use.
■ Everything is so much more expensive in the USA. Everyone knows that!	*But*	■ Petrol is still only half what it is in Europe.

European misconceptions about the USA may be just as misleading, for our images come from a steady diet of musicals and horror films, cop adventure shows and such modern yarns as the *Die Hard* movies and *CSI* television shows. Unfortunately these media images repel as many people as they attract. Endless violence, materialism, urban sprawl and drugs seem to cloud many foreigner's views, as do equally misleading images of easy wealth, limitless opportunity and beautiful weather.

Of course, each stereotype can be substantiated. Commercial television can seem impossibly overloaded with adverts, the USA is considerably more violent than Britain or Northern Ireland, and though cheap the New York city subway can seem as chaotic and under-capitalised as London's underground. But if you are prepared to look more widely the stereotypes can be put into some kind of perspective. After all the USA is almost a continent, with about 304,000,000 people of every kind. Knowing a little about where to go and what to avoid, what to buy and what not to, can make all the difference.

For most would-be visitors the outstanding feature will probably be the USA's great variety of people and places, plus the incredible extremes of wealth.

THE USA: DISCOVERING PEOPLE AND PLACES

The USA is about half of North America, one of the world's major continents, over nine million square kilometres (some three million square miles). Today the USA stretches beyond the mainland 48 states to the Arctic wastes of northern Alaska and the tropical forests of Hawaii. There is also one federal district (Washington DC), plus the Caribbean Commonwealth of Puerto Rico and assorted island colonies. Being mostly temperate but with little of the polar or equatorial extremes found in other countries such as Canada or Russia on the one hand or Brazil or the Congo on the other, the USA is one of the most fertile slices of any continent anywhere.

North–South v. East–West

During the nineteenth century the newly independent USA spread westwards from its original colonial toe-hold along the Atlantic coast, over the mountains and rivers of the continental interior to the Pacific. This produces an essential feature of American geography: the mountains, rivers, weather systems and even migrating birds tend to move north and south, but the USA spreads against and across the grain. The attempt to forge a great north–south trading system to exploit the lay of the land and the southward movement of the main river system failed when the Mississippi River lost out to the growing east–west railway networks last century. Nevertheless, the overall physical structure of the USA remains north–south. But this physical variety is only a start.

Physical, social and economic variety

Despite the superficial similarities of a common currency, a federal constitution, and one legal tongue, English, the physical (geographical) variety is compounded by a social variety and economic variety. The native peoples spoke many languages. Their variety of lifestyles echoed that of the physical environment within which they lived. But the great eras of European settlement imposed a degree of variety far beyond that of the natural order. Imperial Spain moved in from the south-west, Russia from the north-west, Britain and France from the north-east. As in Africa their territorial carve-up paid scant regard to the original inhabitants. Territories were swapped for reasons of big-power politics. France was defeated by its British rival, but left behind a French-speaking, Roman Catholic population to the north of the USA's north-eastern border, but only after its explorers, trappers, traders and priests had opened up the whole continent, teaching the native peoples such games as divide and rule, drunkenness and a desire for European goods. The British retired north of the Great

Lakes, south to the Caribbean islands, or the Atlantic islands of Newfoundland, the Bahamas and Bermuda, or changed into Americans turning their back upon Europe as elsewhere would the Dutch of South Africa. Russia sold up for cash.

The **vastness** of the American continent is beyond our island imaginings. Crossing from New York to Los Angeles means crossing time zones and a score of state lines each with their own police, drinking laws and parliaments. Some execute killers, others let them rot in gaol. Some states are hot and wet as a steam room, others dry as the Sahara. Snow falls while flowers bloom. And beyond Los Angeles lies the Pacific Ocean where Hawaii lies as far to the west as Ireland does to the East of New England. The vastness is not that of unmitigated sameness. Quite the contrary – the topography changes in every direction, though in the midst of the plains the eye can refute this intellectual notion, so flat it seems. The rivers are trapped in deep gorges, winding across wide plains taking hundreds of miles of lazy turns to cover merely ten, pollution ridden, full of white water tourists, or disappearing into desert wastes. So vast is the land that it covers an expanse from alligator-ridden bayous along the Gulf of Mexico to permafrost deserts along the Arctic Ocean. Hardwoods give way to farming where once was only prairie grass. Desert threatens to spread again, like the African Sahel, into the southern high plains. Along the Pacific the earth moves, Mount St Helens spews forth a vision of hell, and sitting on the Pacific ring of fire has Angelenos awaiting the shuddering earth that may yet destroy the seventh largest economy ever known, that of California.

Early settlement

To the east are the Appalachian Mountains, long worn down to mere stumps, though high enough (Mt Mitchell is over 2,000 m high!), wide enough and forested enough to thwart generations of settlers until new travel technologies opened up such gaps as existed. The Mississippi interior was opened up originally by military adventurers, explorers and finally traders. Settlers soon carved up the grasslands into some of the most fertile farms ever created. Miners carried the sweep into the Rockies of the Far West. Not one range, but a whole series of mountains and basins, these western ranges contain both the highest point in the country, outside Alaska, Mt Whitney (4,418 m) and the lowest, Death Valley (-86 m).

The vast interior desert between the Rocky Mountain front ranges in Colorado and the Sierra Nevada mountains of California is so isolated that it was here the Mormons were finally able to establish their new Promised Land in the middle of the nineteenth century. So out of the world is the landscape that it was in these barren wastes that NASA's moon-buggy practice took place in the 1960s.

To the south the states of the Gulf of Mexico are vast areas of fertile farmlands, once covered with forests in the east, grasslands to the west. Hot and humid for much of the year, snow and ice are a rare

When the NASA moonbuggy training was underway a passing Navajo Indian shepherd asked what they were doing. When he heard that they were bound for the moon he asked to record a message for any Navajo already on the moon. His recorded message for the lunar Navajo was finally translated. It simply said: 'Sign nothing'.

surprise. Once inhabited by settled, farming Native Americans these areas were cleared in the 1830s for European settlement. African slaves were brought in to work the expanding cotton plantations. The Indians were driven into the barren areas across the border, later to become reservations under US control. Only in the western deserts could the native peoples survive on their traditional lands, though hedged around by the US authorities.

Industrial development

As the USA expanded westwards to the Pacific the country changed economically and socially. From a once rural society of farms and small towns emerged an industrial giant of huge cities. Factories that both provided the rails and barbed wire for the western farmlands and required the increasing bounty of foodstuffs and raw materials needed more labour than the USA could provide. People poured in from all over Europe. Where once they had originally come mainly from Britain and similar northern European societies they now also flooded in first from Ireland, then from Italy, Poland and Russia, Jews and gentiles alike.

The USA today is only superficially a child of the British Isles. Rather, mainstream Americans come from mainly continental stock, the torrent of urban and entrepreneurial peoples that flooded in before the First World War. Trade and manufacturing of an unprecedented scale developed, linking the products of the US interior with the wider world. Mostly east and southern European, these immigrants took up American English only in so far as it gave them access to political and economic power, plus social clout. They preserved the skin of America, but totally changed its core, not so much becoming Americans as changing the definition of what it was to be American.

Modern urban pluralism and rural conservatism

The 1860s Civil War population of 40 million rose to over 100 million by the First World War. By then it was too late for the older America to turn back the tide. The immigrants, and particularly their children, had created a society so buoyant, so materially prosperous that they could now simply ignore much of this older, rural America of the Midwest High Plains and the Bible Belt. The brash society of the cities had little time for and even less contact with the increasingly resentful survivors of the countryside. Sometimes the White Anglo Saxon Protestant (WASP) countryside would fight back, such as pushing through the outlawing of alcohol (prohibition) and voting to end further mass immigration. But with an ever larger proportion of consumers and voters living and working in the cities such measures were far too late. The cities were liberal, pluralist, atomistic and comparatively secular. The countryside remained WASP, small town, devout and outraged. These two countries have been jousting for control of the USA ever since, even as new waves of newcomers arrived from former communist states, the Middle East (see the opening scene of *The Siege*), and especially Latin America.

THE WEATHER

Where you decide to stay or to live may well depend purely upon what holiday packages or jobs are available. But the USA is so vast it helps to know what you may be letting yourself in for. The weather in the USA is not something that dominates conversation, as in Britain, but the extremes are such that the weather cannot be ignored completely except by the foolhardy. And sometimes just knowing when it'll get dark can be important (*aa.usno.navy.mil/data/docs/RS_oneday.php*). Generally the USA is further south than the UK, so daylight is transformed into night rather more rapidly than most Brits expect (it's got something to do with being nearer the equator).

A continental climate

The USA is continental in scale. The climate is as varied as you would find across all of Europe, from the Arctic north to the desert south. Much of western Europe is surrounded by water, whether the Atlantic or its North Sea, Baltic or Mediterranean offshoots. Though the USA is surrounded by the Atlantic, the Gulf of Mexico, the Pacific and the Great Lakes, vast areas are far from their influences. The result is great extremes, not just in the interior but even along many coastal regions which are themselves influenced as much by the land mass behind them as by the water offshore. It can easily be 43°C (100°F) or −40°C (−40°F too!).

Summers are generally hot, and may be very humid as warm wet air moves northwards from the Caribbean. Winters can be as harsh as any in the inhabited world. In between these extreme seasons hurricanes or tornadoes afflict many areas where great air masses collide. Only in Maine, the Pacific northwest and perhaps Wisconsin can anything approaching a northern European summer be experienced you'll be pleased to know.

Making comparisons

The Pacific northwest alone will seem familiar to a visiting Brit in winter. The recurrent deep snows of New York City would be more familiar to a resident of Moscow than Lisbon or Rome. Los Angeles has a generally Mediterranean climate, Denver the climate of the Russian steppes, New Orleans and Washington DC a humid subtropical climate similar to that of Hong Kong (though fortunately without quite so much rain). Yuma in southwest Arizona has less rain than Alice Springs in Australia's central desert, and Miami has a tropical climate similar to that of Kisangani on the Congo River. Alaska is much like Scandinavia in both climate and topography.

Midwest warning

In **summer** the weather of the Midwest can be quite confusing. This vast expanse from the Rockies to the Great Lakes can be dull, grey and overcast, but usually it will also be very hot and humid, though the windy city of Chicago can manage at times to be as cold and uninviting as any British seaside resort in a poor summer. In **winter**, however, the Arctic air sweeping down from Canada can make the Midwest treacherous, with chill factors (temperatures plus the wind-induced extra chilling effect) being well below zero. A blue sky in winter means heat loss, and so sunburn *and* hypothermia are both possible without care. Minus 40°C is not uncommon on the Prairies where six months earlier it could have been plus 40°C. Those not adequately prepared for these extremes will, and do, perish. Appropriate hats are worn in all seasons.

Winter precautions

Winters are generally colder and longer than in Britain, with the possible exception of those areas around the Gulf of Mexico, and along the Pacific coast. Be prepared for more snow, more ice and more chilling winds than in inland Britain. The bad winter Britain gets once every 20 years is fairly standard over much of the USA every

Seeing a sprinkling of snow this intrepid writer left home an hour earlier than usual to walk to his new job which started at 8.00 am, only to find the university closed: a 'snow alert' had been called. Always listen to the radio or watch breakfast TV for such announcements.

year, even those areas of the interior so hot in summer. If you are used to crossing the Scottish Highlands on the A9 in winter you will be quite at home in an American winter, drifts and all. But in the USA, heating in homes and buildings, public and private, tends to be appropriate for the seasons, if not excessive. Be prepared to strip off into summer things if spending long in such places. Wear padded clothing if possible out of doors, even if you feel stupid looking like an explorer. Hats, gloves and boots are essential for survival, as is the ability to recognise when things are too bad to travel. The opening credits of the Coen brothers' Oscar-winning film *Fargo* (1996) probably provides all you need to know about midwestern winters.

COPING WITH AIR CONDITIONING

Summers are generally hotter, which is okay in the dry and often high south-west, but can be very sticky elsewhere. Air conditioning in a car is not really a luxury if it means that you arrive able to work, or if it means families can survive long journeys. Sceptical hard types will say: 'Just open the window!' Fine, but don't expect to be able to breathe what comes in. And try being a backseat passenger rather than an upfront driver for a while – you will soon get air conditioning.

The only snag is that much air conditioning can be fierce. Take a pullover or sweatshirt with you to work, to the movies, even to the supermarket or art gallery. For an interesting summer experience watch a summer movie (such as *Jaws*) in the chilly air conditioning of a movie theatre. To get the full effect stay dressed for the 35°C weather outside.

When first arriving in a hot and humid summer the temptation is to spend as much time as possible wherever air conditioning can be found, loitering over the shopping, developing a passion for great works of art or the movies. Assuming this doesn't give you a summer cold, this 'cure' can make the problem worse if it means failing to come to terms in some way or another with the problem. A change of behaviour may well be called for, if only keeping out of the sun, walking in the shadow of high buildings, and taking plenty of liquids. Of course if children start to pass out waiting in the lines at Disneyworld, which happens, then you need to get them into the nearest air-conditioned room. But wearing a hat, not sitting out in the sun, and lots of drinks may be necessary drills for all the family, along with an appropriately high factor suncream.

Air conditioning, however, has meant that lots of people from the north have been able to face moving to the sunbelt in search of work and retirement. The telephone system and the Internet helped integrate the South into the nation at large. People and businesses can now keep in touch wherever they are.

*For the **current weather** see USA Today's web page (www.usatoday. com) or the Weather Channel's page (www.weather.com)*

WHERE TO STAY

Let's look at a couple of areas beyond the usual New York, Florida, California triangle.

One of the most spectacular sights anywhere in the USA has to be **New England in the Fall**. When you see the leaves change you know why they don't just call it Autumn. State of the foliage hotlines exist in most states. For the Massachusetts Berkshires, which tend to peak in the first half of October take a look at *www.BostonCentral.com* from mid-September to the end of October each year. For those who don't wish to walk out in the wild call the Arnold Arboretum in Boston where you can enjoy the 14,000 trees change in something approaching comfort. Any website dealing with Fall colours will suggest great viewing spots but they can then become crowded. Just drive up Route 100 through Vermont to escape the crowds. But don't expect to book at the last moment: the Fall in New England is a major tourist event. If you try to book a New England week without success you might try just over the Quebec border where the colours are every bit as spectacular and the crowds are fewer. In November try the Appalachians west of Washington DC.

The Rockies are increasingly accessible given BA's daytime flight to Denver, a direct flight cuts about three and a half hours off the previous routes via changes at Washington Dulles or Chicago O'Hare. Denver International (opened 1995) is ten times the size of Heathrow and handles 49 million passengers per year. This means that as it is still under used it provides speedy baggage retrieval and customs and immigration. Even if you go for the scenery or the skiing see Denver which, like Seattle, has been reinvented with warehouses, bars and restaurants over the last 30 years. The local economy is now based upon financial services, and what is now known as the 'back office'. Sub branches of international corporations perform vital but could-be-anywhere services such as customer 'information factories', while HQs remain in more expensive premier-division cities with up-market addresses (Manhattan, Atlanta, San Francisco). Some 20 British companies now have such branches in Denver for their US customer base. Fancy a world-class museum? Try their collection of North American art. On the other hand perhaps you prefer America's only downtown amusement park. For a two-week stay, skiing prices are not all that more than the equivalent Alpine holiday, though most US packages are room only where continental holidays tend to be half-board. Remember though that ordinary living expenses in the USA tend to be much cheaper than in Europe (meals, petrol, replacement clothes). *Baholidays.com* provides a range of Denver-sight-seeing and hotel information. If you don't want the drive out to a resort such as Aspen (an extra four hours onto an already long trip) a shuttle is scheduled for those transferring from incoming BA flights.

Hotels

The range is enormous, from the flea-pit to the luxury resort. Hotels are more expensive than motels, which tend to be more uniform in facilities and price.

Beware that prices quoted are always *before* **tax.** In Manhattan there are city and state sales taxes plus a hotel occupancy tax, so a budget $119 double at the Manhattan would actually cost $144.29. Doubles in a fashionable SoHo hotel would cost from $349 plus taxes, being $423.17 in reality.

Many US chains can be contacted directly in the UK:

- Hilton (*www.Hilton.co.uk*);
- Ritz-Carlton (*www.ritzcarlton.com*);
- Sheraton (www.sheraton.com).

US hotel discount agency **Quikbook** claims its rooms are 40–65 per cent cheaper than brochure rates for Atlanta, Boston, Chicago, Los Angeles, New York City, San Francisco and Washington DC.

Motels

Motels usually have two double beds, toilet and shower, plus a television as standard, often with cable TV, and a pool (although you must check there is a pool, especially at the bottom end of the market). Prices at recognised chains start at about $80 per night, but prices are per room, not per person, so for families or groups of friends this is good value at $2 pound. The Premier Inn chain in the UK is the nearest in price and facilities to the US norm. Breakfast is traditionally not included, though as competition heats up a 'continental' breakfast snack frequently is. Chains exist for a variety of price levels with great price variety even within a particular chain (between tourist areas and less popular regions). **Best Western** and the **Holiday Inn** are plusher, and pricier than **Super 8 Motels** or **Econolodge**, more like the UK's Travelodge chain. **Howard Johnston's** have built-in coffee shops. Most motels don't have food service, but fast-food outlets and family restaurants are usually next door, often with a discount arrangement if you show your key when paying the bill. Motels are usually cheapest in the Midwest, with family motels off the freeway $15–20 cheaper than brand name motels adjacent to freeway off-ramps. The cheapest are in Las Vegas where discounted accommodation attracts gamblers. Shop around for $36 a night (and all you can eat may be included).

Good news

The mid-1980s saw a massive amount of motel construction leading to a series of price wars which still continue. This means that in towns with an over-abundance of motel construction, chains may reduce their prices below that charged elsewhere. Check their prices on the huge billboards visible from the main roads, phone, or just drop in and ask.

Also, much of this new construction has been to catch trade passing along the new roads, freeways and bypasses. The older motels on the older, now bypassed, roads are often far cheaper and may well have bargains, like special mid-week prices. These can be a considerable saving (if you can avoid thinking of Psycho).

B&B

Bed and breakfast establishments do exist, but are traditionally only accessible through published lists rather than roadside signs. American B&Bs are generally quite expensive and must be pre-booked, though this can now often be done over the Internet. Over the border, Canadian B&Bs are more common and more reasonably priced. 'Tourist Accommodation' signs attract the casual visitor, especially in resorts such as Niagara Falls, Ontario particularly off-season. Many US towns now have their own freephone series and websites. The days of printed guides are nearly over. Today this is very much a web-based business.

■ *www.bbonline.com* has over 2,000 categories on file, which can be searched by various categories such as state, terrain (mountain or coasts), even building types (e.g. whether on the National Registry of Historic Places). You can access individual properties with a picture of both the building and the hosts until you find something you like (and can afford).

■ *www.bedandbreakfast.com/usa.html* has photos and descriptions for a wide range of options.

Inns

Many traditional inns cater for those who can afford something classier than motels. *www.innsofusa.com* provides access to a growing list of American inns, usually up-market, family-run enterprises.

Self-catering

Self-catering apartments are widespread in the USA. They have all the mod-cons you would expect in any motel (double beds, showers, TV and a phone) plus as standard a fully fitted kitchen with dishwasher. Some motels now seek to attract self-catering travellers, so look for kitchen facilities in motel listings. It's unlikely that any other services would be available, like room service, but a coffee shop may well be part of the complex, or merely next door or across the street. Expect to pay at least $500 a week for a two-person studio apartment, though with considerable regional and seasonal variation. The Marmara-Manhattan on the Upper East Side of New York City has 102 'extended-stay' apartments for periods of at least one month. Rates start at $5,000 per month (2008), which is comparable with a basic SoHo apartment. If you think you have arrived anywhere at a slack period be prepared to ask for a special long-stay rate. It is usually, of course, cheaper to stay in a regular motel and eat out, but if you are based in one place for a while, say while house-hunting, and would like something a little more like a flat, self-catering may well be for you.

■ *Arthur Fromer's Budget Travel Magazine* provides regular suggestions for globetrotters, including US information. Subscriptions from *mybt.budget travel.com* ($32 pa).

■ *Essentially America* provides quarterly travel and lifestyle information. To subscribe call 01778 391190 or check out *www.essentially.com* for their travel guide and £3 subscription offer.

Hostels

You can stay for as little as $20 a night in some hostels, located in lighthouses, farmhouses, ranches and private houses. But you need to be careful. Some are heavenly, others horrific. The following guides can help with your choices.

■ *Hotels USA* is an unofficial and often opinionated guide by Evan Halper and Paul Karr, published by Globe Pequot, offering comprehensive at-a-glance ratings for 340 hostels across the United States. Along with the usual indices such as prices and cleanliness, it takes special care to note a variety of other factors such as which hostels are located near natural settings, which have superior kitchen facilities or are particularly good for family visits. However, the unabashed low-down on every hostel is what makes this rating guide worth five stars. For example, Bell's Mountain Hostel in Tennessee is 'kind of weird for those of us who never ran off to weekend retreats with a church youth group'. Those new to hostels will find the basic information enlightening: hostels are not merely cheap hotels, being a different sort of lodging altogether. As such, hostelling isn't for everyone, but this guide is surely for everyone who hostels. It's technically now out of date and out of print, but is still available from Amazon. It is still recommended.

■ *The Hostel Handbook* lists over 600 cheap places to sleep with information on driving cross country and on bus, airline and train services. It appears to be the most complete list in one book of hostels regardless of affiliation across North America, including Hostelling International's hostels, independent hostels and backpackers' places. *www.hostelhandbook.com* is the place to start serious planning.

■ *At Home in Hostel Territory: A Guide to Friendly Lodgings from Seward to Santa Cruz*, Janet Thomas, published by Alaska Northwest (1994), features hostels with a homey atmosphere from Alaska to California. For those who want to find out what the philosophy of hostelling is all about, this is it. Compare this with a booking website to get the best of both worlds. Amazon's site allows you to read select pages for free.

■ For those with a vehicle, try *Road Trip USA: Cross-Country Adventures on America's Two-Lane Highways*, by Jamie Jensen, Avalon, a comprehensive guide to driving away from the interstate freeways. Jensen's guide takes the pain out of the road trip, be it across the continent or a Sunday jaunt. With directions to pit stops, scenic routes, bizarre museums and the best apple pie stands, all you have to do is drive. Simply avoiding the interstates opens up a parallel two-lane world of monuments marking the actual sites of things Americans last heard about in high school, or souvenir stands advertised by giant dinosaurs. This is a travel book for those looking for something a bit different from McDonalds and Disney: Route 93 from Montana to Mexico, Route 2 from Washington State to Maine, and Route 66 from California to Illinois.

Camping

The US is a campers' dream, whether your ideal is the north face of some mountain in the latest hi-tech super tent or in a state park with all mod cons and vast family tent that puts the kind of tents the British find on French sites to shame. But there is a down side: all too often you cannot just turn up. You need to book for the most well-known sites, particularly in world-famous ones such as the Grand Canyon. Such sites can be booked months in advance. If you want to camp at just such a site in the long summer holidays, particularly between May and the start of September, you need to book as the whole of American suburbia seems to have taken to the woods and mountains.

There is a wide array of sites. At one side of the spectrum there is the site with the full works: hot showers, laundry and a pool. These are usually privately owned (though may well be part of a chain such as Kampgrounds of America – watch for KOA signs) and are comparable with staying at a motel where you have brought the cabin with you. Most users will come with their RVs (Recreational Vehicles), which travel across country in search of the sun or distant relatives like a new species migrating until the occupants die in harness. For anything between $10 and $50 a night you will be able to find a pitch. At about half that price you can find space in the vast array of public campgrounds, usually found on public land. Prices are as varied as train prices in the UK, so try out the KOA website to see the array of dropdown menus and categories. The most well known outside the USA are undoubtedly the national parks, but there is also a vast array of national forests (often the land around the national park that stands at their core). Even more available, as there are far more of them, are the state parks and forests. Each state has a wide selection of sites, and they are often excellent, though a little on the basic side compared to the larger private sites. Along the great trails such as that following the Appalachian Mountains from Maine to Georgia there are even more basic facilities, accessible only on foot, often little more than lean-tos that are maintained by trail clubs or state parks. Space is available on a sleeping platform and if you are lucky there is a chemical toilet out back. Latecomers pitch their tents as best they can around the site and join the throng. Bill Bryson will try his best to put you off this form of accommodation in his Appalachian trail book *A Walk in the Woods*. Even these most basic sites will probably have a barbecue pit (if only to ensure people don't light fires outside safe designated areas). Fires are a major issue in the woods, so do as the locals do (within reason). If there is a substantial fire risk open fires may be prohibited. Normally the only problem of using smaller sites is that you may well have to explain to bemused fellow campers where you are from (a country many will be surprised to learn still exists as they only hear about it in terms of eighteenth-century American history). Animals may be a more certain hassle; make sure food is locked away in the car or, if on foot, lift food inside a secure bag off the ground (rope over overhanging branch, then pull – you'll soon get the hang of it). For tips and advice on getting away from it all try the US version of Backpacker (www.thebackpacker.com).

Booking in organised sites can be easy or difficult. KOA has a central booking facility and takes credit card payment from overseas (001 406 7444). The National Parks Service (NPS) also has a central booking agency (001 800 365 2267) and a web page (*www.gorp.com/resource/us-national-park/main.htm*). CampNet has camp-ground information on its site (*www.campnetamerica.com*). Sites specialising in RV facilities can be found on the Go Camping America! Site (*www.gocampingamerica.com/main.htm*l).

US National Parks

Booking accommodation from abroad has long been somewhat of a hassle, so a recent Internet facility is to be much appreciated. There is a secure website at *http://reservations.nps.gov* which allows visitors to book up to five months before travel, as well as providing much useful information on facilities available within the parks.

WHERE TO LIVE

The USA is continental in size. Prices and standards vary accordingly, especially for housing. The most expensive places are in the major cities, such as Georgetown (in Washington DC) or in fashionable suburbs (such as Montgomery County, Maryland, just outside the capital). As in Britain the cheaper areas tend to be far out in the countryside, or in the less than fashionable parts of the city, which can include some adjacent suburban areas (such as the older built-up areas of Prince George's County also just outside Washington DC). The same housing can be ten times as expensive in a booming, fashionable area as in a declining industrial town.

Even within a metropolis, such as Washington DC, you will not know where to find a good place to live without help, a lot of money, or a willingness to make awful mistakes, the latter being a 'learning experience' only single young people should undertake. The social geography of the American conurbation is also constantly changing as areas are gentrified, as racial lines of demarcation shift, and as subway lines are opened. Of course, like most Americans, you might hope a low area you buy into will rise, to your advantage, but it's a major risk even for those well tuned into the city. For a newcomer it's a lottery chance.

But a home in a certain area will not only influence your settling down as a family. It will also influence your standing with colleagues and those you meet, almost like an accent in Britain. Getting housing right is not only one of the most crucial decisions to be made but also one that needs to be sorted out quite quickly if motel fees are not to erode your savings when you first arrive.

Rental sector

This is far larger and more varied than in Britain. Though buying is seen as much the same kind of profitable investment as in Britain, many people do not wish to be tied down to being responsible for property upkeep. Many people move from job to job and prefer to rent locally, moving by rental van in an almost semi-nomadic way. Many more developers build for rent, though many have sold out to sitting tenants, in response to rent control and tenancy security legislation. The end of rent control in New York City results in considerably higher rents than previously, even though in the long run more properties may be built for rent. Those who seek to ape the late Alistair Cooke or the TV characters in *Friends* may find it very tough going in the new rental market. Once a tenant in a rent-controlled apartment dies the place is often gutted, refitted, and on the market at five times the old rent within weeks.

How to find rented accommodation

- Via college/firm's notice (bulletin) board.
- Via specialist, fee-paying agencies.
- Estate agents (*realtors*).
- Small ads in the local newspaper.
- Driving around likely areas and calling in at the rental office within each rental development.

Knowing the lingo

Before you start out on your trek you need to know the lingo which can be quite tricky:

■ Flats are deemed **bachelor, studio** or **efficiency** when small and single room (plus bathroom and kitchen).

■ A **walk-up** is something like a bedsitter in a block without a lift.

■ **Cold-water apartments** are precisely that – you need to install your own water heater (though normally America's big city blocks have traditionally had hot water provided by the landlord rather than the tenant).

Initials abound:

■ mbr = master bedroom
■ wbfp = wood-burning fireplace
■ fdr = formal dining-room
■ .5 bath = toilet and basin, not bath.

Unless you are single or moving in with friends you will probably not want to move into the subdivided, older and larger houses in the poorer neighbourhoods, nor would you want to become involved with **urban homesteading** unless you are already a master craftsman and could transform an abandoned property bought from the city for $1.

If you move into a post-1945 development the chances are you will have access to a couple of communal facilities:

■ Laundry-room, with huge commercial wash and dry machines for renters' use only – take a pile of 25c pieces. Costs are pretty good, and the time (especially the dryers) is much lower than domestic equivalents.

■ Pool, available for key-holders and guests. In heatwaves this can be a great boon.

Houses may also be available for rent, much more easily than in Britain. These are often available through real estate agents for set periods.

Condominiums

During the 1970s the rental market changed quite markedly. Many developers decided to get out of the rental market, often by way of selling to other developers who wanted to redevelop blocks even though they might be full of sitting tenants. Many blocks were redeveloped at great cost, which turned out to be a back-door way of raising the rent legally. Hence such redevelopment became a way to get sitting tenants out of potentially prime sites.

City councils initially liked the improvement to the housing stock. Too late it became evident that the poor, and then the lower reaches of the middle class, were being priced out of their own flats, with the pool of accommodation they could afford declining.

This introduced a new verb into American English: **to condo**. Apartment blocks were transformed into **condominiums** (quickly shortened to **condos**).

In effect condos are now little more than blocks of individually-owned flats, the only trace elements of communal ownership being communal party rooms and sports facilities (plus the pool and laundry room). The TV series *Frasier* is set in a Seattle condo.

Buying

Mortgages are even more likely to be fixed rate rather than flexible as in Britain. This is good news for those buying when rates are low, so protecting the purchaser from further rate rises. For those having to buy, though, when the rates are high a slump in interest rates is of no immediate benefit. Many house buyers attempt to overcome this by refinancing their loan at the new lower rate, a practice still far more common than in the UK.

Unless buying a new property it may be possible to take over (assume) the existing mortgage for the amount outstanding for the remaining term, so avoiding the costs of setting up a new mortgage. If you have no US-based credit history this may be the only way to get into the housing market in middle age.

General US practice is to agree on a sale price and for the buyer and seller to respect it for 14 days, with a 1 per cent down payment. During this time the buyer completes financial arrangements and obtains a survey. If finance is not forthcoming or the property proves to be defective the buyer can withdraw and the seller can place the property back on the market or accept a waiting offer. The buyer has to move quickly in the USA, but the seller will *not* pull out once the deposit has been paid. Scots will not notice too much of a difference, but the English and Welsh certainly will. But beware: each state will have slightly differing rules on this, so get professional advice.

Savings and loan associations ('thrifts') are similar to building societies. Once upon a time they only gave mortgages to certain racial and ethnic groups, but since the 1960's civil rights campaigns this has supposedly ceased. Mortgages are supposed to be available on the basis of being able to repay the loan (plus interest) with the property as collateral. Tell that to those who lost out in the credit crunch of 2008!

What needs to be done?

- Buy a good local guide to property purchase and property financing. Ask at a public library for a recommendation.

- Consider using a house-finding agent.

- Get good local legal advice before committing yourself to purchasing.

- Check out the viability of the 'savings and loan' (many have gone bust).

Location taxation

In the days before the British poll tax was mooted the assessment for local taxation in the two countries was very similar, though in the USA rates are called what they actually are: **property taxes**. They can be high, so check it out! If you should consider a mobile home, check as to how it will be taxed, whether as a fixed property or as a vehicle.

Housing types

Being continental in size and variety, US housing is more varied than outsiders often realise. The first surprise may well be the widespread use of **wood**. Timber-built houses (increasingly popular in Britain due to price advantages) are often called frame houses, though they often have wooden walls too, and in some areas even wooden 'tiles' called **shingles**.

Terraced houses (here called **row houses**) are less widespread in US cities. Baltimore, however, is actually famous precisely for its row houses, unfortunately often covered now with 'Baltimore stone' (pseudo-stone cladding) clearly evident on screen during television's *Homicide* and *The Wire*. Many industrial towns of the Appalachian coalfields have town houses perched on hill-slopes much like in the Rhondda Valley in Britain, though wood rather than brick or stone is likely to predominate. Immigrant areas of the eastern cities had vast areas of tenements, many stories high, now often abandoned as urban and redevelopment decay eat out the heart of the once industrial and trading cities.

Far more than in Britain the middle-class and much of the working-class ('blue collar') housing is detached, free-standing in its own lot. In older, generally midwestern or eastern cities, houses are often more European-like, with fairly small rooms. Out west, however, rooms tend to be larger, and many lower middle-class 1940s–50s houses seem very like the farms the owners had left back on the Great Plains of the 1930s Dust Bowl days, like farmhouses without farms, all packed together, yet each on its own plot of land. As the middle classes have moved on to new property such areas have been bought by minorities so that often very poor ghettos appear, at least superficially, middle-class to European eyes.

House prices

By 2004 the average price paid for a three-bedroom, single-family house was over $185,000 for which the average US family paid about a quarter of their income in mortgage repayments. Housing therefore remains a major demand on people's after-tax income into the new millennium. To get a mortgage on such an averagely priced house it will soon be necessary to earn $75,000 a year. But what can you buy for under $200,000 in the real world of a housing market spread out over a vast country with widely different house prices reflecting hugely different levels of prosperity? Figure 1 shows how varied the prices are across the country.

The USA is, however, so vast that national figures will mean very little to anyone seeking to buy within a particular city's housing market. Figure 1 gives an idea of average house prices in seven major cities relating them to the local cost of living which varies widely. In Indianapolis, a standard mid-western city, the price of an average house is above the national average, but as the overall cost of living is lower than most other cities, $100,000 can buy far more for your money than elsewhere. In these major cities the cost of living is way over the national average. At opposite ends of the country New York City and Honolulu approach *twice* the US average.

	Three-bedroom house median price	Cost of living index
Anaheim	$696,100	167.4
Honolulu	$577,800	183.0
Los Angeles	$474,800	153.1
New York	$506,800	188.7
San Francisco	$726,900	177.0
San Diego	$605,600	141.0
Washington DC	$429,200	137.8

Fig. 1. Average house prices in 2007.

Los Angeles, by contrast, has a cost of living almost 'reasonable'. Prices vary widely across the USA not just from town to town but also from neighbourhood to neighbourhood. When considering high wages it is essential to consider them in terms of what they will buy locally. A college professor with a family to support might find $100,000 okay in upstate New York but inadequate within New York City and impossible within California's Silicon Valley with its many millionaires pushing up the price of almost everything. Nursing staff in particular should note that large US salaries offered to encourage emigration usually involve living in very expensive parts of the country such as New York City (which may be why the hospital cannot find Americans to fill the posts!). However, elsewhere in New York State the same wage might well be viable, though the hospital may be in a deeply unfashionable town, such as Poughskeepsie or Syracuse (though even these distressed towns have world-class universities).

For specific city-by-city information see David Savageau, *Places Rated Almanac*, Prentice Hall, New York (annually). This is essential reading for anyone relocating within the USA. Its fascinating array of statistical information is intelligently explained: a must for all outsiders. For those with web access try looking for financial information sites (such as *www.money.com*).

Utilities

Utilities, especially electricity, gas and hot water, may or may not be included in any rental prices. Traditionally all utilities except the phone were included in the rental paid. As these costs rose (especially for central heating and air conditioning after the oil price rises of the early 1970s) they became separate items. If charged directly by the utility companies, bills are usually monthly, with the sanction of being cut-off if you don't pay (or your cheque bounces).

Beware

Being paid every two weeks but being billed every month can get you as out of phase as being paid monthly but having quarterly bills to meet in Britain.

The telephone is worth an early mention here, if only because 1980s changes complicated a system once fairly easy to use and understand for domestic users. The Bell system was broken up into regional companies with rival long-distance carriers, making long-distance calls, especially across country, quite complicated and expensive. The domestic rental often includes local calls with long-distance calls being separately itemised (a good idea). But even in off-peak hours long-distance calls, especially those just outside the local area, can be quite costly (like Washington DC to Baltimore, which though a shorter distance than Manchester to Birmingham is deemed long-distance at a rate that makes the two cities seem to be in different countries). This only becomes a real problem when trying to use a call box and being asked for $5 of 25c pieces before the operator will connect you. This problem is disappearing as with almost universal availability of mobile (cell) phones, pay phones are fading away as in the UK. Domestic telephone users should watch out for special deals on long-distance calls that may be advertised by your companies. They often have loss-leader rates (to encourage you to get used to using them for long-distance calls). For more details see pages 64–68.

Buying in Florida

It is possible that you may see in the British press advertisements for property in Florida. This is no longer as far-fetched as it might once have seemed. Flying into Orlando is now one of the easiest ways of entering the US for people travelling from northern Europe. The number of British visitors means that people in the Orlando area are no longer fazed by people coming from overseas in general and the UK in particular (yes, business people will recognise and use the term UK, almost unknown elsewhere in the US). Flights are readily available, and the modern airport and its immigration and customs facilities are good. I no longer dread arrival as I used to. And it is increasingly possible to use the services of people in the UK familiar with the situation in Florida.

The thought of blue skies, warm temperatures and friendly people tempts many Europeans over to the sunshine state of Florida. Add to that superb golf courses and the many excellent attractions, such as Disneyworld, and a great swathe of central Florida is increasingly seen as a perfect place for families to holiday or buy a second home.

It is also one of the better places for a second home to pay for itself. With approaching 50 million visitors a year, it may well be possible to cover the running costs of your second home, though you do have to ensure that you buy in an area that is zoned for short-term rentals: that is, one or two weeks at a time rather than over a month. Many communities in the main centres allow second homes, but forbid sub-letting. These communities make their money from hotels, and they aren't going to let you take the bread out of their mouths. You may have to move over the county line to find a community that permits sub-letting, Orange County does not permit short-term lets to preserve the profitability of the hotels, so it is essential to check out first that a property can be let for holiday lets.

Many of the established Florida property agents in Britain also run or can access management and rental services for second homes. Florida Homes International (*www.floridahomes.co.uk*), for example, has set up a Florida Homes Owners' Club to help market and co-ordinate booking for its second-home owners.

American mortgages are usually given with a long-term fixed rate of interest and this can be offset against rental income. Agents specialising in Florida properties will recommend the use of a reputable adviser to explain how the tax, mortgage and rent works. Then you need to go over for an inspection trip, staying in a property similar to the one you'd like to buy, to see if it is what you really want. Doing this, British buyers are often surprised at the value for money they can purchase. American homes are far more spacious than those we are used to and it is not unusual for a 3,000 sq ft house to have only three or four bedrooms.

Many projects have golf courses, a communal pool and tennis courts as standard. The detached homes usually border onto the golf course or back onto wooded conservation land, with prices for three- to seven-bedroom furnished homes going for $300,000 and up. The area immediately around Orlando tends to focus on time-share developments because of the obvious tourist attractions, but many one-time visitors are now moving further afield, often along the Gulf Coast from Venice and Fort Myers north through the Tampa-St Petersburg area north to Inverness.

Four-bedroom houses with two-car garage and pool cost around about $350,000, though it is still possible to find quality homes for far less, but the trade-off is that where property is not expensive it is less likely to be in the sort of area where tourism rentals can help defray the costs. Many second-home owners enjoy such properties themselves, sub-letting to fellow Brits. Expect visitors to be prepared to pay $1,400 a week an hour from Disneyworld. We answered an advert in a local newsagents, and then found the owners were building up a clientele of villagers who returned to hassle-free Inverness northwest of Orlando from time to time. Aiming to have sub-letting making the investment self-financing is not unrealistic, though it may take a few years for even a well-chosen place to make that kind of return on a regular basis, and you remain hostage to oil prices and people's continued willingness to fly long distances in a recession.

How can you buy a property in Florida? The apparently easy, but possibly more difficult way in the long run, is simply to go on holiday and look around. And you won't have to look far. As in Spanish resorts, many people will try to sell you condominium apartments, time-share, with the bait of a free meal and look-see, or even cheap tickets to Disney (I should know, I fell for that one). But if you want something less fraught, there are now people in the UK who can help. Firstly, there is the companion book to this that sets out a range of advice. Then there are the UK-based businesses that specialise in selling US property.

HomesOverseas is the magazine for would-be second-homers overseas (not just in the USA) visit *www.homesoverseas.co.uk* for details.

For further advice

For general points to consider when moving abroad see Michael Furrell's Daily Telegraph Guide *Living and Retiring Abroad*, published in London by Kogan Page. It also has a small section on the USA, as does Roger Jones, *Retire Abroad*, How To Books, 2002. Specific details age, but both provide interesting discussions about what moving abroad entails for those who are no longer in the full flush of youth.

More detailed considerations are raised in David Hoppitt's *Overseas Property Guide: The Do's and Don'ts of Buying a Home Abroad*, published by Telegraph Publications of London. Though the specifically US material is rather thin and only relates to Florida and California and needs up-dating, the general issues raised are important and need to be dealt with wherever property is bought. These include when to obtain professional advice, ground rules for property purchase, time-sharing opportunities and pitfalls, with details on the legalities of purchase and the securing of the necessary financial backing. A useful place to start is the Internet (try *www.money.com* which has 'Best Places to Retire' and 'Best Places to Live' pages with cost of living information, city data, and lots of good advice on making those vital decisions). For a wider consideration of buying overseas to let have a look at Dominic Farrell *The Jet to Let Bible* Lawpack, 2006. For a range of similar guides look below Amazon's entry for this book where similar volumes are recommended or advertised.

FOOD AND DRINK

Eating out

Fast-food from recognisable companies is readily available, often with extras such as gravy grits and mashed potatoes or a scone-like piece of bread reflecting local taste. **All-day breakfast** or **salad bars** may well be part of the war between competing hamburger outlets. Breakfast is probably the best bargain, though all-you-can-eat meals at any time of day are good value (though to be avoided if you are on a diet).

For city restaurants you can find any style and pay any price you like, though in country areas steak may be all that is available.

Americans now eat about half their meals away from home, and this increasingly involves the kind of family gathering you might expect in people's homes. Budget accordingly.

Eating in

Supermarkets vary, but chains are usually excellent for price and exotic choice, including delicatessen items, alcoholic drinks (if locally permitted) and serve-yourself salad bars. Food is priced at familiar European levels, with steak generally cheaper, but with lamb more expensive (and usually frozen from New Zealand). More details on shopping, including shopping for food, are given on pages 55–61.

Incidentals

Drinking in **cafés** and **bars** can be uncomfortably expensive. A cup of coffee can easily cost a couple of pounds (as at home). Prices in **diners** and **coffee-shops** (especially in drug stores) can be very reasonable, often with free coffee refills (if you like it weak). **Cocktails** (where alcohol is permitted) can cost from £5, though half that in the late afternoon – early evening **happy hour**. Cigarettes may cost over £3 for 20, though prices vary greatly to reflect states' individual tax rates, and all prices are rising with regular federal tax increases ('hikes'). But where can you smoke these days?

Tipping

The British have a usually well-earned reputation for being mean tippers, especially in the USA. Tom Wolfe wrote *Bonfire of the Vanities* around just such a British 'tight wad' (though the film version lost the British aspect). Americans over here tend to be seen as over-generous. In the USA tipping is much more important than in Britain. Those in the food and drink business are usually very under-paid. In fact they usually rely upon tips to survive. Watch the US television show *Friends*! As a general rule be generous for good service.

You'll have to use your judgement over how much to leave. Taxi drivers are notorious for their contempt of those who leave less than 10 per cent. About 15 per cent is probably right for bar staff and those serving food. In bars you'll often get a bill each round, though if you become known you'll be able to run up a **tab** to make one payment when you leave. If you pay for each round and leave only the exact money you will probably get ever poorer service. Watch what others are doing. If in doubt ask your friends.

If you are paying by credit card you may notice that when the slip is presented to you, you find the total amount left blank. You are being invited to add something extra for a tip. If you've left a tip at the table make sure you don't end up paying twice.

Alcohol

The story of alcohol in the USA is the story of these United States in all their variety. Over the years America has been a refuge for those fleeing from the gin-sodden old world to a new world of freedom and temperance, and for those who arrived expecting the freedom to do, to eat, and especially to drink, whatever and whenever they liked. These two traditions have fought over and over again, and after the US Constitution had been amended (1919) to outlaw the sale, manufacture and distribution of alcohol it seemed that finally the blue meanies had won out over the boozers.

Rise of the prohibition-era gangsters soon turned public opinion, and as part of Franklin D. Roosevelt's New Deal the US Constitution was re-amended in the mid-1930s to allow things to return to what they had been before. This still enabled local communities to rule whether alcohol should be available in their particular locality. College towns are often 'dry', though the first place over the county or even state line may well have bars, liquor stores and little else. In the Appalachian mountains it is possible if lost to tell whether you are in a Tennessee county (wet) or a North Carolina county (dry) by looking out for a petrol station – if they hang out a beer sign you're still in Tennessee!

No state still remains completely 'dry', though if several adjacent counties are it may start to feel that way. But even in Mormon Utah liquor stores exist, and you can drink with your meal, though you may have to bring the vodka in with you and get a 'set-up' – a Bloody Mary with everything except the vodka, which you add to taste.

As a response to the rising tide of alcohol-related road fatalities, especially involving teenagers, the general trend is to raise the age of drinking to 21, which makes drinking in a college town very inconvenient. Colleges rarely if ever allow alcohol to be sold on campus anyway (the British student union bar is unknown), *but* you'll need proof of your being over 21, hence the cry of 'you got ID?' You can be 40 and bald and still not get a drink if you haven't got an ID and the barman takes a dislike to your face (or accent).

Bars and pubs

Bars, pubs and other dives may be disappointing. They are often little more than drinking places, with perhaps picking up sexual partners as the only added attraction. Even bars which may be recommended to you may well turn out to be ill-lit, deep, narrow and uninviting. Beer on draught plus cheap drinks during the late afternoon happy hour with a chance to meet friends after work may be their only extenuating features. Fortunately US domestic beer is improving, with Sam Smith's Boston ale in draught ('draft') now available all over the country. Bars often do reasonable snacks, steak sandwiches and the like, plus Irish coffee. Have no faith in the kitchens.

Don't expect anything special from bars with the word 'Pub' written outside. They *may* have imported, even European, beers, but at best only Guinness. Other beers, though with exotic names, are usually locally neutered versions (like so much 'foreign' beer in Britain).

A favourite watering hole on Connecticut Avenue in Washington DC used to have a rat come strolling through from time to time. Several months later the place was bolted and barred: 'The public health department finally caught up with them?' 'Hell no, he didn't pay his taxes!'

Places you could safely eat in, apart from the expensive bars in the equally expensive hotels, without fear for your health are likely to be dry, like the Crystal Palace in Disneyworld. Seaworld does, however, serve draught beer to those also eating.

Restaurants

Which leads to restaurants. In rural areas family ones may not allow alcohol of any kind. Though this will hardly inconvenience those going in for the all-you-can-eat breakfast, at the other end of the day after a long time on the road it may come as something of a disappointment to leave your motel room for the restaurant over the way, order steaks, and then find you can order neither beer nor wine (though on your travels you could yesterday and will tomorrow). Rootbeer is an acquired taste (aka mouthwash).

Many communities consider that if you must have alcohol you should buy it elsewhere, and drink it only in the privacy of your own room away from God-fearing folk and their innocent children. As you watch people gorging themselves, blowing smoke everywhere as they eat, and downing Coke like there's no tomorrow, you may feel somewhat annoyed about not being able to get a glass of beer. But tomorrow night in another town the waitress will appear and ask 'Anything from the bar?' and you'll know that you've crossed an important line somewhere out back on the road.

Posher restaurants almost always serve, or permit, alcohol. Presumably such places are deemed for 'grown-ups', who are beyond redemption. Smoking, though, is increasingly frowned upon (and is now illegal in California, Maryland and New York restaurants).

If in doubt ask people you are visiting what the situation is locally. Even dry areas have people who want to drink and these people know all the dodges. They'll know where the nearest available wet jurisdiction is, and where you can take a bottle of drink with a meal without hassle. They may well stock-up themselves once a month when going into the city or over the line, and have a fridge-full ready to be shared with visitors.

If you have any doubts about the seafood, call the US Food & Drug Administration hotline on 1-888-Safefood (almost 50 people have died in Florida from bad oysters over the last ten years).

ENTERTAINMENT

As disposable incomes are generally high, Americans spend a lot on going out. The rich love to sponsor and to be seen at cultural events so world-class **orchestras**, **opera** and **ballet** companies are found in most major cities, though tickets may be hard to come by.

Rock concerts abound, and you may well be able to see not only US groups but major British ones in those huge sports stadia that all cities and most college towns have. Bluegrass, blues, country, folk and jazz festivals abound, often outdoors in summer. They are generally excellent, and not over-expensive for the experience they provide. As gatherings dear to so many Americans they are worth visiting, if only for their colour, food and drink.

Theatre is still mostly associated with Broadway in New York City, or in the regional theatres that take travelling productions. Some cities have stock (repertory) companies which are often enthusiastically supported locally.

Cheap theatre tickets

Same-day cheap tickets are an essential part of the urban experience, a delight for students and budget travellers alike. If you would like to experience New York theatre but cannot afford box-office prices, visit Duffy Square, traditionally at the north end of Times Square but due to construction relocated to the Marriott Marquis Hotel. Established in 1973 for the betterment of theatres and theatregoers alike, TKTS sells unsold tickets for half-price on the day of performance for all Broadway shows. The electronic signs in front display what shows are available for that day. Get in line early, especially during good holiday weather. Box Office Hours:

Evening Performance Monday to Saturday 3.00 pm to 8.00 pm. Matinees Wednesday and Saturday 10.00 am to 2.00 pm. Matinee and Evening Sunday 12 noon to 8.00 pm. Confirm opening hours on their website (*www.tdf.com*).

There was a less well-known TKTS branch at 2 World Trade Center, the same tower with the observatory now located at South Street Seaport. Box Office Hours: Monday to Friday 11.00 am to 5.00 pm and Saturday 11.00 am to 3.30 pm with matinees available the day before. Payment by cards not accepted.

Tickets may generally seem expensive, especially in large cities. Bookings are conveniently made in person at *Ticketron* (see the phone book for location and details, or check online).

Cinemas are generally either for films on general release (about $10) or for old classic re-runs (about $7). New York City and Los Angeles have tomorrow's films today, to test audience reaction (at least $10). Smoking is generally banned in all cinemas, and until recently there have been no on-screen commercials. Audiences can be very raucous. In summer the air conditioning can be fierce, so take a sweater.

Museums and **galleries** are usually free, though may cost a dollar or so. As in Britain specific exhibitions can be rather expensive extras. Beware though: the onset of any federal budget cutbacks can rapidly end most evening openings of publicly-funded institutions, such as Washington DC's Smithsonian Institute (including the Air and Space Museum).

Concerts and the **theatre** can cost at least $50, at least twice that and more for Broadway hits on the New York stage, twice again for big name events at places like Madison Square Gardens.

Entertainment parks vary enormously, from $50 (Dollywood in the Great Smokies of eastern Tennessee) to $300 for a high-season week in Disneyworld (though if part of a package holiday Disney may be much cheaper and, being prepaid, seem an almost painless cost).

DRESS SENSE

It is tempting to view the USA as a more relaxed, unfussy country as far as what to wear goes. The national costume seems to be the T-shirt, jeans and trainers. Such generalisations, however, can be confusingly misleading. There are dress codes (a phrase you may never even have heard before arriving in the US). They just aren't the same as elsewhere.

In New England, those states between New York and the Canadian Maritimes, people tend to be more formal, even stuffy, than you'll find elsewhere. Though casual wear may be okay for the garden or the beach, visiting a restaurant casually dressed would raise many an eyebrow, and in expensive restaurants service would be refused. For work most men wear suits and short neat hair. Women do not generally wear trousers ('pants'). But the suits may turn out to be yellow plaid, if not at work then at church socials or town meetings. Casual dress is more acceptable out west, especially in California, in all but the most expensive places.

However, don't be lulled into believing anything goes. Topless bathing hasn't as a rule arrived, even in areas climatically appropriate. There are militant nudists and naturist bathing areas, but nowhere is nudity as casual as, say, on a summer's day in Danish parks and beaches or around the pools in the south of France. That isn't to say there won't be a lot of exhibitionism on beaches, but the rules will be known by all, and if you cross the line you'll soon find out. Watching what others are doing remains a good rule of thumb. Beware: many public beaches frown upon, or even prohibit, changing on the beach. Use the changing rooms provided. Meanwhile, in the Texan resort of South Padre Island there's a byelaw prohibiting visitors from wearing neckties. Ties were proving to be a discordant, non-relaxing diversion to the ordinary business of seriously relaxing. Who would want to relax in a tie! Who would even bother to ban wearing ties!

CULTURAL EXPECTATIONS

Two stories from the Washington suburbs illustrate differences between American and British cultural expectations that permeate everyday life.

Easy familiarity

A reasonably well-dressed British professor is walking through University Park near the University of Maryland, a neighbourhood of well-maintained detached homes, each with open front lawns. No fences or hedges here. Trees line the sidewalks, and though inner-city problems are but a dozen miles away here all is sweetness and light. In the distance a small child is pedalling like fury towards the pedestrian. Their paths cross and the child looks up at the adult and says 'Hi' with no hesitation or affectation, an outburst of familiarity that takes the British pedestrian aback. Before he can think of anything to say the child has pedalled on and away, bound presumably for home or for a friend's.

With careful politeness and easy informality the child has both confused the visitor and at the same time confirmed a very American experience. It has obviously never occurred to the child, particularly on its own turf, to be silent, or to wait to be spoken to. On the sidewalk of life a child and a passing adult are equal. Such a democratic assumption would never have been made in the academic's own youth back in careful, deferential Britain. In a small way this tiny episode confirms what so many Europeans find so endearing about the USA. And yet that Christmas the same situation was reversed in a not dissimilar suburb not that far away.

No pedestrians here

It is getting dark, and a Scottish family have spent their sixth American Christmas opening presents, watching television and overeating, much as must be happening across the land. But though it has been a cold day there is no wind, and so the assembled revellers decide to brave the chill to walk off their turkey feast, the better to make room for home-made Christmas pudding. The air is so still and bracing no one makes a sound as they crunch their way down the path to the road and set off to walk around the block. No one speaks, it is so cold. Thinking of their forthcoming treat they hurry along wishing there were sidewalks in such residential neighbourhoods.

No provision is made for pedestrians in such new neighbourhoods: no one ever expected any. Which is what the neighbours must have thought when they looked out of their windows and saw four or five figures moving silently down the street. The quiet is only broken by the arrival of the local police, who are neither happy to be called out on such a night, nor sympathetic to the proffered explanation of a pre-Christmas pudding ramble. To the local cops the scene is so bizarre there must be something untoward going on. No one walks in such a neighbourhood, and certainly not in the dark, and most definitely not on Christmas Day.

The moral is...

Is there a moral to be drawn from these two incidents? Only that America too is a mass of contradictions, but ones that may only be evident to a foreigner. How you respond to such differing ideas about something as initially trivial as walking down the road can make all the difference to your stay. But it's the common language that makes us expect the Americans will be like us. When they are not we are offended, as if they have no right to behave like foreigners.

Living in the present

Americans love and ignore the past. There is an almost pathological obsession with the present and particularly the present as harbinger of the future. To say that someone is 'history' is to consign them to the ultimate waste bin. But aren't Americans obsessed with nostalgia? Yes they are, but not with the past in all its confusing and contradictory detail. Put on an exhibition at the Smithsonian in Washington DC which outlines what really happened when Americans moved out west and every patriotic organisation in the country accuses the museum of being unpatriotic, for insulting the flag, for undermining children's faith in the righteousness of the USA and its history.

The positive side of the militant amnesia is that Americans rarely worry about where someone (or at least a white person) is from, only where they are bound. Few ask about where you went to school or college. Even fewer ask about families, unless they have already met with them. Families are in the past. It is the here and now that counts. So the past is only useful to the degree that it helps boost our entry into the future. Leaders who can capture this sense of movement can get away with almost anything else, witness John Kennedy, Ronald Reagan and even Bill Clinton. Where some may want to rake up the past, most Americans respond to appeals to look forward to the New Frontier or just Tomorrow. Candidates who seem to look backwards, such as Dole, Kerry and Gore are 'history'.

Ideals and ideologies

It is traditional for Europeans to berate Americans for their failure to live up to their own high ideals. Slavery and race relations have long been used as a stick with which to beat the Americans. And yet the USA went to war with itself to retain slavery within the Union where it could be dealt with rather than allow the slave states to leave and go their own way. And though American race relations may indeed seem less than idyllic, few other countries have so publicly addressed the issue.

Despite massive economic inequalities, Americans still desperately try to provide education and employment mechanisms with which the poor can work their way out of poverty. And nowhere else have gays and lesbians been so successful in changing the nature of the debate over private and public sexuality, despite the presence of a massive and powerful religious right wing which abhors them.

In a country that seems totally secular, in that there can be no official celebration of the religious (as opposed to the pagan) dimensions of Christmas (the official White House tree has no manger), more people believe in a supreme being and regularly attend a place of worship than in any other developed country.

How such contradictions are sustained within the one country without open war breaking out is a constant source of amazement. The present unruly behaviour of various militia suggests that deep divisions are not always as well dealt with as many would like to believe. But, despite a history of lynching, gangsters, riots and chronic deaths by gunshot wounds, the United States does generally manage to hold together more than perhaps it is generally realised by pessimistic locals and snooty outsiders. Distance has something to do with it, as well as a deeply held general belief in the Constitution, one of those paradoxes when a land seemingly so lawless and focused upon the present professes such faith upon a legal document from deep in America's past.

Passion and opinions

American enthusiasms often manifest themselves in rampant overstatement, quite the opposite of British understatement. Where the beer glass is definitely half empty, for the American the same glass is half full, a far more positive, primary-colour view of the world. With a vigour and simplicity that can bewilder Europeans, Americans argue over divine creationism or Darwinian evolution, race and IQ, choice and abortion, with passion that, though it can break out into street violence, more often than not remains theatrical, like the rabid sermons and political advertisements that would be frowned upon, if not prohibited, in more pastel-shaded European countries, where we prefer to hedge our opinions behind notions of privacy and compromise. Perhaps Europeans have seen the face of Nazi extremism too recently to stray too near the edge. But for a visitor, naked passion American-style can be both invigorating and frightening. For a sample, view almost any of Louis Theroux's television programmes from the USA.

Dodging the issue can seem an unacceptably dangerous form of prevarication compared to the full frontal crudity of American naiveté, which can often become evident in what appears as plain American rudeness. As a student in the 1960s I was given a fantastic present by my sister: my first hippie jeans. To celebrate my going to America she took the pair and sewed enormous triangular patches into the legs, opening them out to become hugely flared. I could see from my mother's face she was not amused, for such alterations had clearly ruined a perfectly decent pair of casual trousers. But she said not a word. Nor did anyone else as I took off to London and away.

Standing waiting for a bus in New York only a few days later, people kept commenting, unfavourably, upon my weird appearance, often to my face. My hair, short by British standards, was deemed far too long for respectable people who felt they had a duty to tell me so, and my two-tone flared pants were an obvious insult to American life that could not go unchallenged.

As the years went by such 'far out' clothes became ever more common across America, and my clothes became of ever less interest to casual passers-by. But I always remembered how similar were the opinions of my mother's generation both in Britain and America, but whereas she had bottled up her opinions, Americans had felt quite at liberty to express theirs. Perhaps the British will one day silently disapprove less obviously and the Americans keep their opinions to themselves more, but I somehow doubt it.

Enjoying the differences

America can be a very exhausting experience for the newcomer. When British visitors arrive it is often very hot and humid and distances are immense. How reassuring that we share the same language and thus the same opinions, expectations and general attitudes towards the world. When Americans turn out to be so very different it can be quite wounding, as if they have somehow let us down, tricked us into thinking they were part of the family, taken us for a ride. But stay in there. The differences can be enjoyed. Some of their ways of doing things might even be better than ours. And once home we may find ourselves appreciating some of our own quirky ways just that little bit more.

Smoking and smokers

The campaign against smoking has now reached the outdoors. Fancy nipping out of the office for a quick puff during your coffee break? Well, many cities such as Davis and Palo Alto in California have now banned smoking within 20 feet of the entrance of any building open to the public. So can smokers hide in the park during their lunch hour? Not in the Houston suburbs where smoking in the park now brings a $500 fine.

Non-smokers who have long suffered colleagues smoking during meetings, over lunch and even between courses at a posh do may well find it difficult to sympathise with smokers being increasingly ostracised. But the whole nature of smoking in the US does reflect a recurrent US preoccupation; when a new idea comes along America tends to take it on board in a big way. Cigarette butts on the beach are not particularly pleasant, though compared to sewage coming in on the tide must surely be a fairly minor problem in the great scheme of things. But in Sharon Massachusetts it is now illegal to smoke in any recreation area, while in New York City it is illegal to smoke in any sports stadium.

Why do so many Americans insist that what they dislike should be made illegal rather than just frowned upon? After all, marijuana is still outlawed, except for medicinal purposes in California. Alcohol was outlawed for years between the world wars in a great experiment that merely handed power to gangsters. Well, partly it goes back to American's very foundation as a series of communities dedicated to establishing new and better communities, little utopias where peer-group pressure to conform was generally confirmed by law. If you insisted as a Quaker on not taking your hat off in the presence of authority you would be expelled from the community, and if you kept returning you ran a serious risk of being executed. The presence of anyone with a radically different view could not be tolerated, for to do so would be to allow the devil, or at least an enemy of the community, to prosper. Do not be taken in by American claims religious toleration goes back to Puritan times. Such toleration as exists in the USA emerged mostly as a pragmatic response to the growing religious diversity evident as the once-isolated colonies became ever more integrated into a USA where people realised that to ensure they were not themselves harassed for their beliefs they would have to agree to leave others alone. Such a pragmatic view of religious toleration is a far cry from the Quaker tradition of encouraging diversity as happened in Pennsylvania, but rarely elsewhere. America is often seen as the 'last, best hope for mankind', and so to act against community norms is seen as deeply disturbing, whether it was radical views in the 1950s or long hair in the 1960s. How can people then be permitted to kill themselves and to threaten the very air others breathe? By this logic smoking is not just a disgusting habit but a threat to the moral fibre of the nation. And that of course has to be dealt with in a formal, legal manner.

It produces some very strange situations: the tobacco state of South Carolina has notices at every entrance of its public buildings reminding people that smoking is forbidden within, even though most of the buildings will have been financed by tobacco sales taxes and taxes on the wages of tobacco workers. It would be like finding a 'No Scotch Whisky Drinking Permitted Within' sign being fastened to every post office, school building, university lecture theatre and so forth across the whole of Scotland. Actually some bourbon-producing counties in Tennessee do not permit alcohol consumption within the county.

SHOPPING

Shopping centres

In the late 1960s and early 1970s going from Britain to the USA was perhaps most dramatic in the contrast between how and where people shopped. The rise of huge British out-of-town shopping centres, hypermarkets and covered precincts had somewhat reduced the contrast by the 1990s.

Learn from others' mistakes: don't let your first bag of US groceries melt into a useless mass before you even get it home!

- *Frozen foods must go straight home by car, in a cool bag.*
- *If you must go shopping on foot do it as late as possible each day, and always keep out of the sun.*
- *Don't expect shopping to be just like home only on a bigger scale. With all the choice you can feel like a rabbit transfixed by oncoming headlights.*

Today the differences for the middle classes are not so noticeable as a generation ago. Tesco's, Sainsbury's and Morrisons have covered Britain with stores, almost, though not quite, like US supermarkets. But whereas in Britain the out-of-town centres (such as Metro Centre in Tyne and Wear) are the exception (and still newsworthy), thousands of such suburban shopping malls exist across the USA. By the late 1980s Washington DC already had more than 15 that made a claim to be malls, half a dozen of which were modern and purpose built.

Downtown

And as such out-of-town shopping proliferated the downtown department stores dramatically declined, squeezed between suburban discounts (boxed hi-fi at cut prices but with no after-sales service) and specialist shops built into malls (on the main axis between two rival supermarkets). The expansion of jobs out in the suburbs took many commuters away from the central business district, and the impoverished inner-city population couldn't support the same level of retail sales. The downtown seemed doomed.

But the last 20 years have seen a rejuvenation of many downtown centres (Boston and Baltimore are two of the most well known). Department stores have been revitalised, speciality shops have been reopened, and conferences, tourists and yuppies have moved in. Even so, the downtown shopping will never dominate the whole metropolis as it once did. Rather, downtown will be just one of many shopping opportunities for the well-heeled and mobile middle class.

The USA is more abroad than most Brits expect

Remember this and you'll not expect things to be quite the same as at home, and so it won't throw you off quite so much when things turn out differently from what you expected. If you are used to a range of small family businesses and shops in a town centre you may find shopping in the USA very strange. If you are already familiar with the fortnightly stock-up trips to your local hypermarket after work you'll hardly notice the difference, except for the wider range of foods. And if you think self-service salad bars in Asda are a novelty, US stores have had them for years.

Opening hours

Opening hours tend to be longer than even the most 'open' of British supermarkets, 24 hours a day seven days a week (often known merely as 7/24 on signs) being not uncommon in large cities (though rare in small towns). Shopping hours in downtown department stores are more likely to be nearer to those in Britain, closing time being about 6.00 pm, though even here a late night opening may be available. Malls tend to close about 10.00 pm, with their department stores remaining open 9.00 am to 9.00 pm. 10.00 pm is a common time for supermarkets to close.

Blue Laws

Just as Sunday opening was for so long a mess in the UK, so in the USA often complicated local options determine Sunday opening. Blue Laws are those laws restricting Sunday opening, not the selling of pornography. Generally, Sunday opening hours tend to be more limited than other days of the week, and though liquor will still be on the shelves, it may only be for sale at certain times. Sunday opening laws tend to be enforced in the USA.

Drugstores

These are more than chemists, though not so unusual for those who have watched British chemists diversify over the years. Stationery, hardware, some clothes, certain foods, perhaps liquor and usually snacks with soft drinks are generally available. Look for the green cross for the pharmacy section (or the Mercurial twisted snake symbol, also in green).

Buying clothes and shoes

The good news:
■ Most clothing, especially where cotton-based, is usually cheaper than in Britain. It may not be American any more (though if it is, a 'union-made' label may tell you so, as on Oshkosh children's clothes). Expect a pair of 501s to cost half the UK price in any factory outlet or mall.

■ British made clothes cost less (a Burberry trench coat will be about a third off the UK price, plus tax at about 9 per cent) – but beware of overpriced luxury goods such as Italian handbags. DKNY bags, though, may be half the UK price.

The bad news:
■ Ignore descriptive sizes. Is 'large' used in comparison to 'small' and 'medium', or 'extra-large' and 'jumbo'? Who knows!? Try clothes on.

■ Women's sizes appear to be but aren't the same as in Britain. A UK 12 is a US 10, and 10 an 8, and so on.

■ For footwear it's the other way around, a British 9 being a US 10 (or perhaps more like a 10½).

More bad news:
■ Average width is often the only shoe fitting available, though these tend to be wider than in the UK.

■ Expect poor standards of service in shoe shops and shoe departments of large stores (remember *Married with Children* is based around a shoes salesman). If you are used to the trained personal service of British shoe shops you are in for a disappointment. The immediate sale is what's important, not cultivating a regular clientele.

Any ways around this?

- If you like fashionable shoes and can jam your feet into average widths, shoe shopping won't be too bad.

- If you can get away with wearing work boots, these are often excellent value (and often imported from Eastern Europe!). US-made cowboy boots are magnificent and with good care can last for years, if not decades. The author's first pair was still being resoled, 20 years after being picked up in a sale.

- Many Americans side-step the problem by using **mail order**. There are specialist firms who meet this problem by offering an excellent service, at a cost, through the post. Increasingly such firms have a presence on the web.

- Keep your eyes peeled for shoes available through factory outlets by the side of motorways. These can turn up in the most out of the way places (like firework stores in southern states). Discounts range from 20–70 per cent, with all the excitement of a bargain.

Clothing sizes

Ladies wear	S		M		L		XL	
UK sizes	8	10	12	14	16	18	20	22
US sizes	6	8	10	12	14	16	18	20
Fits bust	31	32	34	36	37	38	40	42
Fits waist	24	25	26	27	29	31	33	34
Menswear	**S**		**M**		**L**		**XL**	
Neck (ins)	14	14½	15	15½	16	16½	17	17½
(cms)	36	37	38	39	41	42	43	44
Chest (ins)	34	36	38	40	42	44	46	48
(cms)	85	91	96	101	106	112	117	122
Ladies' shoes								
UK sizes	4½	5	5½	6	6½	7	7½	8
US sizes	6	6½	7	7½	8	8½	9	9½
European	37	38	39	40	41	42	43	44
Men's shoes								
UK size	6	7	8	9	10	11	11½	12
US size	7	8	9	10	11	12	12½	13
European	40	41	42	43	44	45	46	47
Children's Clothing								
Approx. height (ins)	39	40	45	48	49	51	53	55
US sizes	4	5	6	6½	7	8	10	12

Mail order

Sears Roebuck of Chicago produce what is probably the most well-known catalogue (nearly a million items). Since rural free delivery was introduced by the US Post Office in 1892, urban suppliers have been able to provide, if not the very latest, at least modern fashion and consumer goods to anyone anywhere. As people moved off the land and into the suburbs they kept their faith in the mail order catalogues. This means that mail order firms generally cater for a more up-market, even specialist, clientele than in Britain. Mail order firms deal directly with customers not via an agent (whose commission would either put up prices or eat away profits). Unlike in Britain mail order is not payment by instalment, but by money order (or today increasingly by charge card over the phone).

Specialised mail order is more developed than in Britain, though if you regularly use garden equipment and supplies catalogues or buy outdoor casual clothes (as from Rohan) you will already be familiar with the general standards and procedures. Specialist catalogues tend to be more exotic than in Britain, and in many states include firearms (or 'sporting goods' as they are often called) as if they were little more than fishing rods and trainers!

Buying non-clothing goodies

The good news:
■ CDs and DVDs remain consistently cheaper in the USA.

■ Cameras are consistently cheaper too.

■ Children's toys are usually cheaper, even for items in Toys R Us that operate in both countries and source their toys from the same manufacturers.

■ Bed linen is consistently cheaper, as are most cotton products.

■ Computer software is usually cheaper and can be used in both countries.

The bad news:
■ American DVDs are group 1, but UK players generally only play group 2 (or require potentially costly adjustments which may invalidate the warranty).

■ US computer software may be cheaper than in the UK but may not be suitable for use over here (tax guides, dictionaries, encyclopaedias with a US focus for its history, geography and politics).

- Electrical goods run off different voltages, so avoid US bargains if returning to the UK.

- Though US bed linen is good value sizes can be quite different, and duvet covers are more difficult to obtain than in the UK.

Shopping for food

Most urban people buy their produce from the fruit and vegetable sections of their local supermarket. The quality is debatable. Certainly fruit is huge and piled high, and is available all year independent of the passing of the seasons. Whether forced giant strawberries have any flavour, though, is hotly argued. Word has it square strawberries are being grown for ease of shipment! And when you get it all home, wash it to get the chemicals off. Some fruits even have a wax covering that needs to be removed.

The good news:
- Many cities have **roadside fruit and vegetable stalls** along the highways in the surrounding counties. Peaches, for instance, can be bought in season very cheaply from these roadside stalls, and it's very common to stop off and load up on the way back home from a weekend away.

- Many cities have **farmers' markets** downtown in a Covent Garden-like hall. Fresh food is brought in from local farms and is often excellent and reasonably priced. Food stalls at such markets can be a great treat – everything from pizzas to oysters (in Baltimore at least, with draught beer too!) Taxi drivers, government employees, policemen and visitors will all nip in for a bite to eat, so the quality tends to be fairly good, with prices reasonable. Towns such as Knoxville, Tennessee, that are trying to redevelop a decaying downtown are encouraging farmers' markets adjacent to downtown malls and theatres as a way of retaining, or attracting back, a sense of activity downtown, so quality is encouraged. If in the national capital try visiting Pennsylvania Avenue SE (behind the Capitol).

More bad news?

- The US is based upon the fruits of mutual distrust. You will often see the sign 'If you broke it you just bought it', hardly the most welcoming of approaches to a casual shopper.

■ CD and book stores often will not let you take any bags into their shops, for fear of shoplifting. Don't take it too personally; they distrust everyone. Security will take the offending bag at the door, usually in exchange for a token.

■ Don't forget that on return to the UK you are liable for VAT and duty for all goods over an allowance of £145 per adult, and that includes clothing, shoes, luggage and those CDs that seemed such a bargain.

Mutual distrust seems to lead naturally enough to lawyers and doctors. As a rule of thumb:

Get good insurance cover
Keep your head down
Get a good lawyer

LAWYERS AND LEGAL FEES

The USA seems to be a society held together by litigation – commerce by other means? The roots of this may well be in the written nature of the Constitution, or conversely the need to regularise relationships in those areas not adequately policed by the Constitution. This is, after all, a free-trade economy operating under the rules of *laissez-faire* capitalism. The USA is overtly and militantly a property-owning democracy. A major role for contract law seems almost inevitable.

US lawyers generally work on a contingent fee basis ('**no win no fee**'). This used to be illegal in Britain based on the fear that it would encourage lawyers to win at any price (else they don't get paid), with a concern not for the case *per se* but for the fee. The advantage the Americans would point out is that in the USA poor people can afford to take large corporations to law knowing that if they lose they will not be stuck with fees to pay. If they win they pay their lawyers a percentage of the awarded damages.

Unfortunately this often leads to lawyers going for vast sums, playing on widespread dislike of larger corporations, such as insurance companies, to boost their take. The result is that insurance premiums, for instance, have skyrocketed, and may now be so high that certain groups can now no longer obtain cover. Commerce by other means indeed! But 'payment by results' is deeply ingrained in the American system. Watch *Ally McBeal* or *Boston Legend* repeats for a view of what this can entail. If you do hire a lawyer on a non-contingency basis expect enormous fees.

As a tourist or medium-stay visitor the only rule of thumb is probably to make sure that you carry adequate **insurance**: health, car and uninsured driver (where you insure yourself against being hit by someone you might have to sue but who hasn't any money or any cover of their own).

HEALTH CARE

US doctors are world famous. Given the amount of debt incurred to get a medical degree high fees are only to be expected. The doctors' 'plight' is helped by the fact that when we are ill everything gets focused upon getting better, so we are vulnerable in the market place – we'll pay what it takes, and doctors know that. To exacerbate the situation most medical fees are paid by the insurance company, so the sick are even less price sensitive. Add to this the doctors' fear of being sued for failure to diagnose correctly something nasty and you have a mass of tests that are deemed standard, are expensive, and anyway the insurance companies will pay up, so what the heck.

To cover themselves most doctors pay over $80,000 in malpractice and accident insurance premiums each year – and that's before any costs! So health care is expensive. Getting the prescription filled, of course, costs extra too! Expect to pay at least $300 a month for a couple for health insurance, and then you still have to pay 20 per cent of the bill. People with chronic problems may not be able to obtain insurance, and end up paying $500 a month for medication, lab work, vitamins and visits to a GP.

Planning ahead

Most British visitors to the USA will enjoy a healthy, hassle-free time. Planning ahead for your health needs can ensure that whatever illnesses you encounter will not be medically or financially catastrophic.

- There are no specific health requirements for the USA, though if you intend to go backpacking or camping out in the wilds it is worthwhile considering a **tetanus** shot. If you were immunised as a child now is a good opportunity to go for a booster shot.

- If taking children whose full course of **vaccinations** have yet to be completed consult your GP.

- If you need **prescribed medicines** check you have the appropriate forms. Fortunately finding a pharmacy in the USA should be no problem. Carry a letter from your GP outlining your drug requirements to ensure passage though US and later UK customs.

■ Avoid over-the-counter cold medicines which contain codeine, a proscribed substance requiring a prescription in the USA.

■ Have a **dental check up**: dental work is very costly in the USA. Any toothache can play havoc with holiday or travel plans.

Insurance

There is NO reciprocal health care agreement between the UK and the USA – so adequate health care insurance is essential. You will need 'worldwide' cover, with $10 million medical cover per person and at least $25,000 legal cover. A three week summer trip for a healthy adult will cost about £25, with special discounts for a family travelling together.

Florida visitors should beware of 'sea-bather's eruption'. This is a large rash caused by jellyfish larvae that sting when trapped within bathing costumes. Bikinis retain fewer larvae than one-piece costumes and so produce less rash.

Elderly visitors may need to approach specialist companies. MRL Insurance (0870 845 0050) specialises in policies for those over 65. Single-trip policies are available as well as multi-trip policies from about £150. The Association of British Insurers has a fact sheet on holiday insurance (call 020 7600 3333 for a copy).

You can now buy your insurance online (and print the documents yourself). Simple-to-use sites include *www.columbusdirect.net* and *www.1stoptravelinsurance. co.uk.*

Further information

Dr Richard Dawood, *The Traveller's Health* (Oxford University Press, 4th edition) or the Cadogan Guide *Bugs, Bites and Bowels* (2006) by Jane Wilson-Howarth.

AIDS

There is no vaccine or cure for AIDS. You cannot catch the infecting virus from everyday contact, from mosquitos, insect bites or from swimming in the motel pool.

Infection comes from sexual contact with an infected person or from infected blood. To protect yourself:

- Do NOT have sex with anyone other than your usual partner.

- If you do have sex with someone else ALWAYS use a condom (US = 'rubber').

- Do not inject illegal drugs, and never share needles.

- Ensure any blood transfusion involves screened blood.

- Have enough insurance cover for first class treatment in any medical emergency.

Medical checklist

- Take a small first aid kit – adhesive dressing packet, insect repellent, antiseptic cream (kits can be bought from major chemists or the AA).

- Personal hygiene is vital – always wash your hands (US = 'wash up') before handling food, particularly if camping.

- Skin piercing (ears, tattooing, acupuncture) is unwise in unfamiliar circumstances.

- Take insect and animal bites seriously – use repellent cream, cover arms and legs in wooded areas. Ask about local poisonous plants such as poison ivy.

- Avoid hypothermia – take padded winter clothing, hats and gloves for all but the most southern states in winter.

- Avoid sunstroke – hats, sunglasses and plenty of fluids anywhere in the summer.

THE US TELEPHONE SYSTEM

The popular view abroad is that the US phone system is the best in the world, being the cheapest and the most efficient. Many Americans might have agreed with you before the break-up of the Bell System. Today the system is more complex and opinions remain divided as to its efficiency and cheapness. Certainly Americans use the phone at least twice as much as the British. Economies of scale should pay dividends for both users and the phone companies. In the big cities such as Washington DC the system is generally very good for the casual user. Push-button and computerised directory enquiries arrived long before in the UK, and most phones can do tricks that have only recently appeared in Britain, such as transferring calls when you are out.

Tones

As soon as you pick up the phone you should hear a constant buzz (unless it's a payphone). The ringing tone is long with long pauses. A short bleep means the number is engaged: you got the 'busy signal'.

Numbers

All numbers fall into a standard system unlike in Britain: typically (987) 654 3210, where the numbers in brackets are the area code and the first three digits the exchange. You may be surprised to find that US phones still have letters along with numbers. Sometimes numbers are given in an appropriate word form: (800) USA-RAIL for the public railroad Amtrack. Be careful not to confuse the number 0 (zero) with the letter O which is the same as the number 6.

The other symbols and * which are still rarely used on domestic British phones are only involved if you want to programme your phone to do things like transfer calls to other numbers. The only trick you'll find useful is to push the * at the end of punching in an international number (it means: that's it, go ahead and call this number).

The main problem for travellers comes from using public phones for calling outside the immediate local area. Local calls are easy. Just dial the last seven numbers. Unfortunately not all calls within the same area code are deemed local. Calls outside the immediate vicinity are called 'long distance' even if you don't consider the distance to be very far. **You need to place a 1 in front of the seven numbers** as in 1-654-3210. For long distance calls with a different area code (as would always be the case if calling another state, and might be the case within a large state such as New York or California) use a 1 followed by the area code plus the seven digit number, as in 1-(987) 654 3210.

Charges

Most calls except from hotel or motel rooms are comparatively cheap, especially within the local area. Long-distance calls from private phones are itemised on the next bill so you can pay back friends precisely what you owe them. Cheap rates apply from 5.00 pm to 11.00 pm Sunday through to Friday, with bargain rates from 11.00 pm to 8.00 am daily, all day Saturday and 8.00 am to 5.00 pm Sundays. Use a private phone where possible as it's considerably cheaper than payphones.

Public telephones

You may have difficulty finding these in certain areas, such as many residential neighbourhoods. Try anywhere people congregate (launderette, gas station, 7–11 store, etc.). Post offices do not generally have telephones as in much of Europe.

Usually you'll need a fist if not a bag full of loose change. You have to put in the minimum fee (which varies from 25c to 35c) just to start the process. If you end up reaching an engaged number you'll get your coins back. The money gets you the dial tone and a local call, still of unlimited duration in some areas. Even to call the operator on a free number ('toll free') you'll need to start the process off with the minimum fee, which you'll get back.

If you dial a long-distance number a voice will cut in to tell you how much more to put into the machine. As the largest coin is 25c you'll need lots of these handy, and your call will be for a three-minute minimum whether or not you want three minutes. Where you get hold of $2.75 in quarters in the middle of nowhere at three in the morning to call ahead and warn your hosts that you've had a flat tyre is not the company's problem. They probably can't understand why you aren't calling 'collect' or charging the call to your own phone account. You may end up having to hope your friends will accept the call. For collect calls within the USA call 1-800-COLLECT.

If you have an account with a US phone company you can use special phone boxes that take US-issued credit cards, but these are usually only available in large airports. Calls based upon price rather than time are rarely available, and again usually only from major airports.

One gleam of light comes in the form of pre-paid phone cards by such long distance carriers as AT&T, MCI or GTI available at airports and some car rental outlets in 10, 25 or 50 units. You can use these almost anywhere by quoting a reference number. Some cards can be recharged by phone. You may have problems using a card for local calls, especially if using a rival company's card. Pick up a leaflet at the rental desks, where you can rent phones (at large airports).

Calling home

The international prefix is 011, which should be followed by the UK code (44), then the British area code minus the initial 0, followed by the number. A call home then might be 011-44-(20) 723 4567. To use a BT chargecard to reverse the charges call 1-800 44 55667 (which gets you through to a UK operator), then give the UK code plus local number in full. For the local US international operator punch in 00 (zero zero) or 10288 00 (if from a non-AT&T phone). But: for direct dials calls punch in 0 (zero) and check out that 'I-triple-D' is available in your area. For local operator chargecard calls ask for the AT&T International Operator Center. For international information call 1-800-874-4000, a free service (as are all 800 calls). As local operators in rural areas may not be able to help you place a call home from a public or motel phone (they may never have been asked for this service before, or if they have you may not be able to understand what they say) this number can be very useful. Telephone boxes rarely have the kind of information about making calls that is normal back home, and telephone books probably won't help either.

Some useful numbers

- Local directory enquiries — 411
- Non-local directory enquiries with the same area code — 1-55 1212
- Directory enquiries for numbers with other area codes — 1-111-555 1212
- To find an area code — 411
- Operator — 0
- International operator — 00 (or 10288 00 if from non-AT&T phone)
- Emergency services — 911
- Wrong number dialled — 211
- Toll-free numbers directory — 1-800-555 1212
- Cash call to UK — 011 44 (plus UK number less initial zero)
- UK direct (for BT chargecards and collect calls) — 1-800-445 5688 (AT&T) 1-800-825 4904 (Sprint) 1-800-854 4826 (MCI)
- UK direct (for Cable and Wireless calling cards) — 1-800-500 0544 (AT&T) 1-800-500 245 (MCI) 1-800-844 4220 (CWI)

Calling from your own phone

Increasingly visitors to the USA want to use their own mobiles. Make sure your mobile is appropriate for the US system. If you just pop into a busy phone shop and ask for a phone that will work 'abroad', you may end up with one that only helps if you happen to be in Ibiza rather than Orlando. Model specifications are changing so rapidly that any particular details will be out of date by the time this book comes out. But if you know to ask specifically about using your new mobile in the US that's half the battle. If overwhelmed by phone shops try the newsagent first and have a look at the wide variety of magazines helping make sense of each new wave of phone technology, such as T3 (*Tomorrow's Technology Today*) which also has a website (*www.t3.co.uk*). You can of course rent a mobile when you arrive, most conveniently at the car rental desk, but of course though you then have the convenience of calling people, with no need to find piles of quarters for public phones, no one knows your number unless you call them first, and all those calls that are going to your existing number are just stacking up for your return.

For a website article 'Why mobile phones can be a challenge' take a look at a delightful site explaining all things electrical: *http://kropla.com/mobilephones.htm*.

WHAT TO READ ON THE USA

There are plenty of general books on the USA. Visit your local public library and you'll find anything from a row to a room full of books on various aspects of US history, geography, politics, literature, economics and travel. But more up-to-date information for the traveller has to be sought elsewhere. The larger the bookshop the larger the choice of up-to-date guidebooks. Large city shops such as Dillons in central London or Blackwells in Oxford may well have a whole wall just on the Americas (North and South) plus as many more on general travel hints. However, since the first edition of this book, even the smallest market town bookshop seems to have acquired a selection that would have been unheard of in big cities only 20 years ago.

A vast influx of British visitors to the USA has grown since the dollar was considerably higher than today with a new wave of articles in papers such as the *Daily Mail*, the *Guardian*, *The Financial Times*, and the *Observer*. Keep an eye on travel pages for up-to-date information (though beware: some articles result from trips paid for by specific sponsors who may well have set a schedule to make the most of their good points). However, more reliable information can be found in *Travel Which?* back numbers which are available in your local public library or, to members online, The *Independent's* Saturday 'Travel Update' is particularly useful.

In trying to decide which guidebook is for you, remember that:

■ Practical information varies in degrees of detail. Guidebooks are most likely to be useful for background information on history, food and the popular sights. If using their practical travelling details check the date of publication as important details can vary substantially from year to year. This is particularly so for library copies, which are usually older editions than in the bookshops. Certain guides are updated each and every year, and usually make this a selling point.

■ Accommodation lists can be detailed and thoroughly inspected, the personal choice of the author, or the result of users' anecdotal reports (unchecked by anyone). You have to check how and when any guidebook is compiled.

Types of guide

The degree of detail varies considerably and deliberately. There are several types of guide:

■ **General travel** – may be a guide to travelling in general throughout the world, where the USA section is small, possibly superficial and only one of many country-by-country offerings, and so is inadequate for any serious traveller. On the plus side they may have information applicable everywhere including the USA if interpreted intelligently. A good example would be Ingrid Cranfield's *The Traveller's Handbook*, published by Heinemann. More specifically see Maggie and Gemma Moss, *Handbook for Women Travellers*, published by Piatkus (London, 1987) which though 20 years old, has important things to say. A website that supports women who travel alone or in groups: *www.transitionsabroad.com/listings/travel/woman/index.shtml*.

■ **USA-at-large sightseeing guides** are useful for general essays on regions like the South, the West Coast, and so forth, plus general essays on US society, history, geography and climate. A typical example would be *Fodor's USA* guide, regularly updated (also available in parts for various regions and cities).

■ **Budget guides** are geared mainly to young people on tight budgets, but their up-to-date practical hints, phone numbers, recommendations and warnings can be invaluable for all visitors. An example would be *Rough Guides* or *Lonely Planet* (*www.lonelyplanet.co.uk*).

■ **Pocket guides** are just that, but they can be very useful, especially if dealing with a specific region or city. Berlitz guides are the most well known example. Beware, though, that some pocket guides assume you are six feet tall with large anorak pockets, not 5′4″ with only the pocket in the back of your shorts.

Specific guidebooks

Here are some of the major guides you are likely to find readily available:

- **AA guides** in the City Pack series are increasingly available for such US cities as San Francisco, Boston, New York and Washington DC. These modern, readable and useful guides are attractively laid out with good photographs, hints for seeing sights and using public transport, plus the general history and geography of the city. Copies are paperback, but in plastic covers (with a useful pull-out city map). They are not cheap, and may be too detailed for a quick visit. Updating is not annual, so beware. Coverage of more US regions is increasingly available through the AA 'Explorer' series. Boston and New England, California and Florida are already available in the bookshops. The AA also provides a 'Touring Guides' series which already includes *One the Road California* and *Touring Florida*. For state maps with detailed Interstate maps the AA issue a *Big Road USA Atlas*, though equivalent US versions are readily available once you arrive in the USA, and they are usually more up to date.

- **Berlitz Travel Guides** are cheap and cheerful; attractive to read, authoritative and carefully compiled. Some are updated each year. They are truly pocket guides, and the Florida volume in particular is good value. The colour maps are a bit garish, but nonetheless useful.

- **Fodor Guides** offer lots of practical information whether on the whole of the USA or on specific regions. They are, however, full collections of facts, though being regularly updated they offer a vital measure of assistance when arriving in a strange city on a countrywide tour. The Washington DC volume is quite useful. The *Fodor Budget Guide* to US cities is an abbreviated version of the national volume with some useful hints for budget travellers. Fodor also provide guides for adjacent areas – Canada, Latin America and the Caribbean. Newly commissioned volumes appear from time to time.

- **Michelin Green Guides** are for those with larger pockets (as in Rohan travel trousers). They cover regions and specific cities, the former for touring by car with an emphasis on historical sights, monuments and famous vistas. The city volumes are excellent, with clear maps and well-translated text (from the French originals), and they are particularly recommended for excursion suggestions, with consideration given for stays of various lengths. The New York City volume is excellent, with subway maps, bus routes and tours laid out, and includes covering material on the various neighbourhoods.

■ **Rough Guides** are, as their name suggests, aimed specifically at budget travellers, particularly the young (and young at heart). They tend to be more upbeat, and give the reader the feeling that the writer has actually enjoyed visiting the place in question. Practical facts are available, as well as historical and cultural information. All visitors may enjoy their concern for off-the-tourist-trail places to visit and things to do. The New York City edition is particularly interesting. Their strong points are that they are contemporary, well researched and at a reasonable price. However, they have a distinctly budget feel about them, compared, say, to the glossy Berlitz guides, which may put some people off. There's lots to see on their web page (www.roughguides.com).

■ **Virgin City Guides** deal with specific cities. The New York guide presents both areas and themes, starting with a neighbourhood by neighbourhood guide (where to eat, drink and shop) and then what to do (eat, drink and shop). If you're into fashion, fun and youth this is for you.

Finally there is a long-standing personal favourite:

■ **Traveller's USA and Canada Survival Kit** which is specifically geared towards young people, especially students able to spend at least a long summer in North America. Compiled by Susan Griffin and Simon Calder for Vacation Work, Oxford, it is periodically updated and costs about £10. There are sections on red tape, currency, health insurance, getting about, where to stay, living it up, and where to find the best buys with a wealth of things to do and to avoid, plus phone numbers. *Moneywise Guide to North America 2000* (BUNAC annually) is also a great Linus blanket if you ever get into a fix. Second-hand copies are available on Amazon.co.uk. *Let's Go USA* by Harvard Student Agencies is much the same, but has been updated for 2007.

What's suitable?

If you are spending some considerable time in one place, like New York City, you may find it worthwhile first checking out the range of books available from libraries. The larger the library the larger (and newer) the selection. Then visit a large bookshop if at all possible and browse for as long as you can. You'll need to ask yourself:

■ *How long in any one place?* If only a few days are involved, say in Florida, a pocket Berlitz will probably be enough. A week or more and a Fodor-like guidebook would be an investment.

■ *Is the guide for the car, coat pocket, or for shorts?* The large Fodor volumes are heavy and are definitely for the car, whereas a Michelin can be carried comfortably even in summer.

■ *How accurate and up to date must the information be for me?* If you are on a pre-paid tour by coach or even in conjunction with a particular motel chain you won't need vast amounts of budget accommodation information, so a borrowed copy giving general sights to see should be enough if you check your copy's date of publication, and make any necessary adjustment for inflation. If in doubt, ring ahead to the resort or attraction for current prices.

Longer stays

As you read such material you will come to realise that most of it refers to being on holiday, whether from a US or a UK base. People do, of course, spend up to several years on working holidays and these guides can be invaluable. But by and large these books don't cater for long-stay visitors' particular problems. For people actually living in the USA with their families a new type of guide is needed. Only gradually are such guides for living in the US appearing. You are reading one now!

For interest try also Roger W. Hicks and Frances Schultz, *Long Stays in America*, published by David & Charles, Newton Abbot, 1986. Despite an excellent cover the text's layout manages to hide a lot of excellent material. This is a book to read rather than to use as a reference source. Don't be put off by the poor quality and the irrelevance of the illustrations, not by its age. This is a roadmap to a foreign land.

Maps

These are not generally available for the USA, except those suitable for the motorist. Town plans in guides are often of little use except in the most general sense (to show the relative locations of the sights). Fortunately most US downtowns, but not all, are on a regular grid system so sketch maps of US inner cities are of more use than equivalents for European cities. Better town plans can be obtained locally or at specialist outlets in the UK. or increasingly online.

■ The Travel Bookshop also sells travel books and guides from its base in Notting Hill, London (*www.thetravelbookshop.com*).

■ Daunt Books (*www.dauntbooks.co.uk*) is an old-fashioned, Edwardian bookshop in Marylebone High Street in London.

- Stanford Map and Travel Bookshop has branches in Long Acre (near Covent Garden) and in Bristol and Manchester (*www.stanfords.co.uk*).

- The Map Shop in the High Street of Upton-upon-Severn has state by state lists (*www.themapshop.co.uk*).

- Bookland in central Chester on Bridge Street (next to Rohan) is a personal favourite with good service, modern facilities and an old shop feeling (*www.bookland.co.uk*).

The 'Let's Go' guidebook series has started to produce city maps that are pamphlet-sized and laminated for bad-weather use. *Let's Go Guide to New York City* also has 40 pages of essential information for under $10.

For those drivers who don't want to rely upon being able to pick up highway maps at petrol stations (and gone are the days when they were both plentiful and free!) the Rand McNally *Road Atlas* is now available in UK bookshops and it covers every state and most cities. It is a wonderful book to delve into, to work out new routes, or just to reminisce. It is very widely available throughout the USA – where you will probably find a cheaper and newer edition.

For details as to how to find local maps see Victor Selwyn's *Plan Your Route* published by David & Charles of Newton Abbot. See particularly Chapter 7 on the maps of the southwestern deserts.

US equivalents to the Ordnance Survey are not widely available to the general public, except in US Parks Service bookshops within National Parks. Topographical maps by the US Geological Survey are excellent if you can find them. US college bookshops usually stock their local maps.

State-by-state topographical ('topo') published in the USA by DeLorme Mapping Company are available in specialist stores and some large Waterstones. Not all states are yet issued, but others are in the pipeline. Their AAA 'Map'n'Go' CD-Rom is excellent. Visit their website at *www.delorme.com,* or try *www.mapquest.com* for maps for a given address or zip code. Coupled with *www.whitepages.com* this can be a powerful tool to find people and where they live. Then look down on them at Google Earth.

Other viewpoints

People from overseas have visited the USA since its founding and have written many guides for explorers, travellers, visitors, emigrants or just the readers back home.

■ Probably the most famous within the USA remains *The Domestic Manners of the Americans* by Mrs Frances Trollope, mother of the *Barchester Chronicles* author Anthony Trollope. Her comments from the 1830s are often unintentionally witty as she surveys the rise of the common man, slavery, utopian experiments and the new cities. Americans hated her. Mark Twain said it was because she'd hit the nail on the head. Later Charles Dickens did the grand tour, recording his impressions in *American Notes*, recently republished by Penguin in paperback. His novel *Martin Chuzzlewit* is also based upon much of this first-hand experience (and has a considerably more developed US section than appeared in the television version).

■ Recent views are numerous, and many are well worth reading. Any Jonathan Raban book is worth reading: he canoed the Mississippi for his *Old Glory*, a Picador paperback. Other academics have used the novel to explore the excitement and trauma of being a Brit in the USA. Malcolm Bradbury (of *History Man* fame) wrote *Stepping Westward*, an Arena paperback which both confirms and confounds the *Dallas* glamour of the West. Later David Lodge explored the late 1960s California through the eyes of an initially staid Birmingham university teacher in *Changing Places*, a Penguin paperback. If you don't manage to read these before you visit the USA you must do so upon your return!

■ Many British journalists have done the US road trip, ranging from Alistair Cooke in the 1940s (only recently published) to Jan Morris and Bill Bryson. All are worth reading (available through Amazon for well priced second-hand copies).

Americans on themselves

But what of Americans' *own* views of themselves? The list is endless. After all, most of what has ever been written in English has been written in the USA. The size and ethnic variety of the USA mean it is impossible really to read about America at large, except that many American writers were often engaged in satirising the narrowness and provincialism they sensed all about them at home.

The nineteenth century saw such great writers as **Walt Whitman**, whose *Leaves of Grass* has a freedom of line and a delight in the vernacular sounds of everyday life that exalt the promise of everything democratic while coming to terms with the reality of the Civil War slaughter. If ever visiting the battlefields read Whitman's elegies for the fallen (which of course came to include President Lincoln in 'When lilacs last in the doorway bloomed...'). **Mark Twain** too explored the quality of US society and what it was to be American (a still popular theme). His classics include the documentary *Life on the Mississippi* from which emerged his masterpiece *Huckleberry Finn* where a white child and a black slave together learn more about the ways of their world than they would wish to know, and in so doing throw into relief both America's promise and failings.

This sense that the US was finding it impossible to mature with honour recurs in **F. Scott Fitzgerald's** *The Great Gatsby* where the romantic view of American promise is shown to have been plundered by the rich, who, by the 1920s, have turned the US into little more than just another country, no worse and certainly little better than elsewhere.

The Great Depression of the 1930s confirmed this for many Americans at large. **John Steinbeck** explored the fate of many ordinary working people in those harsh times in *Of Mice and Men* (1937) and especially *The Grapes of Wrath* (1939), an epic struggle of the newly landless to survive the Dust Bowl of Oklahoma and their crushing disillusionment with the Promised Land of California. Both the book and the subsequent film (with Henry Fonda) remain classics.

This theme also affected much popular music. **Woody Guthrie's** *Dust Bowl Ballads* are still heard in the music of Bob Dylan in the 1970s, Ry Cooder in the 1980s, and Billy Bragg in the 1990s. Bruce Springsteen returned to this theme in his recent album *We Shall Overcome: The Seegar Sessions.*

Since the 1940s American writing has expanded beyond all bounds. Richard Wright's *Native Son* and Ralph Ellison's *Invisible Man* have opened up the black experience to an ever wider audience, though possibly the most eye-opening account remains Alex Haley's *The Autobiography of Malcolm X*, the posthumous story of the slain radical. Evan Hunter's *Streets of Gold*, a Corgi paperback, explores the New York immigrant experience more realistically though perhaps less commercially successful than Mario Puzo's *Godfather.*

This leads into mention of the **movies**, for *Godfather II* (1974) is one of the most accessible explorations of New York ethnic diversity life on the big screen, though Spike Lee's *Do The Right Thing* (1989) is more contemporary.

But New York City has been seen in many lights. All offer a glimpse that can lift the visitor into a world of both imagination and concrete reality: *The French Connection* (1971), *The Taking of Pelham 123* (1974), *Marathon Man* (1976), and *Midnight Cowboy* (1969), not to mention the disturbing *Taxi Driver* (1976). Even the *Stepford Wives* (1975) explores one threatening image of the suburbs as seen by the big-city enthusiast. *Three Days of the Condor* (1975) is very strong on downtown Manhattan and Washington Heights, though it is possibly television's *Law and Order* that best explores what many see as being the actual and threatening reality of New York City. Movie buffs can compare such television interpretations with the movies *Fort Apache the Bronx* (1981) and *Assault on Precinct 13* (1976) (though the latter is actually set in Los Angeles). Watch *Seven* (1995) if you dare. No wonder so many viewers prefer *Seinfeld* or *Friends* for their weekly view on New York's lighter side.

For a reminder that America is far more than New York or even New England try Carl Hiaasen's black comedy *Tourist Season* or Nicholas Evans' *The Horse Whisperer*. Southern society comes through in John Berendt's *Midnight in the Garden of Good and Evil* or any of Patricia Cornwell's forensic novels (not for the squeamish).

Learning about the USA

For those wanting a more structured and academically-based introduction to the USA there are courses available both here and in the USA.

■ Courses on a wide range of topics are put on by the **American Studies Resource Centre**. Enquiries can be made via:
The American Studies Resource Centre
Aldham Roberts Centre
Liverpool John Moore's University
Mount Pleasant, Liverpool L3 5U2
Website: *www.americansc.org.uk*
Tel/Fax: (0151) 2331 3241.

■ If you contact the **Adult and Continuing Education Centre** at your local university or college they may well have short courses on topics such as American Film, Presidential Elections or American Literature.

■ For **courses in the USA** contact the International Study Programmes Department, Council on International Educational Exchange (*www.ciee.org*) which offers a comprehensive advisory and enrolment service for courses and programmes for summer sessions at US universities.

■ You could go the whole hog and take a degree in **American** (meaning primarily US) **Studies**. The major teaching departments are East Anglia (Norwich), Keele (Stoke-on-Trent), Nottingham, and Sussex (Brighton) though most colleges now have some American Studies courses. A well-used option is to take American Studies not as a single honours degree but as part of a joint honours programme. At Keele, for instance, American Studies can be studied alongside: Biochemistry, Biology, Criminology, Economics, Electronic Music, English, Geography, History, International Politics, Law, Music, Philosophy, Politics, or Psychology. Keele sends 150 students to North America each year. For further details contact:
Student Recruitment,
Keele University, Keele,
Staffordshire, ST5 5BG
Tel: (01782) 734010
(Website: *www.keele.ac.uk*)
or
Admissions Tutor
American Studies
Keele University, Keele,
Staffordshire ST5 5BG
Tel: (01782) 733010

So what else can I read?

Books on the USA can and do fill libraries. Useful readable introductions to its history, geography and economy are less easily found at reasonable prices. A general introduction to the contemporary USA can be found in David Stuart Ryan's *America: A Guide to the Experience* (Kozmik Press, London 1986) available in some public libraries. For an hilarious read try Jane Walmsley's *Brit-Think Ameri-Think: A Transatlantic Survival Guide* (Harrap, London 1988). Did you realise that the only difference between us and the Americans is that they think death is optional?

US history books tend to be huge, heavy and expensive. Reasonably priced and recommended paperbacks include Peter N. Carroll and David W. Noble, *The Free and Unfree* (Penguin, Harmondsworth 1989) and Hugh Brogan's *The Pelican History of the United States of America* (Penguin, Harmondsworth 1990). The latter was long a bookclub selection, so there are many second-hand copies around.

Contemporary issues are explored in a recent Edinburgh University Press paperback series, including Liam Kennedy *Race and Space in Contemporary American Culture*, Robert Williams *Political Scandals in the USA*, and for a reasonably priced look at America as a place try Stephen F. Mills, *The American Landscape*.

For a practical guide to places of historical interest try *The Smithsonian Guide to Historic America* (in 12 volumes) published by Stewart, Tabori and Chang, New York 1989. Each volume costs about £12, but copies are available in public libraries.

A British expatriate's view worth a look is *The American Century* by Harold Evans, a 2000 paperback.

There are plenty of magazines that address our continuing fascination with all things American. Probably the most well known remains *National Geographic*. Once only available to members, in recent years subscriptions have become readily available and copies can be bought from most newsagents. It is considerably cheaper by subscription. Many people still rely on picking up copies at car boot sales and second-hand bookshops. The magazine has suffered from a long standing patriotic reputation that made it somewhat difficult to take in anything but short bursts by readers overseas, though the photographs have always been first class. Since the 1960s the range and tone evident in the stories has changed, with excellent material mixed with travellers' tales. Though a majority of articles are usually about countries outside the USA, there are always American articles which offer a good introduction to America's physical and cultural variety. Many articles deal with current environmental and social problems, with excellent maps and diagrams. Back issues are now available on CD-Rom from any large PC store. The insert maps usually disappear from second-hand copies no matter how pristine and unread they appear to be, so their recent availability on CD-Rom is welcome. Every copy that has ever been issued, back into the days before colour photographs, is now available for printing out from any reasonably powered PC. For readers who would enjoy a painless introduction to the vast cultural and physical variety that is America the *National Geographic* is indeed a delight.

Essentially America, published quarterly covers areas and sites of interest across the USA and Canada. Current subscription details are on their website (*www.essent iallyamerica.com*).

Seemingly US news magazines can be somewhat disappointing. Though *Time Magazine*, for instance, seems to be American, most of the magazine available in

Britain is actually a general European edition with little of the local material found in the US edition. Try the British published *Economist* for a world-class coverage of the USA.

Something lighter?

But on holiday we probably seek something less serious. For those going to Florida try Carl Hiaasen's black comedy *Tourist Seasons*. If specifically bound for Disneyworld try Hiaasen's *Native Tongue*. Visitors to glitzy Miami might enjoy seeing how it used to be in Elmore Leonard's *La Brava* or Charles Willeford's *Miami Blues*. Further up the Atlantic coast but no less humid Savannah has been put on the map by John Berendt's elegant *Midnight in the Garden of Good and Evil*. For a more forensic side to southern heat try Thomas Harris's *Red Dragon, The Silence of the Lambs* or Patricia Cornwell's *The Body Farm*. John Grisham's legal thrillers such as *The Chamber* are an equally humid read. His *Pelican Brief* adds an environmental dimension, though for a more vicious eco-thriller read James Hall's *Under the Cover of Daylight*.

3

Preparations at Home

'She's leaving home, bye bye!'

Paperwork done in good time can make all the difference when going abroad. But besides everything involved in getting entry into the USA you also need to make certain arrangements at home:

- selling or leasing your home, or terminating the lease;
- storing or transporting household effects;
- getting yourself and your family over to the USA (see Chapter 5);
- sorting out any tax implications of changing countries (Chapter 8).

THE HOUSE

If you are leaving for a sufficiently long time, if not quite for good, you may need to consider selling your existing house. As your major capital asset you will probably need to sell in order to buy another in the USA. The Consumers' Association's self-help guide may be helpful in this.

With estate agents, solicitors and surveyors offering ever more comprehensive services, selling is not quite the hassle it once was. As you are not simultaneously a buyer you are not so deeply enmeshed in the chain of buyers and sellers that bedevils so many. This should make your property quite attractive to certain people, such as first-time buyers who are not themselves part of any chain.

Certain fundamental questions need discussing though.

Should we keep the house rather than sell?

If you intend to return to the UK it may make a lot of sense not to sell but to lease the property while away. Then there's somewhere to live upon returning.

BUT – if you need the equity tied up in your house you'll probably have to sell. If this is so, remember that when you do at last return, house prices could conceivably have risen a good deal, so you'll need to return from the USA with much more than you left with, just to stay even, never mind better off.

Should we lease the house?

If you can afford to leave your equity intact then do so, but leaving it unoccupied can be a recipe for disaster:

- Your mortgage still has to be paid.

- Your insurance is usually based on the assumption that the house is generally occupied (and by a family NOT students).

- It may become a target for thieves and vandals.

- You'll find the garden overgrown, yourself very unpopular with neighbours if you haven't made adequate arrangements for the grass to be cut, and leaves swept and so forth.

Unless you are going away for only a few months do not leave it unoccupied. Even if you are only away for the summer it is still highly vulnerable so:

- Cancel the milk, papers, coal, etc and get a neighbour to push mail and circulars completely through the letter box.

- Arrange for the garden to be kept neat and tidy.

- If possible arrange for a housesitter. A student relative writing a thesis might love the peace and quiet in exchange for mowing the lawn (and feeding the cat!). Or maybe friends would like to stay for a couple of weeks while you're away, using it as a holiday base?

- Join an exchange system: vetted foreign visitors use your home and car while you use theirs. Details from: INTERVAC on (01225) 892 208; Worldwide Home Exchange Club on (020) 7589 6055. On the web try *www.nethomexchange.com* for an American perspective.

How do we lease our house?

If you are going on a staff exchange a simple house plus car swap may be possible, to everyone's advantage and convenience. Even if you aren't going on an exchange you may be able to contact someone who is coming to Britain much as you are going to the USA. Academic staff from the USA often stay at UK universities over the summer or when on a term's leave and require suitable accommodation while they pursue their research – check with the notice board of local universities' senior common room (SCR), staff house or equivalent staff room.

Ensure your building society will let you lease out your house. If you explain the situation in good time, particularly if it is for a set period, they may well be agreeable (as it's better than an empty vulnerable property).

Use a reputable agent, or rent via a reputable college. Accommodation is always needed by colleges, but you'd need to enquire as to what controls, if any, the college would exercise on its students living in your house. Contacting someone who has rented via the college may help to allay (or confirm) your fears.

Any snags in leasing out our home?

Assuming your building society raises no insurmountable objections, you need to consider:

■ *Will the rent cover the mortgage plus reasonable wear and tear?* If you don't know – get out the calculator and work it out!

■ *How will the rent influence our income tax liability?* Again you need to talk to your tax office.

■ *What possessions to leave out and what to store?* If you are exchanging with known people you may feel it necessary only to empty wardrobes, storing what you are not taking with you in the attic in labelled boxes. If you are letting on the open market you will probably want to put into storage a lot more, such as your collection of jazz records and the hi-fi itself. It might be worth storing such items elsewhere, such as the in-laws' attic. However, the more your stuff is left in the house the more self-evidently it remains your house and home. This may be important when you return and seek repossession.

■ *How will we obtain repossession upon our return? What if we return early?* A good agent may be able to help here. Getting awkward tenants out of accommodation, even furnished accommodation, can be time consuming, though if it is quite obvious that you are returning to live rather than to sell with vacant possession this can usually be managed without too much of a problem, particularly if it is explained to would-be tenants *before* they settle in. The 1988 Housing Act introduced Assured Shorthold Tenancies to ensure owners can move back in at the end of the agreed tenancy.

A few further considerations

■ Don't be tempted to put everything in storage, rent as unfurnished, and then expect to move back in at a moment's notice. Rent controls and security of tenure legislation could make repossession against a tenant's wishes very difficult, expensive and troublesome. It may be possible to arrange a licence rather than a lease if you feel unfurnished is necessary. Set a definite date for your return to repossess and the licence should, if done correctly, enable you to exclude the tenancy from the terms of the Rent Act.

■ Remember that you don't know your tenants as well as you might think, if you know them at all. Even family friends will now have children who may have perfected the art of wear and tear. For some families dirty shoes aren't allowed beyond the front step; for others dirty feet on the sofas go quite unnoticed!

■ A general book that may nevertheless help the expatriate is Robert B. Davies's *Profitable Letting*, published by Fourmat, 1989. The specifics age but the general points remain vital.

■ For general information contact The Association of Residential Letting Agents (*www.arla.co.uk*).

■ For blank Assured Shorthold Tenancy agreements visit the legal stationers Oyez (*www.oyezforms.co.uk*).

Alternatives to leasing your home?

If you wish to close up your house for 10 to 12 weeks without leasing it out, you need to consider a systematic preparation of the property:

■ Have neighbours check the property daily.

■ Have the exterior regularly cleaned.

■ Inform the police and the neighbourhood watch co-ordinator.

■ Fit burglar alarms with appropriate deterrent lights, heavy bolts and five-lever mortise locks.

Home insurance brokers such as the AA can provide specific coverage for lengthy absences so long as the contents are worth less than £40,000 with few if any high value individual items. Premiums should be no higher than normal, though there may be restrictions on leaving the property empty for very long periods. For specialists in older people's distinct needs consider Saga (*www.saga.co.uk*).

House swapping

To search for suitable home owners with whom to swap, think Internet. If you put your mind to it you can download details, think about what's on offer, and make connections, all within just a couple of hours. Then there's time to email with photo attachments, suggestions for including each other's cars and perhaps camping equipment, and finally agreeing on an exchange.

But is house swapping the holiday for you? If you are going to spend your two weeks in San Francisco worrying whether the people in your house have spilt ash on the carpet or scratched your car at that nasty turn in Tesco's underground car park, house swapping may not be for you. But for growing numbers of visitors, house swapping is a great way to see America for little more than the household bills and spending money you'd run up just staying at home, plus a return ticket. Worries about how that nice couple from Manhattan are treating your suburban semi tend to disappear when you realise you are holding their expensively restored apartment to ransom, and that you are more likely to damage their only asset than they yours.

It is hardly surprising that the already popular house-swapping companies have taken to the Internet. Their stock in trade has always been their ability to market a database of would-be swappers, and clearly the best form of worldwide distribution and manipulation of any such database is now through the Internet. The advantage for the traveller with a PC is that once a potential swap has been identified on one of these sites you can then exchange emails and images of your respective houses and cars to your heart's content, until both sides of the swap are happy with what they are doing. Then it's just a matter of getting onto www.ebookers.com for a cheap flight and warning the neighbours that this year they don't have to feed the cat while you are away, and that you are not being burgled by wayward Americans.

Probably the best known commercial house-swap company is Homelink International (*www.homelink.org*), with more than 12,000 members. The site teases with a glimpse of its listings, but you need to join to obtain details necessary to make contact. Be prepared to shell out £115 for international membership. Have a look at this site first as it is the model which prepares you for judging what its rivals have to offer. It used to be quite evident that Homelink had simply transformed its massive directory that came in the post onto its website, though the site is now changing to take advantage of web pages. You can search for properties by area, and can specify what your needs are (such as a car or wheelchair accessibility). As with all accommodation adverts Americans love abbreviations, so you need to know that *ub* means there is the use of a boat, *mk* modern kitchen or that *bs* indicates a babysitter is available, though pop-up translations are available. Similar services are provided by Intervac (*www.intervac.com*), Green Theme International (*www.gti-home-exchange.com*) and International Home Exchange Network (*www.homeexchange.com*), the latter being particularly good for US houses. Other US-focused sites includes Digsville (*www.digsville.com*) and Trading Homes (*www.trading-homes.com*) which also offer message boards where swappers can write about their neighbourhoods.

If you feel intimidated by such matters, ask around for someone who has already done this – there are more than you may think. Once you feel confident with the web pages, you will find obtaining suitable information is relatively straightforward.

There are of course increasing numbers of interest groups on the Internet. Many have sites geared to travel and house exchanging. If Christians have discovered house swapping (*www.christianhomeexchange.com*) so have Jews (*www.jewishhome swop. com*). Can it be long before Saga get in on the act? Meanwhile what Americans euphemistically call 'Seniors' have their own site (*www.seniorshome exchange.com*), as do teachers (*www.teacherstravelweb.com*). There are specially adapted homes to choose from on a site specifically for travellers with physical disabilities (*www.independentliving.org/vacaswap.html*).

So what's it like to do an American house swap?

People have mostly good experiences, though there are risks, just like any other holiday. But it is particularly vital to swap with someone whose attitudes you can identify with. Taking three pre-teen children used to a rough house at home into a childless couple's house full of fragile antiques is a ticket to hell. If you find the other side of the exchange are very finicky about who is responsible for scratches and tears to the curtains you might want to swap with someone less house proud and more like yourself.

Spending several weeks in someone else's home can be strange for many people, particularly at first, like wearing a dead relative's jacket. Don't think about what's going on back home. There's nothing you can do anyway, the insurance will cope with most things, and the idea of going on holiday was to rest not worry. The most fraught aspects can be setting up the exchange initially, and gazumping is not unheard of as people get a better offer and leave you in the lurch. Most families are pretty scrupulous about making sure the house they borrowed is at least put back in shape before they leave, but there are some who treat your house like a motel and just walk away from it at the end of their stay. But the greatest challenge has to be how to respond when you get to your destination to find that everything is far grander than you have been led to expect, putting your own house fairly in the shade. Enjoy the novelty of your temporary home – the Americans are probably so enthralled with the village pub and being able to get to Stratford in under an hour that they haven't noticed that they've swapped their mansion for your shoe box. Of course you may find they leave having forgotten to mention the large dent on the back of the car, but that's part of life's rich pageant.

Own up to anything you'll never get away with. If your inability to use their barbecue led to a burn on the deck it's not just good manners to let them know when they return, but a good strategy to let them know before they find out. Some exchangers have worried about red wine on the carpet all holiday, only to find that it had been spilt there the day before they arrived! There is no ultimate insurance that you have not exchanged with the family from hell, except that most people will be well-meaning types just like yourselves, people just as apprehensive about being in your home as you are about their being there. And don't forget: you are in their home. If you have long been thinking about having some antique sent away for cleaning, or even stored at the bank, just before a house swap might be a good time to do that, for the benefit of all concerned. It's really not fair to leave unsuspecting house guests with something that ought to be in a museum.

Don't underestimate the paperwork involved. Just be glad that as long as you aren't staying for more than three months you won't also have to apply for a visa as well. The present **Visa Waiver Program** will do nicely.

What if the other side of the exchange backs out at the last minute? Relatives do die at the most inconvenient times, and then you are stuck. Make sure that you have insurance on the travel side, though of course you cannot get compensation for losing somewhere practically free to stay. Ask a particular agency when you sign on whether they have any arrangements for dealing with sudden last minute pull-outs that would leave you stranded. What's the worst that could happen when you turn up on their doorstep? You might find their children have moved back in from college having known nothing about their parents' plans to let someone else live in the family home. This is unlikely, but it has happened.

Initially you will be sent (or complete online) a form that outlines the property you are offering – number of rooms, en suite facilities, preferred dates, your occupation. Applications are accepted at face value as agencies cannot possibly vet everyone (or anyone really). You get a copy of the agency's next directory and/or access to the private parts of the online directory. Remember the exchange agency does not arrange your exchange, merely provides the notice board that makes it possible. Then it's up to you to find something you like whose owner you hope will like yours. The agencies try to ensure that you don't spend all your time contacting people who have already made swap arrangements by updating their listings. Old hands seem to believe that October is the best time for seeing what's available for the following summer.

If you do not want to be approached then you can keep your name out of the directory and simply rely upon contacting someone whose property takes your fancy, though if everyone did this the system would collapse. The fee though will remain the same. If nothing happens you may have to pay an extra fee, say £20, to re-advertise in the next printed directory, though agencies estimate that fewer than 10 per cent need to re-advertise.

You are not totally on your own once your advert goes in the directory. Intervac do provide you with some pointers and suggestions with checklists of arrangements that you need to clear before the exchange takes place (who looks after the cats and dogs, what happens if the car dies). Once your entry goes in you need to have an extended version available should someone contact you. You may need to promote your location, especially if you are from a less than well-known area, Birmingham needs to be located within an hour of Stratford on Avon for most Americans! It's also exchange etiquette to provide a folder of things to do and places to visit (as might be available in a hotel room).

Once you receive a directory or can go online it is probably best to contact someone whose property appeals rather than wait for someone to contact you. It may be a good idea to have some photos of both the inside and outside to send off in answer to enquiries. Try using attachments with emails before you need to send a picture of the house to Seattle! As you may not be the only person who has applied you may have to do a bit of soft sell to get taken seriously (that's where saying that Birmingham is within an hour of Stratford becomes a trump card). If you start up a correspondence you should certainly expect to provide far more details than initially. If all goes well you confirm the details in an Exchange Agreement which comes with the directory. It sets out dates and so forth, plus who is responsible for the lawn, the cats and so on. One copy you keep, one goes off to the potential visitor, with one to the national organiser.

Once things are arranged you will need to inform your insurance company that you will be having non-paying guests staying between specific, stated dates. Similarly check that your car insurance covers the new arrivals.

- Green Theme International (*www.gti-home-exchange.com*).
- Home Base Holidays (*www.home-base-hols.com*).
- HomeLink International (*www.homelink.org*).
- Intervac Home Exchange (*www.intervac.com*).

SHIPPING POSSESSIONS TO THE USA

Travelling to the USA may turn out to be the easiest aspect of the whole saga, once the paperwork has been completed. At least you are unlikely to lose anyone *en route*. Moving your possessions can be quite another thing, and a hassle-free move will require careful preparation and a certain amount of luck. Certain questions need to be asked.

Who is paying to ship everything over?

- *Your new employers?* If so, they may have a preferred carrier. Check before committing yourself elsewhere.

- *Yourselves?* Check the rates very carefully. What minimum load is involved? If 200 kg is the minimum might it not be cheaper to prune things down to an absolute minimum and take them on the plane with you rather than involve a different carrier? And who is going to pay to bring your things back at the end of your contract, when the exchange is over, or just when you decide America's not for you?

What will it cost?

■ Door-to-door rates for 5 ft^3 (large size) tea chests from about £160 (1995), with discounts for sending several to same address at same time (four chests for about £300).

■ Door to (major) port rates are considerably cheaper, up to half door-to-door, but only of use to those able to reach New York City, Miami, Los Angeles or San Francisco.

■ Collection within UK can add further cost so check inside/outside M25 rates. Different operators may have differing operational bases with different rate structures.

■ Insurance will cost from 3½ to 5 per cent of replacement value.

■ For operators see your local *Yellow Pages*.
Interpack Worldwide (0800 0393093 or www.interpack.co.uk).
Seven Seas (0800 21 6698 or *www.sevenseas.co.uk*).
ExcessBaggage (0800 082 1985 or *www.excess-baggage.com*).

■ Airfreight is also available to large US cities, either to the airport, or direct to a local address. For Atlanta that's £3.65 per kilo for you to collect at the airport and clear it through customs yourself, or £5.65 per kilo where the company clears it for you and delivers locally. Expect a 25kg minimum per shipping.

How bulky or how heavy?

■ Check with the various carriers carefully. Bulky items in non-standard shapes may well incur penalty charges with one firm, whereas the weight may be more crucial with another.

■ What's included in the price? Is insurance? Is packing? What about door-to-door service? These items cannot be too carefully checked and cross-checked. Even then you may get an inconvenient surprise once you arrive if nothing shows up.

Excess baggage is one way to take necessary goods with you: two bags, each a maximum of 23 kg per person (if length + depth + breadth aren't greater than 158cm) generally goes free with tourist fares across the North Atlantic (though this may be liable to a charge on cheaper flights to Newark). Anything over 23 kg goes at the excess rate, which can be very expensive if charged by weight rather than by piece. It may be possible to send extra baggage by cheaper freight rate if booked beforehand. US-bound allowances are higher than journeys elsewhere (by US law), but with security scares allowances are liable to last-minute changes. British airports (2008) allow two hand items per passenger, but one scare and this could change again.

An anecdote of warning!

A metal trunk (US=footlocker) was packed with college papers and summer clothes, sealed with the required US Customs declarations and the keys given to the shipper as instructed, some six weeks before required for the 24 August start of the new semester at the University of Maryland just outside Washington DC. Six weeks later nothing had arrived at the other end, even though the agreement was door-to-door for a specific date.

On contacting the shipper it turned out that the trunk would be awaiting collection at College Park railway station. This, it turned out, no longer existed. Then the shipper said it was still on the docks at Liverpool, but should arrive for collection at the docks in Baltimore (30 miles to the north) within the month.

Six weeks later the US Customs issued a notification to collect or be charged $50 a day from Dulles International Airport in Virginia (30 miles in the other direction). The paperwork had gone astray so the trunk had to be claimed and taken through customs in person, during office hours. The loan of an SUV (sports ultility vehicle) made this possible. Their invoice said the trunk came via Canada and New York by land and sea, but in fact it was stored with other items that had just been flown in from London Heathrow.

Five years later the same footlocker was booked in as excess luggage on the trip back to Heathrow, but on arrival at Heathrow it turned out still to be in Dulles awaiting the next day's flight, necessitating a further trip to the airport. Even the best laid schemes...

What should I leave behind?

Remember all those holidays where you came back with half the clothes unworn, half the CDs unplayed, and half the toys unused? This time you have no room for anything that isn't absolutely necessary.

■ Most British **electrical goods** are useless on the US 110V (60 Hz) supply. Even a 240/110V converter will mean the motor speed will be of no use for tape decks and record players except those powered off a USB lead directly from a laptop or PC. Whereas immigrants to Australia or New Zealand may find it worthwhile to ship out household goods like dishwashers, due to electrical compatibility and the high local prices, this is not so for the USA where goods are generally cheaper and need no adaptation for US-sized rooms. For a view of all things electrical than can plague people abroad take a look at www.kropla.com, a simple and effective site that does what it says on the tin.

■ **Furniture** is cheap and readily available for the newcomer in the USA. Garage sales are a usual way for all sorts of people to sell off excellent furniture at rock bottom prices to avoid the shipping costs within the USA before they move. British arrivals will be amazed at what's on offer, or what may even be given to you by people glad to be able both to help out and to clear their own garage of spare beds, sofas and so forth. See the Goldie Hawn and Steve Martin comedy *The Housesitter* for a garage sale that could be anywhere in the USA.

Of course shipping out **fine furniture** is another matter, whether it is antique or modern: if you can afford to ship it you'll be the envy of your colleagues. However, beware: the humidity range is quite unlike that in Britain, which may affect fine furniture considerably. Expert advice on preservation is as worthwhile as advice on shipping.

What should I take then?

During the Second World War the slogan was 'Is your journey really necessary?' Something along these lines needs to be asked, and you need to limit yourself to items that are:

very special
very useful, or
very personal.

■ *Personal effects:* from ornaments to books via records to jewellery. If you don't expect to return, or at least not for several years, you'll probably want your favourite Beatles EPs, your photographic albums, and your wedding souvenirs. If your stay isn't too long these could all go into storage.

■ *Household goods:* though most US accommodation comes with cooker and refrigerator, buying all new kitchenware, pillowcases and duvets (even where available) can be very expensive, even if you become a great garage sale devotee. Don't bother with the garlic press you've never used, though your Edwardian parsley-cutter may be decorative enough to take along for display in your new kitchen.

■ *Clothing:* a great opportunity to leave most of what fills your drawers and attic to your local Oxfam. You might like to fit yourselves out with new shoes before you go. Many Britons seem to prefer Clarks shoes to what's available over there.

Even if you leave all your furniture and concentrate upon lesser chattels it is quite likely you'll still end up with 500 kg per grown up. That's half a tonne each. If you intend to take books this figure will be easily reached. If your library is an essential part of your professional tool kit you may need to negotiate a special arrangement with your new employer to ship them *en masse.* Fortunately the US mail permits books (as educational material) to be shipped overseas very cheaply – if sent by the mailbag load to a single address. So the return move, even if at your own expense, isn't so expensive, though my trick of double the load at half the price doesn't really help.

What should we put into storage?

Find out how much it costs to store and insure (and who provides the packing cases and the shipment to the place of storage). If the cost of storage is greater than the replacement value you alone can decide whether or not the sentimental value is worth this extra expense. Most people returning to their stored possessions find that too much rather than too little has been retained, so storage preparation is a great opportunity for a mammoth clear-out. 'Triage' is the name of the game: three piles, one for essentials to keep, one of things to be disposed of and a third pile for the rest. The hardnosed would say store only the one pile of essentials! Get rid of the rest: chairs you know you'll never get around to repairing, flared jeans, and old school textbooks. Now might be a good time to donate your grandfather's Royal Flying Corps diary and pay book to the RAF Museum – at least you'll know it is in safe hands.

If your new employer offers to shift all your goods and effects rather than pay for a preset amount it might be worthwhile shipping everything over and putting the whole lot into storage over there while you look for somewhere to live. Self-storage lock-ups have long been common in the USA. A row of miniature 'garages' will be enclosed in a compound, with a resident guard, so things should be quite secure. If you must leave valuables, such as antiques, in such a depot don't advertise or talk about the fact. Any security can be broken if the price is right!

CUSTOMS AND EXCISE

UK

Private household goods can usually be exported from Britain without too much hassle. Export licences will normally be granted for privately owned, albeit valuable, items if they are not being taken abroad for sale.

■ If you have any doubts talk to your shipping agent and make enquiries from your local office of Customs and Excise. Officially they are now known as HM Revenue & Customs (*www.hmrc.gov.uk*).

US

Customs will allow in bona fide household goods, clothes and personal effects. Though a container-load of micro chips will not be let in despite your hobby as a hacker, a load of obviously household and family goods will, if you can show the necessary papers to support your arriving with the kitchen sink. Do not arrive with all your worldly goods (unless you can get everything into two suitcases) and expect to be allowed in on the Visa Waiver Program for short stay visitors.

■ It may help US Customs and yourself if you list everything as you pack it (it helps if a box does go astray to know what to claim for). Any item could be taxed on its value, so you need to estimate some figures, though you can guess some, such as 'Sports gear $50').

■ You can download free inventory templates from Microsoft that will run either in Excel or Access. Take a look at Microsoft Office online, and click the templates tab for 'Home contents inventory database'.

■ To obtain an early sense of what's involved, download US Customs forms 'Declaration for Free Entry of Unaccompanied Articles – 3299' and 'Supplementary Declaration of Unaccompanied Personal and Household Effects – C128'.

> **Remember**
>
> *Meeting and dealing with incoming families and their belongings is hardly something new for US Customs, so they'll know both what they want and what they want you to do to make your arrival easy (if only for their convenience).*

Entradas

Visas

Depart.
Sorties / So

DEPARTMENT OF HOMELAND SECURITY U.S. CUSTOMS AND BORDER PROTECTION

ADMITTED

52

1404

Class
Until

4

Visas and Immigration

These States are the amplest poem
Here is not merely a nation but a teeming
Nation of nations.

Walt Whitman

A SOCIETY OF IMMIGRANTS

The USA is not like the Old World, a place of relative permanence and continuity, adapting only so far as it preserves what has been. The USA continually reinvents itself, turning 'them' into 'us'. It is a nation that does not grow from affinity with the soil or even with one language whose origins are lost in time. Instead the USA is polyglot, an ingathering of all the races, peoples and religions of the earth. It has always relied upon attracting peoples from elsewhere. Even the native peoples (mistakenly taken for 'Indians') came from Siberia in the dim and distant past.

Recent newcomers

Europeans came initially to dominate the modern influx, but just as the British came by the turn of this century to be outnumbered by peoples from eastern and southern Europe, so too this once novel combination has recently been overtaken by a continuing influx from Latin America, south-east Asia, Africa and a post-communist wave from Russia. The dominant black and white mix has recently given way to browns and yellows.

Forty years ago most immigrants came from Europe or from Canada. Since the early 1990s most have been Mexicans, Filipinos, Vietnamese, Koreans, Indians, Chinese and West Indians. They arrive on jumbo jets; they walk across the border; they are washed ashore on the Florida Keys.

Fears and suspicions

A flickering fear says aliens are overrunning the country. If the USA is a lifeboat in a world of trouble maybe it is in danger of being swamped. Racism re-emerges, fuelled by fears of recession returning. Even current prosperity involves great disparity between different regions and different sectors of the economy, with many ordinary people losing their jobs. The long-standing mutual fears and suspicions of blacks and whites give way to mutual apprehension that those browns and yellows recently let in will throw open the gates to one and all, levelling down, with English but one of many possible tongues.

But this has always been the fear. Benjamin Franklin feared that the Pennsylvania of the 1750s would be overrun by Germans. In the 1840s the Irish seemed about to swamp the towns and, while digging the canals, the countryside too. Later Jews, fleeing Czarist hostility, brought their Yiddish language, their Hebrew writing, and their Saturday Sabbath into the growing cities which many Americans feared were being turned into foreign countries. Working for the good of their children, immigrants stood together when necessary and plunged into the mainstream when possible, learning English, voting, investing their lives in almost any job that would keep the family intact.

Beginning life anew

John F. Kennedy, son of an Irish family made good in the USA, saw his country as 'a society of immigrants, each of whom has begun life anew, on an equal footing'. For him America's secret was that it was 'a nation of people with the fresh memory of old traditions who dared to explore new frontiers'. It was in his memory that the USA abandoned the old 1920s quota system which, if too late to keep the USA White Anglo-Saxon and Protestant (WASP), at least had kept it predominantly European. Since 1965 new waves of immigration have brought newcomers not just from Europe but increasingly from the Third World. Of over 1,266,000 legal immigrants (2006) the largest number came from Mexico (about 174,000) and the Philippines (75,000). In 2005 about 96,000 people from Muslim countries became legal US permanent residents.

Recognising the changes

For British settlers (or even visitors) recognition of this change is essential. The British have a very ambivalent attitude towards the USA. The temptation is to see it as a richer, larger version of the south of England with more snow and more sun, but still recognisably British (if not quite English). If this were ever true the mass influx from southern and eastern Europe of Italians, Slavs, Jews and Poles during the 19th century has long since swept over this British heritage. The countryside is full of people originally from Scandinavia and Germany, as the place-names of the Midwest tell us (see Harrison Keillor's *Lake Wobegone Days*, Penguin 1986, for a loving but caustic look at such people in Minnesota or watch the Coen brothers' *Fargo*).

Today's Third World influx is changing the very language and landscape of America. Where once there were small ethnic enclaves like San Francisco's Chinatown, now there are vast Spanish-speaking neighbourhoods in most cities. The Governor of New York City may be African American (David Paterson, 2008), but city mayors are likely to have been born in the Philippines or in Cuba. Each year the US Citizenship and Immigration Services (still generally referred to as the INS, after its old name) catches over a million illegal immigrants. The US Census Bureau reckons they missed between two and three times more. Most are from Mexico, crossing the land border in a dash from the conditions of Bangladesh to those of Switzerland in one night.

No wonder that the INS requires visitors to provide proof they intend to leave. A cynic might say that the less the INS can control the 2,000-mile land border to the south the more it needs to demonstrate its authority where it can with those coming openly into the USA at airports.

TOURIST, LONG-STAY VISITOR OR IMMIGRANT?

It used to be that few British or Irish people ever went to the USA except as emigrants. US entry rules still reflect the fact that until comparatively recently few if any arrived as tourists or on business. Even if you have an interest in settling down permanently in the USA it helps to understand the wider immigration-based system for handling incoming foreigners. As a long-stay visitor you fall between being either a tourist or an immigrant, and so you need to understand your paperwork so that US officials don't manage to confuse you, and a confused arrival seems like someone on the make. The port of entry, nowadays of course, is usually an airport, though it might just be a small border crossing if you have already been to visit relatives in Canada. If at all possible make your initial entry by one of the big airports, but if you must enter by land use a main crossing point which will have all the facilities and officials who have dealt with people like you before, say where the Montreal–New York City freeway crosses from Quebec into New York (scene of the final shoot out in *Die Hard with Vengeance*) or the Vancouver–Seattle freeway crosses the 49th parallel. Avoid small road crossings into rural Vermont used by local farmers and lost American tourists – you may be the first European the official has ever had to process and it can take forever as they check everything with their regional office over a busy phone line (believe me, I've crossed over this way and regretted it). And don't even think of using a back road to avoid having to show your papers. You need your passport and visa officially dealt with to be in the country legally.

If you want to settle in the USA permanently you will need a good guide. The ideal situation would be to have a US lawyer who specialises in immigration cases accessible from the USA before problems arise. Fortunately a couple of US-based lawyers provide just such a service:

■ Richard Fleischer, *Applying for a United States Visa: a practical guide to the New Immigration Law,* International Venture Handbooks, Plymouth, (1993). Given the post 9/11 situation this needs updating, but remains a useful introduction to the sort of processes involved.

■ Henry G. Liebman, *Getting into America: the immigrant guide to finding a new life in the USA,* How To Books, Oxford (2003). This does incorporate some of the post 9/11 changes.

Both can be ordered through a good bookstore or ordered secondhand from Amazon (*www.amazon.co.uk*). Larger public libraries may well have one of these in their reference collection (phone ahead to find out if making a specific journey).

What follows in this chapter on immigration and visas is therefore a necessary introduction to the complex questions of getting an immigrant (or any other kind of) visa, and may not provide definitive answers to specific questions you have about your particular case. This chapter should enable you to make general sense of the main features of what's involved, preparing you for the more complex details provided by guides dealing only with the visa process, which in turn will prepare you for either the forms themselves, or a lawyer who can help address your own particular circumstances. Remember most of us use a lawyer when moving just down the road. How much more advice do you need if moving countries?

Travelling into the unknown

The USA has always offered immigrants a prize: land, a job, or freedom of expression. But it has rarely been an easy bargain. The streets have never been paved with gold. Those who expect gold have been severely disappointed. Just being alive is a risk. We are all immigrants in the sense that we are all travelling into an unknown. To go to the USA is to compound that. You are going into someone else's future, which you must make your own. The familiarities of home, relatives, bank holidays, the passage of the seasons, cup finals, TV programmes, *The Archers* or *Desert Island Discs* will all vanish to be replaced by the occasional long-distance telephone call, harsher seasons (or no seasons at all), cable-TV with 200 channels spouting religions and languages you don't recognise, not to mention more advertisements that you thought possible. You may think that you can keep up to date by listening to BBC Online, and so you will initially. But, when no one else at work listens to *The Archers*, after a while, neither will you, except if there's a crisis of some kind back home (air crash, flooding or bombing). From all this novelty you'll have to carve out a new routine, a new set of familiar surroundings which you'll have to be prepared to jettison at a moment's notice when promotion means leaving Portland, Maine, for Portland, Oregon. And you may see the children even less than before.

Coping with further changes

Arriving in the USA it may be tempting to see yourself as remaining essentially who you have always been, though with more money as befits being within a wealthier economy. Feeling like this many immigrants have been very bewildered when they were asked to change their lives again and again. The company may be taken over and all existing staff fired. The department of history may be closed as a university cost-cutting device. The union may call you out on strike, and you lose.

Such traumas are of course increasingly likely back home. Indeed changes such as these may be what encouraged you to leave for the USA! But the price of that extra pay, the extra promotion prospects, the better-funded library or laboratory may be the greater risk. If your company gains a military contract you will have to go along with that or leave with no other job in sight. Being offered promotion may be on the 'up or out' principle (take it or leave the company) which may leave you in a part of the USA you'd never intended to visit never mind settle in with your children.

Being flexible

Great courage and flexibility will be needed in this kind of situation. If you really do want to stay in the city where you've started to settle down, greater flexibility in job selection than you've ever had before may be necessary. Teachers drive cabs, act as tour guides, write freelance, and even work for political candidates in the hope that their election will lead to a job in their office.

As there is less of a safety net in the USA, networks of friends and family take on ever more importance, and hard work and commitment are essential, with an enthusiastic endorsement of the US's 'can do' attitude, rather than the more pessimistic 'what if it doesn't work out?' US attitudes to success and failure, while rewarding success more, also encourage risk and so don't take failure to be a mortal sin. It is not a sin to be knocked down. It is only a sin to stay down. By having taken the leap of faith necessary to become an immigrant you are already making a stake in becoming American, and may find flexibility more appealing and less threatening.

Moving on

All members of the family should have talked the options and implications over though. If after staying for a year in one place a move seems imminent it will again need to be talked through, and if all were aware early on that this might happen the house can be treated like a long-lease summer cottage and all the further packing, saying goodbye, changing schools and so on can be seen as a further adventure so that the family can stay together rather than a rude awakening.

GETTING A VISA

There is a bewildering array of visas, and the appropriate regulations can and do change at any time without notice (though any major changes will usually be accompanied by considerable media publicity). For up-to-date information it is essential that you visit the US Embassy website (*www.usembassy.org.uk*) also available at *http://evisaforms.state.gov/*.

Don't phone if you can avoid it, as you will most likely be put on hold, and may be merely directed to the news update section of the Embassy website. If you must, call 09042-450-100 (accessible only from within the UK) Monday–Friday 08.00–20.00 and Saturday, 10.00–16.00 for 'Operator Assisted Visa Information Service' (not available on UK public holidays). **Beware:** calls are charged at £1.20 per minute. Written information is also available. Write to The Consular Information Unit, United States Embassy, 24 Grosvenor Square, London W1 1AE.

But what is a visa?

A visa, issued a US Embassy or Consulate outside the USA, entitles the holder to apply for admission on arrival in the USA. It is usually attached to the holder's passport in much the same way as the holder's details were originally added by the

UK Passport Office – a laminated page setting out the necessary details in visible and machine-readable forms.

Who needs a visa?

Anyone who is not eligible to enter the United States visa-free under the Visa Waiver Program, or is not exempt from the visa requirement, needs a visa.

What types of visas are available?

- **Non-immigrant visas:** A non-immigrant visa is required by anyone seeking temporary admission into the United States who is not eligible to travel visa-free under the Visa Waiver Program, or is not exempt from the visa requirement. Non immigrant visas cover visits for tourism, business, work or study. Non-immigrant visas are essentially for those intending to return home at some time, rather than to stay and settle down.

- **Immigrant visas** are for those wishing to settle permanently in the United States. Upon entry into the United States, an immigrant visa holder is processed for what is commonly called a 'Green Card' but which officially is called a 'Permanent Resident Card' (PRC). The holder of a PRC may reside and may work in the United States. Though this is a necessary stage for becoming a US citizen there is no legal requirement that the holder of a PRC must apply to become a naturalised US citizen; he or she still retains his or her overseas citizenship and passport until such time as naturalisation takes place. PRC holders seeking to become naturalised US citizens may file an application after five years (three years if married to a US citizen). Many such 'resident aliens' never actually take out citizenship and so never qualify for a US passport, though children born in the USA be Americans and will receive a US passport as a matter of course.

In practice, however, there are many intermediate statuses, some of what can be changed once awarded, and some of which cannot. So it's essential you know what status you want to achieve, and what the limits and potentials are of the status with which you enter the USA. To be absolutely sure you need professional advice.

Application fees

Congress requires the US State Department to introduce newer and more complex immigration procedures the better to protect the USA's borders, but each patriotic Congressperson is determined his or her constituents should not have to pay for such arrangements to be put in place and carried out, especially when the beneficiaries are foreigners. You, the user of this 'service', will have to pay, so while taxes may not be going up, user fees most certainly are. Every visa applicant is required to pay an application fee: there are no exceptions. The 'non-immigrant visa application processing fee' from January 2008 starts at $131 (non-refundable).

The visa application form may be obtained by downloading form DS156 from the US Embassy London site (*www.usembassy.org.uk*).

The immigrant equivalent (Form DS230 is $335–$400 depending upon status. There are cheaper and easier procedures for students and short-term exchange visitors ($100 as of mid-2008) payable electronically.

Please be aware that if you don't in the end apply for a visa, or if the worst comes to the worst and a visa is not issued, no refunds are possible. The fee is for using the service, not a price for a visa, which the US authorities still insist is free, the required fee notwithstanding. If you remain puzzled by such a US Government linguistic sleight of tongue be thankful you are not caught in their equally bizarre distinction between who is an 'illegal combatant' and who is a 'POW'. Regardless of whether a visa is ultimately issued or refused there will be no refund of the fee.

You need to read the US Embassy's page on visa types and fees, especially if you are doing it by yourself without professional advice (as provided on intra-company transfers by employers or by universities for exchange students or visiting scholars).

New US visa application requirements

The US government is implementing new visa application procedures worldwide. Since 1 August, 2003, almost all applicants have to schedule a personal interview with a consular officer at the US Embassy. Everyone else who isn't eligible for the Visa Waiver Program (mostly tourists who have no arrest records) has to be interviewed for a visa – and that especially includes students going as part of an exchange programme whether organised by their own UK university or not, and those UK students going to work for the summer (BUNAC, etc). UK passport holders who were born in any of the seven countries designated as state sponsors of terrorism are also required to apply for a visa in person. If in doubt, and for further information, consult the embassy website (www.usembassy.org.uk) and click on the clearly marked areas dealing with consular matters and visas.

But that's not all: as part of the current Homeland Security campaign to monitor access to the USA, visitors entering under the Visa Waiver Program must be in possession of a machine-readable passport.

Machine-readable passports can be identified by the presence of two typeface lines printed at the bottom of the laminated page containing all your personal details which can be read electronically and checked against details held on a computer.

For some years the Visa Waiver Program was merely a pilot programme liable to be cancelled by Congress if it were felt to be undermining US security. But on 30 October, 2000, the programme was made permanent when President Clinton signed into law the Visa Waiver Permanent Program Act. If this bill had been left for another year it is doubtful if, in the light of 9/11, it would have been passed. But it was and it allows primarily tourists from nations that do not require Americans to have visas to enter their country to enter the US without visas. As all foreigners entering the USA must have visas this is technically not a no-visa policy but a 'visa waiver program', for Americans a real, albeit subtle, distinction.

Those visitors seeking to take advantage of visa-free travel must meet all of the following requirements: the traveller must be a citizen of one of the 27 approved countries, travelling on an unexpired, machine-readable passport. A passport indicating that the bearer is a British Subject, British Dependent Territories Citizen, British Overseas Citizen, British National (Overseas) Citizen, or British Protected Person does not qualify for travel without a visa, nor does a passport which states the holder has Right of Abode or indefinite leave to remain in the United Kingdom; travelling for business, pleasure or transit only; staying in the United States for 90 days or less; holding a return or onward ticket. Finally, those entering the United States aboard must travel with a shipping company or an airline that has agreed with the US Immigration and Naturalization Service to participate in the programme. Finally, travellers must present a completed form I-94W, which is the card unofficially and somewhat misleadingly called a landing card that is handed out to passengers on approaching the USA. If you are entering the USA over a land border there is also a fee of $7.00.

It is vital to appreciate that some travellers may not be eligible to enter the United States visa-free under the VWP. These include people who have been arrested, even if the arrest did not result in a criminal conviction, and those with criminal records, (the Rehabilitation of Offenders Act does not apply to US visa law). Others who may not use the VWP include those with certain serious communicable illnesses, those who have been refused admission into, or have already been deported from, the United States, or have previously overstayed on the Visa Waiver Program. Such people may enter the USA on special restricted visas, but may not attempt to enter visa-free. If they attempt to travel without a visa, they may be refused entry into the United States and sent home immediately at their own expense. Do traffic violations mean that participation in the VWP is out of the question? Visa-free travel is available in the case of minor traffic offences which did not result in an arrest and/or conviction, provided they are otherwise qualified. If the traffic offence occurred in the United States, and there are fines left unpaid or you did not attend your court hearing, there may be a warrant out for your arrest, which can complicate attempts to enter the USA. Before travelling to the USA it may be necessary to contact the court where you were to appear. Court addresses can be found on the web (*www.refdesk.com*).

It is often thought that passports must be valid for six months beyond a visitor's planned return from the USA. If travelling under the Visa Waiver Program, the passport must be valid for at least three months from the date on which the holder enters the United States. If not, the holder will be admitted until the expiration date on the passport. UK passports whose validity has been officially extended for two years are valid for travel to the United States. What is equally crucial though is that the US Citizenship and Immigration Service (USCIS) officer at the border believes the traveller will return home shortly, evidence usually being a return ticket, though students may need to show that they have to return home to complete their studies. If the officer is not satisfied that the traveller meets the qualifications required, the traveller will be denied entry and returned home as quickly as possible.

It is crucial that those who plan to study, to work, or to stay more than three months however legally do not attempt to enter the USA on the Visa Waiver Program. Such people must have the appropriate visas. Any immigration officer who suspects a visa-free arrival is intent upon formal study, work or staying longer than three months will refuse admittance to the traveller. Even someone who merely appears to be entering to study or work will be examined very closely and may be refused entry. Travellers who regularly enter and leave the USA can be questioned for a very long time if the examining officer suspects someone has come, for example, to earn money. I know: I have been questioned at great length when officers thought I was in Florida for more than a family holiday, and colleagues who have been in and out for years have suddenly found themselves excluded when an old traffic violation finally came to light on new computer systems.

How do I know which visa I need?

The non-immigrant or immigrant distinction seems pretty straightforward. Unfortunately it isn't always quite so simple:

- *Going for a look around prior to applying for a job?* You'd probably do best to go in as a tourist (see next section). But if you tell the welcoming Immigration officer that you are on a job-hunting exercise you may well be refused entry. Enter and leave as a tourist. Then apply for an appropriate visa to re-enter later.

- *Not wanting to commit yourself to settling down but wanting to enter the job market free to change jobs at will?* An immigrant visa is necessary. Visas given for those with specific job contracts stipulate that you must leave if you end your contract with the sponsoring employer. However, once legally inside the US it may well be possible to change your status (say, for instance, if you've married or have had children while living and working in the USA). You will almost certainly need a US lawyer who specialises in immigration law for this.

NON-IMMIGRANT VISAS

There are 13 types of non-immigrant visas (each with a different letter prefix). All applications must satisfy certain conditions. Applicants must be sound in body and mind, have no drug or dependency problems, with no criminal record (which includes advocating polygamy!), must not be nor have been a communist (or Nazi collaborator!). And of course applicants must be not entering the USA to 'overthrow, by force or violence or other unconstitutional means, the Government of the United States or of all forms of law'. Or as the US guidelines sum up:

'In short, aliens who do not measure up to the moral, mental, physical and other standards fixed by law are, with very few exceptions, excludable from admission even if they have the necessary documents.'

Important point

A US visa is not permission to enter the USA. It is merely a statement by the US authorities abroad that the bearer seems to have met the necessary criteria and that they know of no reason why the bearer shouldn't be permitted to enter. Admission is actually granted by a USCIS officer at the port of entry. Arriving on a valid tourist visa with all your worldly possessions and all the family (including grandma and the dog) would suggest to the most hard-pressed USCIS officer that you might be entering the USA for more than just a few days at Disneyworld.

If you fail to declare a reason why the US authorities might want to exclude you (such as a prior conviction) you can be removed from the USA without a court hearing, and be excluded permanently.

The conditions which applicants must satisfy are set out in some detail on the USCIS website (*www.uscis.gov/portal/site/ISCIS*) where there are lots of dropdown menus and hot links to play with. Actually, this site is okay, having both general information and ways to check an application status.

Visa types

There are 13 basic types. When applying it is essential you know which category is appropriate or your application will get rejected, which can add to the already lengthy process time that you can ill afford to lose:

A diplomats and consular staff with authorised families
B visitors for business or pleasure (but see visa-free proviso later)
C transit visas
D ship and aircrews due to leave soon
E businessmen or investors
F students to 'pursue a full course of study at an established institute of learning'
G diplomatic visas for international organisations
H temporary worker, defined as an alien who is to perform a prearranged professional or highly skilled job for a temporary period, or to fill a temporary position for which there is a shortage of US workers; the employment must be approved in advance by USCIS in the USA on the basis of an application filed by the prospective employer
I bona fide media people
J student, academic or nanny to join a recognised programme
K fiancé(e) entrance, valid for 90 days only prior to marriage and change to permanent resident status
L intracompany transfer
Q international cultural exchange participants who will be employed but whose primary purpose in the US is to share their cultural tradition with Americans; this might involve folk musicians working in a museum programme approved in advance by the US authorities.

Most visa types permit spouse (and children under 21) to go with the applicant, though care needs to be taken as to whether or not they can then work. For instance, the spouse or children of a student (F) visa may not work or even apply for permission to work. Intracompany transfer spouses and children may only work if they've successfully applied for work visas in their own right.

Documents needed to support an application depend upon the visa type sought, and whether or not the issuing official suspects fraud. Proof of intent to return home is necessary. But how can anyone prove intent? Well of course you can't, but you can provide evidence that returning home is more important than staying on in the USA:

- The need to return to complete a degree or to further a career:
  - a statement from your college saying you must be back by a specific date or forfeit your place
  - a statement from your company setting a date by which you must return or forfeit promotion.
- A return ticket (rather than just money or a credit card) suggests an intent to return home by a specific date.

The more footloose and fancy-free you appear to be to the US authorities the more necessary it is to show you have a compelling reason to return home.

Someone with a mortgage, children in school, an established career and a return ticket plus a package tour to Disneyworld is less likely to be asked for further proof of intent to return than a recently graduated single male with no return ticket, or a single female with child care qualifications and a single ticket to a wealthy suburb (who would appear to the suspicious USCIS as a potential and illegal nanny).

Electronic System for Travel Authorization (ESTA)

As of January 2009, all incoming passengers who intend to take advantage of the Visa Waiver Program will be required to register online before departure for the USA at least 72 hours (three days) in advance rather than complete a form on the plane. This new requirement is intended to bolster the US sense of security while providing travellers with the convenience of a registration valid for multiple entry over two years. As with visas and visa waivers, successful ESTA registration will not guarantee admission at a US port of entry, merely authorising a passenger to board a carrier for travel to the US. Immigration officers will continue to make the final decision at the ports of entry. For additional information read 'Know Before You Go' at *www.cbp.gov/travel*.

Organising the paperwork

There are lengthy procedures, much undertaken by others.

Applicants for A, G, H-2, H-3, most I, and L visas will be handled by someone else, usually an employer (or would-be employer). K applicants, of course, will have a fiancé(e) to help them with the necessary papers. E and I visas are special cases, dealt with as such, and F and J visas involve the appropriate college providing evidence of status.

If a visa petition has been submitted to the USCIS in the USA to establish a preferential status, say for an immediate relative, the paperwork comes from the overseas applicant's US contacts to the USCIS for approval. If successful the USCIS forwards the paperwork directly to the consular office dealing with the applicant overseas. For certain employment visas (H-2, H-3 or L categories) the 'intending employment party' must file, whereas professional or 'exceptional ability' status applicants file with the USCIS themselves via the local US embassy.

IMMIGRANT VISAS

The first great age of mass immigration came to an end in the 1920s following the arrival of an unprecedented number of people from eastern, central and southern Europe. A system was then introduced with high quotas for the countries of northwest Europe, and low quotas elsewhere. In the 1960s this was recognised to be a system inappropriate for a nation attempting to rid itself of the legacy of a deeply racist history. Instead, immigration was ended for everyone, except for those able to present themselves as legitimate exceptions. The guiding principles for being allowed to enter became:

■ refugees;
■ family reunions;
■ to help the USA (skills, investments, etc).

In theory at least there are no special preferences beyond these necessary for the ordinary conduct of business, commerce, trade, tourism, certain humanitarian concerns and the needs of the US economy. In practice, though, reality is a little more complicated.

Refugees

These have an automatic right of entry. In practice anti-communist refugees (such as the first wave of Vietnamese boat-people) have been welcome (if they had some US link), whereas those from right-wing regimes are not (hence Cuban refugees are welcome but not those from Haiti). Economic refugees are most definitely NOT welcome these days.

Family reunions

There is a complex preference system to allow in about half a million immediate relatives of US citizens (children, spouse and parents). Children must be unmarried and under 21.

The preference system was reorganised in the 1990s, with complex transitional arrangements. Even so, the US Congress can and will change precise numbers and quotas. There are strong immigrant lobby groups, such as the Cubans and the Irish, who can and do exert pressure for rule changes as important elections approach. So the preference systems outlined below are presented only in their barest formats, to suggest how complicated the rules have become, and why so many people use a specialist lawyer.

To help the US economy

Applicants whose arrival within the USA would substantially benefit the US economy have specific quotas. About a quarter of a million skilled and professional workers, plus investors, can be recruited overseas, though usually to fill specific job and investment shortages.

Skilled foreign professionals have always been welcome within the US economy – a brain drain that has invigorated the US job market for generations. But the number of visas issued can change dramatically as the US attempts to match the number of arrivals to the number and type of jobs available, or worse still, that will probably be available. Even those with once appropriate skills can suddenly find they cannot enter the USA, whereas they could have done last year and might be able to next year. These H-1B visas are given each year to foreign workers whose specialised skills are sought by US companies. During the technology boom, the H-1B visa program, provided a gateway for thousands of people from the Indian subcontinent who came to work in the United States, especially in Silicon Valley. Of course the level of applications also changes with the state of the US economy in general and the health of certain sectors in particular. In 2002 the number of H-1B visa applications dropped by 75 per cent, reflecting the downturn in the dot-com sector and the elimination of certain technical jobs. On the other hand the L-1 visa, used for transferring staff within international companies has no quotas. This has become a live issue as critics of the programme argue that US corporations are using it to replace US employees with less expensive foreign workers from places like India and the Philippines. Some have even called for scrapping the H-1B visa, a reaction against the increasing trend of sending technology, call room and back-office jobs overseas, though any reduction in the visa limit may gradually diminish the US's ability to attract the most talented workers, important as baby boomers retire and the numbers of Americans graduating in technologically sophisticated areas declines.

For a glimpse of the complexities of the preference system for both family reunions and 'employment-based' immigration, take a look at a major immigration website (*www.foreignborn.com*) which explores the various and often confusing categories.

The lottery

If the preference applications have been filled and there are still some spare places, others from designated countries may be invited to apply on a first-come-first-served basis. No job is necessary at the time of initial application, but must be on offer in writing with appropriate 'Labor Certification' as per the preference system applicant if the visa comes to be issued. You may well have heard that there were 50,000 visas to distribute each year by lottery. You may even have read advertisements offering professional help obtaining just such a lottery visa, at a price. But:

■ lotteries are not held every year;

■ most UK citizens are not usually eligible (eligibility is country-specific and reflects ethnic group lobbying on Capitol Hill to ensure overall immigration exhibits 'diversity');

■ initial applications do not require professional help with the form;

■ costly 'professional advice' usually means merely copies of forms available for free from the US Embassy;

■ for the 2008 lottery (for 50,000 places) there were 6.4 million applications. Maybe that's why they call it a lottery?

Using your visa

Once an immigrant visa has been issued you need to use it within four months if you wish to establish 'permanent residence'. This status doesn't mean you can never leave the USA, but that if you do so without first having taken out US citizenship you may lose your right of re-entry if you stay abroad too long.

OVERSTAYING

If, as a visitor, you overstay for a few weeks don't expect to find the FBI after you, but if you should be unlucky enough to get caught you may find it goes against you should you ever try to return. If you leave by way of Canada make sure the Visa Waiver stub is collected by the Canadian officer who scrutinises your UK passport . If you have overstayed on the US side the Canadian authorities will want to know that you are leaving straightaway: they don't want to be lumbered with you as the US won't take you back.

If you want to stay legally you will need to contact the USCIS website to check their location and times of opening. As they will assume you are trying to stay to work you should take all necessary papers with you. The best thing to do if possible is to take a US relative or friend along to vouch that you are staying on for family reasons, have a place to stay, and intend to return home. You'll need to complete the USCIS form *Application for Issuance or Extension of Permit to Re-enter the USA*. Written proof that you have to be back home to start a job, enter college, or some such would be very useful (as would a return ticket).

If you want to change your status you will need a lawyer. Initially, though, you need to know what a lawyer can and cannot do for you. Petition forms change regularly and it is always best to check the latest versions, available on the US Citizenship and Immigration Services (USCIS) website (*www.uscis.gov*).

EXPECTATIONS – YOURS AND THEIRS

Despite a tradition of immigration, polls show that less than a third of Americans agree with the idea that 'America should keep its doors open to people who wished to immigrate to the US because that is what American open door heritage is all about.' Some two thirds now believe that this philosophy is no longer feasible. Though a majority still approve of offering sanctuary to those oppressed overseas, almost as many now believe legal immigration is both too high and from the wrong parts of the world.

If Americans are uncertain as to how they should respond to continuing immigration how should would-be immigrants respond to the USA? In the past British emigrants have been able to disappear into the White Anglo-Saxon Protestant mainstream. Many adults lose their British accents almost as quickly as they pick up US words and phrases. Children make the transition in weeks. But what if the USA turns out to be more like *Law and Order* than *Sex and the City*? Most legal immigrants will rarely, if ever, even glimpse the world portrayed in such movies as *Falling Down* (1992) never mind *Seven* (1995).

Slotting into place

The very rules that require immigrants to be skilled, educated and going to a specific job or family reunion mean that most British people will slot right into workplace and neighbourhood with little more difficulty than if they had merely moved to somewhere at the other end of the UK. In fact, moving to another EU country might well be more confusing with language and legal systems so different from the US-UK traditions. Some people, however, find a move within Europe less traumatic than one to the USA. Continental countries are so obviously different and foreign, whereas the differences within the USA may only creep up, as when there's an illness, or there's a sudden need for assistance and you turn out to be the only person in the car park who can speak English. Of course if you treat the USA as a foreign country, which it is, such problems may seem less bizarre and unexpected when they do occur. Prepare for America's strangeness by reading E. Wanning *Culture Shock! USA* (2005).

Responding to US expectations

British immigrants will be caught in a cross-fire of US expectations. A British accent means you are stuffy but sophisticated, swinging but old-fashioned, staid but cosmopolitan, and so forth. You'll be expected to play darts, golf and soccer, drink only warm beer, stout or G and Ts, and eat only fish'n'chips and roast beef. And of course you'll be pressed to drink tea even if you'd prefer coffee or even a beer! Enjoy it or ignore it. Just don't complain that the water wasn't hot enough in the tea (or that the coffee is very thin by European standards).

As an immigrant you may have to be prepared to be more serious about life than those settled back home can be. But this can make the adrenalin flow, that most American of juices.

For British arrivals, though, experience suggests that the more highly skilled, the more firmly middle class, the greater the chances both of making good in the USA, and of becoming American. For the USA the immigrants' greatest value is as a leavening agent, yeast to reinvigorate society and the economy. Economically, immigrants generate more than they themselves consume. Socially, they add variety for which the US is famous, acting as an antidote to the blandness otherwise enveloping much of the USA.

Straddling two cultures

Ironically, most immigrants, or at least their children, seek to merge with the mainstream. And the British arriving as part of the brain drain have not gone into exile in the same way as the Vietnamese, the Cubans or Soviet Jews. The exiles didn't so much abandon their countries as feel their countries abandoned them. The brain drain scientist can always go home for visits, for funerals and wakes, or even to return. The exile cannot.

Both groups, however, straddle two cultures. They leave behind a train that continues on its way regardless. The Britain they leave will not spin its wheels awaiting their return. Yet the emigrant/immigrant can never become a true American, for that requires more than even citizenship or allegiance to a set of ideas. It requires the experience of growing up in a country, the sense of 'my home town'.

ENCOUNTERING THE HISPANIC AMERICAN SOUTHWEST

Many British immigrants are in for a series of big surprise. They often have some sense of the rich and poor divide and its racial dimensions, but the high profile of the African-American middle class, especially in government or education, can be quite unexpected. But it is reasonably easy to adapt to the realisation that certain people are more rather than less like yourself. It is quite another thing to find so many people who are neither black nor white and who rightly consider themselves American.

Whereas the large number of Russian-speakers in parts of New York merely seem like a hangover from the last century rather than something totally unexpected, in the southwest things are quite different. **Spanish** is the coming language. The immigrants are mostly from across the border, not from across an ocean. Mexican-Americans are living in what was their country until the USA took it from them in the early nineteenth century, but unlike the Native Americans they have as their homeland one of the poorest, fastest growing, urbanised countries in the world across an increasingly defended land border. Maintaining their links back across the border Mexican-Americans are gradually outnumbering (and so outvoting) white residents who seem to have forgotten that they have only held this land for about 150 years.

In south Florida the Hispanic population is primarily from Cuba, though whether the American-born children will ever want to return home remains to be seen.

To Hispanic Americans, recently arrived British immigrants seem like bizarre outsiders, people who should adapt to the changing cultural politics of the southwest or go some place else. British immigrants can be disorientated particularly where the very notion is decaying that public life is always in English. Where once public notices would be only in English now they are more likely to be in Spanish. The English-speaker can feel very out of things in shops and offices where Spanish is the norm rather than the exception.

5

Getting to the USA

This chapter provides information on the range of fares, carriers and packages available for travelling to the USA. Fares change so rapidly that it is vital to keep an eye on newspapers and websites that will keep you up to date.

BY SEA

It used to be fairly straightforward to travel to the USA by sea. This was often cheaper, avoided flying for those who still feared this method of tempting fate, and large amounts of baggage could be taken along at reasonable rates. Containerisation has undermined traditional freight services that provided such passenger accommodation. However, some travel by **freight vessels** is still possible. The Cadogan Guide *Travel by Cargo Ship* was out of date the day it was published over ten years ago, but its general points are still valid. It deals with 120 itineraries to 300 destinations worldwide, with details of companies and fares. There are a couple of web portals to look at: the Internet Guide to Freighter Travel (*www.geocities.com/ freighterman.geo/mainmenu.html*) and How to Travel By Ship (*www.thetravelers notebook.com/how-to-travel-cargo-ship*). You may have to see the world to reach the USA, but if you have the time (or want space in your life to write a novel) this may be the way to do it.

Only if you want a cruise en route and they offer you a good baggage rate (so you can take all your boxes in the hold) should you consider going over by **transatlantic liner**. Some cruise liners bound for the Caribbean do go over to New York City first of all (to pick up the bulk of their passengers) so you might be able to find a place. Cunard have a Transatlantic Timetable on their main site (*www.cunard.co.uk*). There is also the Berlitz Guide *Cruising and Cruise Ships* (2003).

Strand Travel on (020 7010 9290) can arrange places on **cargo boats** sailing from Thamesport for what they call 'Travellers not Tourists' (*www.strandtravel.co.uk*).

If you want to go to sea and visit America you might consider working on a cruise ship.

BY AIR

The North Atlantic is the most heavily used long-distance route anywhere. So the good news is that there's plenty of flights. The bad news is that the fare structures are very confusing (even for those who use it regularly).

No summary can hope to do justice to the complex web of prices. Try looking at the Sunday papers' travel sections for a sense of the range of travel possibilities and varied prices. The web and increased competition have changed the market out of all recognition since the first edition back in 1988.

The main variations are:

- ordinary full price;
- economy tickets;
- charter fares;
- economy airlines;
- courier flights;
- last minute deals;
- package tours;
- round the world (RTW) via USA.

> **Note**
>
> *Since 1997 there have been new airport departure taxes, but they should be included in the advertised prices of all flights.*

Ordinary full-price tickets

These provide great flexibility as any ticket is almost as good as money, being exchangeable with and between airlines. Tickets can be cancelled without penalty, and there's a generous baggage allowance with good service. If your employer will pay for this, then well and good.

Who buys ordinary tickets? Those for whom money is no object and where flexibility is essential.

Economy tickets

These are what used to be called APEX tickets (Advance Excursion).

Charter fares

These are supposed to be for interest groups booking together, though travel agents have been known to cobble together passengers of no common interest except that of a cheap ticket. There's always the danger of being stranded if your firm goes broke (or hasn't paid its bills). Increasingly though chartering firms are airline subsidiaries or package holiday firms.

Who's for a charter? Those who can't resist the chance of a bargain, and who will not be too inconvenienced if things go wrong, such as single people. You need to be young enough to sleep on airport floors if things go wrong, which seldom happens in transatlantic travel (thanks to US regulation of carriers).

Last-minute deals

Companies have ways of filling seats still unsold at the time of take-off. Aiming to be your first port of call is *www.ebookers.com* where almost all services are available if you can pay by credit card. Also try *www.lastminute.com* and *www.expedia.co.uk.*

There are two incompatible ideas about last-minute bookings: it is better to give away tickets to fill the plane, prices fall just before a flight; the convenience of booking last-minute should be paid for, and thus it's the very early tickets that are cheap, the last-minute ones expensive (as on the trains). Delay making a booking and modern web pages clearly track prices, going up the nearer to the flight the booking is made.

Economy airlines

These have been instrumental in forcing the larger companies to increase their flexibility, helping make economy fares a normal feature of air travel. Though People's Express and Laker have disappeared, Virgin Atlantic still provides scheduled services with and without frills. Their low-price reputation may mean that they are booked up long in advance for the holiday season, though at other times you may be able just to book on the day. Though once associated with second rank travel, Gatwick and Newark rather than the more popular Heathrow and JFK, such days are gone and all the airports have been substantially upgraded in facilities and flight connections. Don't forget to try airlines that are not so well known in the UK as Atlantic carriers, such as Air India (01753 684828), El Al (020 7957 4100) or Air Kuwait (020 7412 0007) via agents such as Bridge of the World (020 7911 0900) or directly from their web pages (via Google).

Travel agents

The 'consolidators' and 'bucket shops' of old have gone, with cut price airlines and people buying online. Such agents as there are offer special services.

See the travel sections of the Sunday papers for the wide array of companies seeking your custom, many specialising in North America. Of course if you only want to see a fleeting glimpse of at most a couple of large US cities there is one further option: as part of a grand tour deluxe.

Courier flights

This used to be the cheapest way to fly. Firms wanted packages hand delivered by the next plane and needed responsible and reasonably presentable couriers. This option became more difficult once the travel pages of most newspapers started advertising the existence of courier services. Then radical changes in courier and shipping services (FedEx, UPS) further reduced the need for amateurs to be involved.

Package tours

The travel sections of the Sunday papers are full of package tours to various sites/ sights, whether fly-drive or accompanied by road or rail.

The Round the World option (RTW)

Most airlines restrict stopovers to a certain predetermined number of locations, usually flying in one direction only. Target prices are about £1,000. **Air New Zealand** (*www.airnewzealand.co.uk*) sees RTW as part of a 'multistop' option, with a special series of pages for 'Round the World Adventure' though getting you to spend time in New Zealand rather than the USA is its aim. There are many specialist operators:

- Round the World Flights (*www.round the worldflights.com*);
- STA Travel (*www.statravel.co.uk*);
- Travel Supermarket (*www.travelsupermarket.com*);
- Around the World Guide (*www.thetravellerUK.com/cheapflights*).

There used to be an array of paperbacks providing RTW advice, but the pace of change in long-distance travel, particularly the availability of web-based information, which is so much more up to date (potentially at least) has meant such books have faded away over the last decade.

INFORMATION UPDATE: INFORMATION OVERLOAD

A caveat to all travel information is necessary: it is now impossible to give concise, accurate and up-to-date information on flights to North America that will not be out of date by the time the information reaches the reader. It is vital to be aware of the range of fares, carriers and packages. The details presented here are merely to suggest the complex range of fare structures that present themselves these days.

Fares change so rapidly it is essential to keep an eye on those newspapers that will bring you up to date. *The Independent*, for example, has a 'Travel Update' section in its Saturday editions, which regularly includes US information. Similar updates can be found in the travel section of *The Sunday Times* or Saturday's *Guardian*. The same paper's weekend section often deals with regions of the USA (such as the Rockies or Texas) including details on travel operators, hints for independent travel, target prices and any new regulations, taxes, etc. An hour spent reading back copies (in large libraries) or increasingly just by going online to a newspaper and typing in the topic of interest – their software will bring up everything they have on it. *Holiday Which?* also has similar updates, but less frequently deals with the USA, so that relevant articles may well be out of date on prices by the time you come across them.

It also pays to phone around these numbers and explore these websites:

American Airlines	(020) 8572 5555	*www.americanair.com*
British Airways	0345 222111	*www.british-airways.com*
Northwest Airlines	0990 561000	*www.nwa.com*
Jetsave	(01342) 327711	
Virgin Atlantic	(01293) 747747	*www.fly.virgin.com*
Delta	0800 414 767	*www.delta-air.com*
Continental	(01293) 776464	*www.flycontinental.com*
Trailfinders	(020) 7937 5400	*www.trailfinder.com*
United	0845 844 4777	*www.ual.com*
Icelandic	(020) 7388 5599	*www.icelandair.co.uk*

WHAT ARE YOUR NEEDS?

Consider your family status: are you really willing to take the same risks with others as you did when you were a student? Or as a student do you really want the frills when a day or so camping out at the airport could leave you with enough money to take the train out to the west coast? Be honest with yourself as to your real needs, discuss it with others, and then make a coolly reasoned decision. How critical would things be if it turned out you had made the wrong decision?

DESTINATIONS

Most Europeans bound for the USA fly into eastern airports, though those bound for the west coast can fly direct into Los Angeles, for an overcrowded and unpleasant experience, or San Francisco. Travellers from the Far East or Australasia will pass through customs and immigration in Hawaii (an attempt to take the pressure off Los Angeles International).

Flying 'direct' and flying 'non-stop'

Don't expect to fly straight to a western or southern destination. For Las Vegas be prepared to fly to San Francisco (for immigration control) and then fly east to Las Vegas. Direct does not equal straight through or non-stop. Direct to Hawaii may mean via Los Angeles, with an enforced stopover possible. Direct to Washington DC can actually mean to Kennedy Airport in New York and then on USAir's 'Eagle' (almost a crop-duster) for a spectacular low-level flight down over the Chesapeake to Dulles International Airport. 'Direct' does *not* necessarily mean Heathrow non-stop to National Airport. With children such changes can add considerably to anticipated angst. Northwestern from Manchester to Orlando actually goes via Amsterdam, an exhausting finale on the long journey home. And as UK airlines change their US partners such interchanges can only get more confusing.

UK connections

Don't forget you may have to fly first to a London airport. Some companies provide free regional airport connections, though usually not during high season. If you have to use a regional airport consider by-passing London all together. Fly to Amsterdam for KLM-Northwestern flights direct to Orlando rather than fly to London, then New York or Atlanta only to have to change for Orlando.

TRAVEL PROTECTION

The bonding situation is complex and potentially bewildering. Keep up to date by watching and listening to travel programmes and by reading the travel pages of the press. The most accessible explanation of the situation is given in *Holiday Which?* (available in most public libraries or *www.which.co.uk*) which has warned that not all scheduled flights are covered by existing bonding arrangements (though if you pay by credit card you may be able to claim against the card issuing bank). If in doubt book with an IATA airline through their official website. Don't rely upon Air Travel Organiser's Licensing (ATOL) or ABTA bonding as these cover only tours or package holidays. For more information see *www.abta.com/benefits.html.*

Travel insurance

About a third of Brits going overseas have inadequate insurance. In the USA you need full coverage, and then some. And don't delay seeking insurance until you arrive. CDs may be cheaper in the USA, but insurance certainly isn't. And buying your insurance package in the UK means that travel insurance will be included, covering cancellation and loss of luggage, besides health and accident liability once in the USA. You will also be acquiring reasonably priced insurance as an ordinary traveller, whereas once in the US already you will have become an exotic, and therefore risky and hence expensive, outsider.

If you feel that exam failure may force a cancellation, checking to ensure there is a cancellation clause is essential. Check what is and isn't covered. Death of a spouse is almost certainly covered: change of mind won't be. Older travellers may dislike increased premiums and higher excess limits. Policies vary though. Some age loadings only apply to those 70 and over, and then only on long-haul journeys over two weeks. Others have no age loading on long haul journeys. Start at *www.travelinsuranceforseniors.co.uk* or *www.instant-online-insurance.co.uk. The Telegraph* online site has regular questions and answers on travel for the over-60s.

It pays to shop around, particularly if you are intent on dangerous diversions such as skiing or climbing. Most insurance sites have sections dealing specifically with such extras:

- *www.britishinformation.com*
- *www.holidayinsurance.com*

And don't forget 'the Travel Shop' at *www.saga.co.uk*, the specialists for all over-60s. Don't rely upon being covered by promises of 'free travel insurance' given by credit and debit card companies, though gold card customers may be offered some useful cover. And you don't have to buy the insurance package offered by the travel agent from whom you bought the fly-drive package agents or airlines. Insurance mark-ups are high, and you may well obtain a better deal from going to a specialist such as Endsleigh (*www.endsleigh.co.uk* for details of your nearest shop), or via an all-purpose site (such as *www.ebookers.com*).

The recent success story of travel insurance is the annual policy, which has become increasingly competitive allowing any number of trips of up to three weeks at a time. A year-long policy will also cover baggage and money within the UK, particularly worthwhile if you take trips at home as well as abroad.

SINGLE-PARENT FAMILY TRIPS

In the US families with only one child have traditionally had to pay adult fares, or only slightly less, for the first child. If there were bulk buying on behalf of single-parent families, prices would surely come down. The Single Parent Travel Club (*www.spta.org.uk*) organises holidays in the UK and overseas, including the USA. Google 'single parent travel' for a range of regional and national groups for more ideas, contacts and group fares.

NEW YORK CITY

London to New York City must be the world's most competitive international route. All major airlines want to run scheduled services between **London-Heathrow** and **John F. Kennedy**, the major terminal on Long Island, or failing that between **London-Gatwick** and **Newark-New Jersey** (just across the Hudson River from Manhattan). Previous restrictions on which airlines used which airport have been eased recently, making guidelines for travellers that much more difficult, particularly with the recent 'open skies' policy.

Kennedy Airport is easier to navigate these days as immigration, baggage reclaim and customs have been modernised under new Dutch (KLM) management. Changing money and getting into town are easy: 24-hour banking and Carey Coaches into Manhattan. Beware of unlicensed (and hence uninsured) cabs.

Newark has just had a massive face-lift to bring improved links with the Jersey turnpike, a monorail connection to Amtrak trains, a revamped Terminal C for

Continental Airlines plus 6,000 new car parking spaces. Work continues on extending the runway to reduce ground delays, which the authorities admit can sometimes be 'intolerable'. A six-hour stopover can range from being miserable to merely boring. Take a good book if delays are possible.

Fare structures are complicated and confusing, but still the best way to keep abreast of new deals is to see the weekend newspapers.

Gatwick (very accessible via Victoria Station, through-trains from the Midlands and North via Kensington-Olympia, or the M25) may be a better source of cheap fares than Heathrow. Don't forget regional airports such as **Manchester, Glasgow** and now **Birmingham**.

Weekend short breaks

■ All major airlines periodically offer a package of return flight, two or three nights' hotel accommodation plus a ticket for a Broadway show at eye-catching prices. There is something approaching a true 'freemarket' in airline tickets on the Atlantic run – hundreds of rival suppliers, low government control and, via the web, an informed public. The price is what the market will sustain when you go to buy. These packages are usually for the low demand season just before the Christmas holidays. After mid-November a Saturday night away may be required. Travel must be completed by mid-December, when normal traffic picks up.

■ A useful website is provided by the city's tourist board (*www.nycvisit.com*).

WASHINGTON DC AND BALTIMORE MD

BA flies direct to Dulles International Airport, which though in northern Virginia is only 20 miles by purpose-built expressway from the White House and Interstate 95, the major north-south motorway along the east coast. Fly-drive packages are available, with pre-paid accommodation vouchers, but you may well need to book ahead for motel accommodation in the DC area due to the number of American visitors to the national capital area, even outside major holiday periods.

The alternative is to fly into Baltimore-Washington International which lies on the freeway linking Baltimore Maryland and Washington DC. It is actually very little further from central DC than is Dulles, and for those visitors for the capital's northern (that is Maryland) suburbs a deal more convenient. Both cities provide access to the vast Chesapeake area, the Atlantic beaches, and the Blue Ridge (only an hour to the west).

SOME OTHER GATEWAY CITIES

■ **Atlanta**. Delta flies from Manchester and Gatwick to Atlanta connecting to Nashville and much of the south east. Atlanta is a major travel hub for road and rail connections onward.

■ **Boston**. Virgin Atlantic, BA, American and Northwestern all have direct flights from the UK to this city that is considerably nearer Europe than even New York. Take the subway into the city centre from this conveniently off-shore airport, or try the water shuttle if only for the view.

■ **Chicago** is the great hub of the interior Great Lakes area. Try American Airlines, or Air India from Heathrow.

■ **Dallas** is served by BA, for links to much of the Great Plains and the Rockies, particularly ski resorts such as Aspen.

■ **Las Vegas** is now served 'non-stop' from Gatwick by Virgin Atlantic.

■ **Los Angeles** has the famously overcrowded LEX to which you can fly directly over the Pole avoiding the even longer flight to the east coast and across the continent. If you come via Asia or Australia you may find you go through Customs and Immigration in Hawaii, relieving the pressure on LEX.

■ **Miami and Orlando** are increasingly major entry points for Europeans and South Americans, though Miami is a day's long drive from Disneyworld. Expedia, Ebookers or Cheapflights will show you the range available.

■ **San Francisco** is now served by a range of airlines. Kelkoo will compare possibilities (*www.travel.kelkoo.co.uk*).

PRE-PAID TOUR OR INDEPENDENT TRAVEL?

If you have already experienced the USA it is more fun to book the fly-drive package and then go where you will, staying at motels as the spirit moves you. But for an inexpensive sample of America a pre-paid tour can be both good value and reassuring.

TIPS FOR THE JOURNEY

If you've never flown before here are a few essential points to bear in mind:

■ It's the safest way to travel (and possibly the most boring).

■ You cannot guarantee a particular seat merely by turning up early at check in. Most seats are now allocated beforehand online. Bulkhead seats give a little extra leg room, but generally go to people travelling with children. Emergency exit seats have to be assigned to 'able-bodied' passengers during check in. In 30 years I've had such a seat just once – so it really is a matter of pure luck.

■ Drink only water, juices and soft drinks. Flying such long distances produces dehydration, which alcohol only makes worse. So save any free little bottles of wine and spirits for later – in some motel late at night when you've just pulled off the freeway you'll really enjoy a well-earned shot of your favourite tipple.

■ If you ordered vegetarian meals say so (with seat number) as soon as you board the plane, or take your own food.

■ If you disregard the smoking ban you can be refused a return flight. As with on-board disturbances, carriers can land and charge the extra landing fees to the offender. Don't be tempted to smoke extra cigarettes before boarding to compensate for a nicotine-free flight – the drop in nicotine levels will be that more intense and the withdrawal symptoms worse.

Getting to the airport

The flight will be stressful enough. Go easy on getting to the airport. Major motorway black-spots such as the M4/M25 near the Heathrow airport access road and the M6 southbound through the West Midlands should be avoided if possible. Birmingham, Manchester and Heathrow now all have purpose-built mainline railway connections. The newly opened Paddington to Heathrow service runs four times per hour, though for passengers coming from the North it may still be quicker to take the airport bus or the underground. And you can now order your duty free online, as well as pre-book your car parking (*www.baa.co.uk*). For a map to BCP car parks check out the BCP page (*www.bcponline.co.uk*). All cars are being actively discouraged not just from the immediate vicinity of arrivals and departure areas but from major airports completely, keeping the roads open where possible to avoid the jams so familiar at Heathrow.

Buying dollars

Take US dollar traveller's cheques (**NOT** sterling) and some currency for when you arrive. You can usually find a Bureau de Change at your UK airport. You can even order cash from Travelex and collect it at the airport (*www.travelex.co.uk*). Post Offices across the UK now sell dollars over the counter at reasonable rates.

Immigration control

Have your passport ready on the plane (not in your luggage in the hold) for filling in the various official US forms. The immigration form asks for your address (a relic of the view that new arrivals are coming to settle down rather than to travel around as tourists). Give a friend's address, or a motel address. (If you don't yet know, make an intelligent guess such as the Holiday Inn, Orlando, Florida).

After the immigration official has checked your form it'll be stapled into your passport above your visa. Keep it like that until you are leaving (when an airline representative will take it and return it to the authorities).

Customs

There may not always be a red/green choice, so every arrival may meet an officer face to face. Keep your passport ready – if only because customs officials seem less understanding for returning US citizens. Be prepared to open *all* your cases as they check for drugs, weapons and fruit.

You may be required to identify your baggage immediately you clear immigration, but it may then disappear for collection elsewhere. Presumably dogs and X-ray equipment have access to the baggage. The process is particularly evident in large airports, and those with substantial links with Latin America (such as Orlando International Airport next to Disneyworld).

Waiting at the airport

The earlier you reach check-in the longer you have to wait, a particular problem for travellers with active children. Most lounges are restricted to first and business-class, so you need to stake out comfortable seats and be prepared to explore the shopping and fast-food facilities.

Insurance: property and health

It is necessary to buy cover before leaving the UK. It is unlikely to be available in the USA (until you become resident, but that's another matter). Check with your credit or charge card company as to whether or not 'free' cover is available for those using their card for booking the flight and accommodation. If you have an 'all risks' household insurance package you may already have 60 days' worldwide cover. Check your policy's small print, and double-check with the agent (and even they may have to check with authorities higher up). Beware of the amount you have to pay before the insurer pays up (the 'excess'). You may need further cover for portable computer equipment or musical instruments. Try *www.endsleigh.co.uk*. For the USA you do need $10 million worth of health cover. Will the policy fly you home if you are seriously injured? Will it fly your relatives out if you are too ill to move? Over 65 years old? Expect double premiums. What's the cancellation/curtailment cover for your trip of a lifetime? Are certain activities such as white water rafting excluded? Can they be included? If you intend to visit the USA frequently consider yearly cover rather than per trip. It may well be cheaper to obtain single cover for health and baggage. Quiz your insurance company.

Returning home

Always confirm your return flight at least a couple of days beforehand. Schedules may be changed for all sorts of reasons – air-traffic controllers elsewhere may be on strike, or bad weather may have trapped planes half a world way. Check in in good time, especially if you have lots of luggage and a family. Getting on board in a relaxed frame of mind is always a good idea, especially when planes are likely to be full. Families will want to sit together, so use online check-in whenever possible. New planes have individual screens providing everyone with a good view. And remember: you can only bring £148 worth of goods back into the UK per adult before VAT and duty become payable.

Luggage claims

Insure your baggage, but keep hold of it at airports. Thefts at New York's JFK continue to increase, mainly when travellers accept assistance only to see their bags take off. Heavy suitcases may be safe on baggage trolleys, but holdalls have been known to be snatched, particularly at kiosks. At Heathrow solo parents and pregnant women can now call for a porter, free of charge, via a Help Point in car parks, terminals and baggage reclaim halls. British trolleys remain free. At many US airports you need US coins or low denomination bills (save these from a previous visit) or a credit card. Kennedy and Newark airports have now introduced self-service luggage carts available free of charge at international arrival terminals.

Being bumped off a long-haul flight

It is standard for airlines to overbook flights to compensate for (or rather take advantage of) 'no-shows', those ticket holders that for whatever reason fail to show up for the flight. If you are travelling on a flight from or between EU countries 'Denied Boarding' legislation provides between €250 and €600 compensation, though as departure looms you may be able to volunteer to be left behind for considerably more. In the USA it is not unheard of to be offered a return flight to anywhere in the USA that the airlines flies (plus of course a seat on the next flight to your present destination).

To avoid being bumped, reconfirm your flight and check in early. Late arrivals, especially those who have not reconfirmed their return flight, are the most likely to be bumped, though if you insist you can ask to travel with the flight crew or jump seats. You may find that having used these seats for take-off you are required to stand the rest of the journey and go without meals (yes, on a transatlantic flight!). Such arrangements are only possible if the captain accepts that there are exceptional reasons for your being at your destination (a funeral might help).

Jet lag

Tired? Nauseous? Just flown across more than four time zones? Feelings of disorientation are not just due to sleep deprivation, or even the thin air (less pressure inside trans-Atlantic crossings is about the same as being at 8,000 feet) but may well have something to do with melatonin, a hormone produced by the brain to set the body clock. Whether synthetic melatonin, available from health food shops and pharmacies in the USA, can eliminate jet lag is still debated. But what is generally agreed is that long journeys should start with a good night's sleep (how many of us stay up late packing only to get up very early to reach the airport just in time thinking we'll catch up on our sleep on the plane!). If you can afford to stay at a hotel near the airport so much the better.

But what else can be done on the journey?

- Reset your watch to the time at the point of arrival on take off.

- Sleep with eyeshades.

- Use earplugs to minimise the effect of pressure changes. Boots sell an up-market version with a ceramic filter to allow air to seep in while protecting the inner ear, and many up-market headphones have noise cancellation ear inserts or similar devices.

- Eat lightly.

- Drink plenty of water before and during the flight.

- Avoid excessive alcohol.

- Get a good night's sleep on arrival. This can be difficult if welcoming hosts insist on celebrating, but from my experience this is the most effective part of any strategy. Staying for a night on first arrival in a motel where you can go to bed when you want to may be $100 well spent, and usually means you are up bright and breezy the following morning ready for a full day, vital if you have to work. Visit friends and relatives at your convenience, not theirs.

If you are going just for a weekend break you can either stay on UK time, getting up and going to bed early even by American standards, or go straight to US time catching up on your sleep once back home – easier on those returning on a morning flight rather than the traditional overnight 'red eye'.

You may have had a big party before coming back home, but don't turn up at the check-in inebriated, or you might be refused a seat. The UK Civil Aviation Authority can seek fines of up to £5,000 or even two years in prison for abusive in-flight behaviour, and airlines would rather avoid problems by leaving people behind.

Check-in

Most flights to North America involve very early starts. Many passengers increasingly find it easier to stay overnight at an airport hotel. Ask if they have any special deals available (which may include free parking while you are away). At Gatwick, for instance, there is a typically wide array of overnight accommodation, such as the Hilton (01293 518080), the Holiday Inn (01293 529991), Forte Meridien (01293 568307) or Travelodge (0800 850950) at about £50 per night.

Manchester has the Posthouse (0161 437 5811), the Hilton (0161 436 4404), the Holiday Inn (0161 498 0333). For off-site hotels call 0161 489 2063. Glasgow has two airport hotels: Posthouse (0141 587 1212) and The Premier Inn (0141 842 1563). Call 0141 887 7220 for off airport options. For Heathrow contact Hotel Reservations (0800 716298) for a wide range of overnight possibilities and shuttle availabilities. Hounslow Tourist Information has an even wider array (020) 8572 8279).

SUMMARY

- Going to the USA is now far easier than for previous generations but paradoxically the very large numbers of ways of getting to the USA, particularly the ever growing number of flights, fly-drive packages and all-in holidays means that any prospective visitor can suffer from information overload.

- This chapter has suggested some of the main ways of travelling to the USA, but which is best can still be difficult to work out. Try coming at the choice from two different directions: what's affordable and what's the realistically minimal convenience needed. If you have these two sorted out, most options fade away to leave a considerably smaller field from which to choose.

- Don't overestimate what you can do as you get older, or with children, or with changing financial circumstances. It is all too easy to become locked into a way of approaching travel that reflects previous, perhaps fitter, single or more flexible days.

- And equally don't underestimate the cost of moving around the USA once you get there. The image remains of cheap travel whether by bus, car or plane. Per mile it may be cheap, but those miles just go on adding up. Take every advantage possible of cheap deals negotiated *before* leaving the UK, whether bus passes, multiple stop-over plane trips, or merely a good deal on car hire through a transatlantic airline.

AMERICA AT THE CLICK OF A MOUSE

When this book was in its infancy there were hardly any books for US-bound travellers, with the sole exception of the BUNAC student guide. Now even the smallest bookshop in the most unfashionable town has both a travel section and at the very least a shelf of guides, not just to the USA but to specific areas and even individual cities. But just as the guidebooks seem to have cornered the market in providing advice everything is changing.

Browsing the web

Today there is the Internet, or as it is more popularly though not quite correctly called, the web. Not only have guidebook publishers started to provide information via the web, so has almost everyone else. Summer camps, transit authorities, the US Citizenship & Immigration Service, motel chains, B&Bs, states, unions, chambers of commerce, all have their web pages. And better still, there are ways of finding their web addresses that don't require you to already have the very information you are actually looking for, as happens all too frequently when using printed sources like directories.

Go to a web browser ('**search engine**') and type in a phrase such as 'US rental accommodation' and you will find that a whole page of people offering accommodation may appear. Scrolling down, it may immediately become apparent that there are just too many people listed, so you have to learn how to give the browser enough but not too much detail. And then you'll realise you are in the wrong category as everyone seems to be offering unfurnished apartments and houses for long-term rent.

If you want holidays lettings in Virginia near the beach try 'vacation rental accommodation Virginia' and only those interested in holiday lets will be displayed. Beware: if you type in 'holiday rentals' you will only find details of rental arrangements for US public holidays such as 4 July. Two weeks off in August is a vacation, not a holiday. You need to adjust to local usage quickly!

But with each refinement the search narrows. Indeed many pages start with a nationwide map, where you just click the state you are interested in, and so on downwards. Sometimes your search will end with a particularly property with associated directions and a map. If you were looking for Bed & Breakfasts you might well end up looking at photographs of the resident owners, with a tour of the property via a webcam.

Getting the details

This ability to obtain great detail can be very useful. If you want to stay at motels while in the Washington DC area, type in the name of a motel chain. You will be offered a list of states, or perhaps a US map. With a few further clicks you can be looking at an array of motels in the District of Columbia area, each with their own street map and directions off the interstate, with details about reaching the main tourist sites. Without a single phone call you can find that there is indeed an Econolodge within easy reach of Mount Vernon (George Washington's home) and that there is also a Travelodge on Columbia Pike along which buses bound for the nearest Metro station pass every few minutes, for those visitors wanting an easy access to the downtown sites without having to worry about downtown parking. Some sites may even have photographs of the accommodation, and each motel will be listed with its own map which you can download and take with you, a great help if you travel using merely a highways map where urban detail is only provided for a few downtown blocks around the downtown.

Making enquiries

Many websites, such as those for B&Bs, will come with not just a traditional address, but also an email address. Send off an enquiry, and when you log onto your mail the next morning there may well be several replies already. It's a lot quicker than the postal service, and you don't have to have a fax machine for an instantaneous connection. If you do intend to send a fax don't forget that as more people switch to broadband fewer people have kept up their fax facility (have you?). You may not read what you had hoped: all the places you can afford may well be full when you want to stay. But at least you know now and not in two weeks' time, and can quickly act accordingly.

Becoming your own travel agent

The web now allows the PC owner to compile detailed information beyond the capabilities of even the most specialist travel agent. You can become your own travel agent and book not just your stateside accommodation but also your transatlantic flight, car rental and insurance. If in doubt where to start, go to *www.yahoo.co.uk* and click the 'Travel' category where departure and arrival times plus dates and comparative prices appear. Then try more dedicated sites such as Ebooker or Expedia.

Beware

If you are trying to find information about services, such as flights or insurance, you are buying over here, make sure you are using a 'UK and Ireland' specific search engine. Yahoo will often default back to its US parent unless you make sure you hit the 'UK and Ireland' button before a search. When seeking US contacts you can, of course, go straight to the US version of Yahoo and its rivals, (of which the world's favourite remains Google).

You can still enquire via the web and book through travel agents, but you may well feel by now that that it is bit too much like having a dog and barking yourself. Airlines increasingly recognise the need to do business direct with the customer. That way they won't have to pay agents' fees for your business. And most flights are now ticketless, so long as you print off your finally agreed schedule.

Making payments

It is possible to email credit card numbers, though you might reasonably feel less than enthusiastic about this. Who knows where the numbers might end up? But money can be wired from banks. Money orders can be sent. Of course, for UK services you just put a cheque in the post. And though web access is not for free (besides the PC you have to have a modem, the right software, and an account with an Internet Service Supplier), once you have the technology in place an email to America costs the same as one to your neighbour, and an hour or so downloading web pages shouldn't cost more than a pound or so if done outside peak hours, particularly if you have broadband. And once abroad you can seek out local cybercafés where you can access further web information.

Useful websites

Before you leave:

American Airlines	*www.americanair.com*
British Airways	*www.british-airways.com*
Continental Airlines	*www.flycontinental.com*
Delta Airlines	*www.delta-air.com*
United Airlines	*www.united.com*
Virgin Atlantic	*www.virgin-atlantic.com*
Health advice	*www.nhsdirect.nhs.uk*
Travel health	*www.fitfortravel.nhs.uk*
Distance calculator	*www.mapcrow.info/*
Online maps	*www.randmcnally.com*
Embassies	*www.embassy.org*
General tourism	*www.visitusa.org.uk*

Accommodation in the USA and across the world:

www.hotelstravel.com (Internet hotel finder)
www.ebooker.com (online reservations)

www.disneyworld.co.uk/trip_planner (Disney reservations)
www.holiday-inn.com (Holiday Inn)
www.radisson.com (Radisson Hotels world-wide)
www.westin.com (Westin Hotels and Resorts)

Youth hostels:

www.hostelworld.com/usa
www.hiusa.org

Getting to the airport:

www.nationalrail.co.uk
www.nationalexpress.co.uk/
www.travellers-world.info/rail.html

Home exchange:

www.homexchange.com/index.html
www.homlink.org
www.intervac.com

Federal Express	*www.fedex.com*
Travel books	*www.stanfords.co.uk*
Travel guide	*www.cnn.com/travel*

Web access to cheap flights

The trouble with all approaches to obtaining cheap fares is that the fares may well disappear between finding out about them, thinking about them, and trying to book them. Other travellers too will be surfing for cheap fares, particularly if there is a public holiday or event involved. As such sites are ever changing it may well be that by the time you read this a particular site may have either blossomed or have disappeared altogether. But if it has disappeared by the time you come to surf the net for cheap fares, fear not, there will be other sites and if you go to *http:// uk.ask.com* ask a question, such as 'Where do I find cheap airfares?' in real English.

Using the web

There are many guides to using the world wide web. A glance across the computer magazines in any newsagent will reveal a plethora of net-specific magazines, many of which now pride themselves on providing a beginner's guide to surfing the net – and often carry up-to-date information on particular travel sites.

6

Travelling About

The USA is continental in scale. Not to experience this is to miss an essential ingredient of the country (almost like Americans visiting Europe and seeing nothing of its historical traditions). But, being so vast, the distances can eat up much of your precious time, whether you are a visitor or a resident. Hence the attraction of flying.

Do not try to see too much, especially in your first trip. Vary your schedule so that though some days may involve 400 miles of freeway, others will involve taking detours to visit historical sights (Civil War battlefields or colonial settlements are excellent, and usually inexpensive). Driving the country roads can be very interesting and a great change of pace. Driving from Atlanta to Washington DC? Try US15 across Virginia, or even the Blue Ridge Parkway, both of which run parallel to major freeways.

Don't expect to visit four national parks in four days. Even if you can manage the driving you will probably get scenic overload (as in 'Oh no! Not more mountains' felt towards the end of six weeks' criss-crossing of the Rocky Mountains). Would you want to 'do' Snowdonia in one day, the Lake District the next, and then the Highlands before Edinburgh *en route* for London-Heathrow?

In the days of YouTube it is easy to find extracts or clips from almost anywhere, but the quality is extremely variable. For a well edited, professional small-screen experience, look at the United States selection at *www.travelvj.com/travel_videos* (I particularly liked Pioneer Square in Seattle. Is that the original Starbucks?)

TRAVELLING BY CAR

For anything but a coach tour a car really is essential for everyone visiting the USA and with petrol ranging around the $4 mark cars are cheap to run by European standards (though don't tell that to Americans). Even a one-resort holiday can be greatly improved by a few days visiting nearby sights, theme parks, or just experiencing the open road.

The USA is larger, and the distances between cities greater, so the time needed to explore is that much greater than in the UK. Costs per mile are still low compared to Europe, but the distances so great the overall costs can still be quite a surprise. There *are* positive aspects though:

■ Local car hire is very reasonably priced.

■ Petrol remains cheap by European standards.

■ Motoring means wide roads and lots of places to park (particularly as Americans start to restrict their travelling).

■ For most of the freeway network driving is actually relaxing due to the legal 65/70 mph speed limits. (Around cities, though, freeways are like bad sections of the M6.)

So a holiday based, for instance, near central Florida's Disneyworld can be both wide-ranging (Florida Keys to the south, Fort Augustine in the northeast, and Panama City to the northwest) *and* very reasonably priced, especially if car hire is booked as part of the flight and accommodation package, or just pre-booked from the UK. Such special rates usually involve collecting and returning the car from the same airport, and may require you to stay within the one state (which may be larger than the UK!). For general information contact:

■ The American Automobile Association (AAA) – known as the 'triple-A' – is actually a federation of state or regional associations with reciprocal arrangements (*www.aaamidatlantic.com*). The 'Triple A' publish useful guides through their website *http://travel.aaa/travelinformation.html*.

■ Jamie Jensen, *Road Trip USA: Cross Country Adventures on America's Two-lane Highways* (2006) is an invitation to be a traveller not tourist.

- Bill Bryson, *The Lost Continent: Travels in Small Town America* (1989) – America out of the rearview mirror.

- Andrew Vincent, *Drive USA* (2002) is an interesting overview by a BBC producer in the light of a career on the road – from using cruise control to options at an accident.

CAR HIRE (US = rental)

A few numbers to try in the UK before booking:

- Alamo: 0870 400 4562 (*www.alamo.co.uk*);
- Avis: 0844 581 0147 (*www.avis.co.uk*);
- Budget: 0844 581 9998 (*www.budget.co.uk*);
- Thrifty: 0808 234 7642 (*www.thrifty.co.uk*);
- Hertz: 0870 846 0013 (*www.hertz.co.uk*);
- Dollar 0808 234 7524 (*www.dollar.com*).

One of the best sources for rental information is Breezenet's Guide to Airport Rental Cars (at *www.bnm.com*) where for each US city best deals are listed, with online booking instructions, including a useful introduction to the jargon and acronyms. The best website remains Expedia (*www.expedia.co.uk*), but do try rivals such as *www.kayak.co.uk*.

Questions to ask

What's the **collision damage waiver** (CDW), **loss damage waiver** (LDW) and the **personal accident insurance** (PAI) situation? US booking clerks will assume you know what these terms (or even initials) mean, and may never have had to explain them before. Ensure that *you* know what they mean!

Without CDW you are liable for collision damage (up to something like $5,000). For peace of mind CDW is probably essential, though costly (an extra that can be up to 30 per cent on top of the quoted or pre-paid costs). LDW covers tyre damage, vandalism, theft and loss of use (if your vehicle is being repaired).

PAI is more modest, but may be unnecessary if you have already bought adequate health insurance for your trip before leaving the UK. Check your policy's small print for whether you need extra PAI. Don't rely on advice from the sales clerks: they won't know, and anyway they make commission on every policy they sell.

> **Remember**
>
> *Your UK car insurance will not cover your trip to the USA so you will need a complete coverage. US clerks are used to dealing with American customers who already have their car rental insurance needs covered by their domestic policies. And complete insurance is expensive if bought in the USA: buy it at home.*
>
> *Don't rely on the £3 million cover in your general travel insurance – its personal liability section covers everything except driving. So in case you are sued by a third party (someone you hit) you do need extra cover. And don't think the free travel insurance you got by paying with a credit card will give you third party cover – it doesn't. Personal liability insurance (PLIS) cover is advisable, to protect you from being sued by third parties in the case of an accident.*

■ Is the car hire restricted to the one state? What about a trip from a Florida base over into Georgia? Is this permitted? Is suitable insurance cover available? At what extra cost?

■ Can the booking be done via the airline company at the time you buy the airline tickets? Pre-booked rates are considerably better than last minute, at-the-airport rates which are always the most expensive.

■ What's the minimum age for hiring or driving a hired car? Premiums may be required for under-25 drivers. Under 21 is usually prohibited.

■ What size of car would be suitable? A family driving any distance (Miami to Orlando is a six-hour drive on the freeways!) should avoid sub-compacts (Punto equivalents) and go for at least a mid-range four- or five-door saloon (or at least a Ford Tempo) which will have adequate luggage space, a good air conditioning unit, and plenty of inside room. Travelling 55–65 mph on the US highways may be smooth, but it may also be very boring, so comfort, room to stretch, and a suitably powered engine (less noisy if nothing else) are essential.

■ Can a trip **start** and **end** at **different** places? If so what are the drop-off charges? These can be very steep: sometimes equal to the initial hire charge. But having driven from Miami to New York City who wants to drive back down I95 to avoid a

> **Remember**
>
> *Travelling just around Florida is like travelling up and down the length of Britain in terms of distances. Travelling around the USA is continental travel. Would you drive the family from London to Athens in a VW Beetle? If you can, fly. If not, use as large a car as you can afford. And don't assume the size and type of car you used as a student is still appropriate as a parent.*

couple of hundred dollars drop-off charge? It may be worth paying the charge to be able to stay and enjoy New York City rather than to end a family holiday with four days driving flat-out on the freeway (plus motel charges that would probably equal the drop-off charge alone).

■ Can **all payments** (except petrol of course) be made **before leaving** for the USA? Or will there be extras, such as state tax or deposits on the vehicle? Taking a 'fly-drive' package from a major UK or US airline may mean low or no deposit, minimum hassle, and priority booking (at an advantageous price). Will there be a fuel charge? This may involve an additional service charge but means no need to refuel before returning the car.

■ Avoid 'fuel purchase plans'. They encourage you to prepay for a full tank, or return with a part-filled tank and pay for what you have used. If you pay for a full tank you inevitably hand some back at the return check in. If you pay for a refill, petrol is charged at twice the retail price.

■ If your **credit card** is used for ID (identification) will it also be used to **block-off** a line of credit as a **deposit**? This question needs some explaining. Even though you may have pre-paid for your care hire (perhaps as part of a 'fly-drive' package) most hire companies will still require Mastercard, VISA or American Express as ID.

So far so good. But beware: they may well use your card to block-off a credit line of several hundred dollars as a deposit. This is not a credit from your account into theirs, to be recredited upon your returning the car intact. Rather it is blocking off a part of your unused credit line.

For instance, if you have £1,500 as your limit with £500 of outstanding debt, then you have a credit line of £1,000 left. If the car hire company were then to block off £200 for the duration of your hiring their car you would only have £800, not the £1,000 you might have thought you still had.

This only becomes a problem if you have only, say, £200 left of your credit line (surely enough for an occasional extra on a pre-paid holiday given all the travellers' cheques you are carrying). All your £200 may well be blocked off, without your being made aware of this. Upon arriving at a motel cash desk you present your card, only to have the central computer in New York say that you have no credit left, not even the £200 you expected. At the end of a three-week stay you may well have spent more than you expected, relying upon that £200 for the last couple of days.

Such inconvenience might even continue after you have returned the car intact – it takes time to unblock a blocked line of credit.

Ask exactly how much of a credit line is being blocked, and if possible, before leaving home pay off as much of the credit card debt as you can to enlarge your line of credit. And do this in enough time for the central computer to have the new state of your account before you use your card in the USA.

For summer 2008 hire firms quoted £100–200 per week for even the smallest car (including CDW) plus tax and personal accident insurance per day. Budget on $30 per day for petrol on long distance trips.

■ For petrol prices across the USA take a look at *www.gasbuddy.com* which tracks changes from state to state with maps to help find the best pump price.

Rentals: any alternatives?

■ **Part holiday hire.** Here you pick up your car only when you intend to travel away from your arrival area. If staying a week at Disneyworld-Epcot before touring it might be worth your while to take a bus or taxi from the airport on your arrival, picking up the car only when you actually need it a week later. You'll hardly need a car at the self-sufficient Disney complex.

Similarly if you intend to spend a final week in central New York City it might be wise to return ('check in') the hired car as soon as you arrive (after perhaps a circuit of the main highway and bridges), travelling by subway or even by taxi to avoid car parking costs (astronomical). *But*, if you want to explore central Florida or New York's Long Island keeping the car will be essential. Don't rely upon being able to borrow friends' cars – they'll probably need them just to function normally.

■ **Delivery driving.** Drive a car for someone flying long distances. Specialist companies, listed in *Yellow Pages* as 'Automatic Transporter and drive-away companies', will link you up with people seeking to avoid long-distance driving. Be prepared to be fingerprinted, photographed and charged a $500 deposit that will be returned when the car is produced safe and on time. The general route will be set out for you, with 300 to 400 miles per

An Aussie leaving Norfolk, Virginia, bound for Sydney by way of Los Angeles got to drive a rock-star's British registered Daimler right across country, complete with peaked cap for driver. His wife rode behind in style!

day expected. In Miami cars may well be available for New York City using I95, with small detours allowed for accommodation. For a couple with luggage this can be a godsend. For a useful overview see the Driving USA section of the packpacker's site (*www.backpackeressentials.com. au*).

■ **Motor homes.** These huge motorised caravans (also called **campers** or **RVs/ recreational vehicles**) give plenty of space for a family of four, though are probably no cheaper than a car plus motel accommodation unless pre-booked as part of a bargain package. All mod-cons are standard – toilet, shower, mains-voltage generator and hook-up facilities for organised stopping sites. Contact Cruise America for details (*www.cruiseamerica.com*).

Unlike cars they usually have to be returned to the place of hire (no one-way rentals), and they only give about 10 mpg. But they can allow you to explore the main highway: US parks are plentiful, well kept and often have hook-up facilities, though parks such as Yosemite in California are now so popular entry has to be pre-booked very early in the year for school holiday periods. Kampgrounds of America (KOA) can be contacted beforehand from the UK (*www.koacamp grounds.com*).

More importantly, staying in such parks allows you to meet ordinary middle-Americans (the famous 'Silent Majority') in fairly relaxed surroundings. Unlike the situation in impersonal motels people do mix in park camp sites, children soon find playmates, and barbecues sound to the music of the banjo and guitar. Officially alcohol is usually banned, but if no one gets silly, beer (and ice!) usually appear from the huge coolers people take with them everywhere.

■ **Motor bikes.** Enthusiasts believe this is the only way to travel across country. It's even possible to rent a Dream Machine such as a Harley-Davidson for use in the US through Ride Free Motorcycle Tours. Riders must be at least 21 years old and hold a full bike licence. There's a website too (*www.freeride.com*). Those of us less adventurous can join a tour over very different terrains from coast to mountain (*www.ca-motorcycletours.com*).

■ **Borrowing from family or friends.** This is not usually a good idea, unless as part of a house swap. The easiest way to outstay your welcome is to have your host's car when their work, shopping and kids' routines all depend upon them having two cars. Having said that, though, Americans are amazingly generous with offering the use of their cars, albeit the second one. However, it's probably only a good idea for an odd day here and there.

If you need one every day you should hire one, or re-think your visit to concentrate upon those attractions with easy car-less access, as with the museums of central Washington DC, well served by the new Metro (but even so only from certain suburbs).

TAKING THE CAR TO THE USA

In a word: DON'T. At least don't unless it is an exceptional, rare or vintage (low octane) vehicle. The shipping costs are only the start:

■ If you normally use 4-star (96–8 octane) you can't buy it in the USA (US 'premium' grade is about 93 octane). Even if you have a 2- or 3-star car the use of 'premium' is expensive (by US standards).

■ If you are staying more than temporarily you will have to meet very strict federal emission regulations (or worse, California's even stricter rules). The only exceptions are for pre-1956 cars (almost vintage in US terms!) for which no modifications are required or for pre-1966 cars for which only minor modifications to the crankcase are needed.

■ Horror stories abound of cars failing to meet US standards being destroyed at the port of entry.

Words of warning:

■ Even importing US-specification cars will require at least a new catalytic converter if the car has used leaded petrol in Europe.

■ Though a European-bought car may get into the USA, such a private import will have no US warranty, which can make repairs expensive.

As a general rule buying or hiring a car is going to be a better bet, cheaper and more convenient. If you still want to ship your car (or motorbike) call a specialist firm such as Autoshippers, a Bristol-based company (at 0117 982 8123 or *www.autoshippers.co.uk*). Don't forget: if you need to ask the cost you can't afford it.

BUYING A CAR IN THE USA

This may be a very good idea if you are staying for any length of time. Foreign cars have swamped the market, are available at good prices, and spares are readily available. For Europeans such smaller cars are probably easier to handle, especially around town. The only snag may be some residual anti-foreigner feeling, though unless you are going to do business with a US car company or supplier, such feelings are unlikely to affect you. In fact as Americans become more used to foreign cars it is quite likely that names such as Nissan will become as 'American' as Volkswagen! BMW are building in South Carolina, so they are becoming American to ever more people.

Range Rovers, Jaguars and Rolls-Royces are available even though owned by non-British firms these days, and driving one of these will stimulate much favourable admiration. If you are using your Britishness as a selling point driving a 'British' car may be a positive advantage. Patriotic Americans expect others to be equally patriotic.

What's good value for money?

■ **Air conditioning** may seem like a luxury to those who think 21°C (70°F) is a heat wave. But in a hot and muggy 33°C (90°F), air conditioning can make the difference between being able to carry on or not.

> **Beware**
>
> *Relying on moving the heat control from hot to cold will not do the job. All that happens is that hot outside air will be blown through the car without being first further heated by the engine.*

There are a few snags with air conditioning:

1. It can easily put a mile per gallon onto your fuel consumption, but at US prices this is hardly worth considering (power-steering also adds a further loss) unless you are fortunate enough to have hit a low exchange rate.

2. In under-powered cars such as the old Ford Tempo, putting on the air conditioning produced a noticeable loss of power. By the 1990s this problem seemed to be overcome though.

3. Again, in under-powered cars the radiator may boil if the air conditioning is left on while taking the car up long mountain passes. Overloading an under-powered car to go uphill is never a good idea. Take the freeway not the old scenic highway if moving home with a U-Haul behind containing all your worldly belongings.

■ **Size** should not be despised. Though the days of the 'gas-guzzler' may well be over, US cars are still by and large bigger than their UK equivalents. If you intend to go across country, especially with family, you will all welcome the space. If you drive a Mondeo in Britain do you really want to drive the equivalent of London to St Petersburg in something no larger than a Punto?

On holiday you may find that it is worthwhile to get a larger car than usual. After all, do you normally spend most of the day in the car with most of the family? A trip over to Salt Lake City from Atlanta is not a dash down the M1 to see family in Nottingham.

■ **Cruise controls** are only recently becoming generally available in Europe. Put simply, the control is pre-set to a particular speed, say the legal 65 mph maximum. You press the button, and that's the speed you keep to up hill and down dale, come what may. To pass you can still accelerate. Braking, or moving into a lower gear, will cancel the control, to be resumed at the touch of a button. So why bother?
1. It does wonders for your mpg on long trips.
2. It avoids the problem familiar to long-distance drivers of gradually speeding up as the miles pass by, leading to a speeding ticket. And this does happen!
3. It makes long, smooth freeway drives less tiring, especially out west.

Buying new

Good news: As with most consumer goods cars in the USA are generally cheaper than abroad. The vastness and wealth of the market mean the economies of scale can be enacted for basic features, and a wide variety of options can be available.

Bad news: The US 'sticker price' is even more misleading than in the UK. The price that caught your eye may be for the most basic model. The car actually available in the showroom already comes equipped with 'optional' extras, and these mount up. This practice is taking quite a hammering from the Japanese whose cars tend to be fully equipped as standard. *Always* check item by item that what you see is actually included in the asking price, even for foreign cars, then 'dicker' (haggle). For the Coen brothers' take on such extras see the showroom scenes in *Fargo*.

Buying second-hand

Many bargains can be obtained in the USA as a result of the far more widespread desire to have the newest model, come what may. *But* beware:

■ Americans by and large maintain their cars far less well than comparable Europeans (ignore that well-cared-for look).

■ Used-car warranties are usually for about a month, and compared to Europe almost worthless, even when from reputable dealers.

■ The statutory protection now available in the UK is not generally available in the USA.

■ Cars in the snowbelt can suffer from killer corrosion due to the vast amounts of salt put down on the roads.
(*Good news:* Where there is no snow, like southern California, corrosion can be negligible.)

■ Spares may be hard to come by for certain foreign cars, impossible in certain areas. Though Jaguar parts may be easy to obtain in New York City, in Manhattan, Kansas, they may be next to impossible (and so have to be sent from New York City!).

■ In certain states sales tax is payable on private sales. So if you buy a second-hand car from a colleague for $5,000 you will have to pay $250 tax (if the rate is 5 per cent). Don't think you can conveniently 'forget' to pay this: when you go to re-register the car you'll be asked for the receipt and the 5 per cent will be required there and then.

■ The AAA 'New Car Service' is available for *all* car purchases for AAA members.

■ The editors of Used Consumer Reports bring out an annual *Used Car Buying Guide* that identifies models with poor reliability or repair records (available from Amazon).

REPAIRS AND MAINTENANCE

Getting your car serviced can be very expensive. As elsewhere many businesses in this field are run by 'cowboys'. To avoid this trap many people resort to using the authorised dealer, though their rates may be so high as to force you back to the 'cowboys'. I tried to keep my VW Beetle on the road using the local VW dealer in Maryland, but eventually had to resort to the local cut-price cowboys just to be able to pay the bills (and going overdrawn on a US account simply produces cheques that bounce at great expense).

A tune up is often the only maintenance that US cars ever get, not counting the car wash. Tune-up chains will, in theory, check the points and the timing, changing the oil and the plugs for you. But as these chains make their money by rapid turnover and the use of cheap and therefore unskilled labour, you may get better value for money learning to do these jobs yourself, or even getting the neighbour's car-mad teenager to do them for you. Otherwise it's just a case of asking friends and colleagues for their recommendations, and once you have found someone reliable, stick to them. Regular customers generally get the more reliable service. The AAA can provide a list of approved auto-repair facilities in any particular area (for members).

If you are just visiting the USA, car hire will take most of the strain. If the fanbelt breaks on the freeway a reputable company will come and collect you (and allow extra time at the end of the hire period to make up for lost time).

PETROL

Petrol is very cheap compared to Europe. Prices are those last seen at home over ten years ago. Though many economists think US prices are too low, given higher world prices, for the visitor this is wonderful. Unless you drive at 90 mph over hundreds of miles daily, your fuel bill will be the least of your worries. Credit cards, cash and usually dollar traveller's cheques (such as Bank America's VISA cheques) are all readily acceptable.

Most gas stations are now self-service. The days of the personal service are generally over, though facilities are still usually good. But you need to turn the pump on when you've taken the nozzle out of the cradle, unlike in the UK. Most gas stations are more than that (as is becoming the case in the UK). In certain states, such as Virginia, gas stations even sell beer and wine.

Petrol is **regular** or **super**, approximately 2- or 3-star and lead-free. Follow your car hire recommendations.

■ Petrol is available everywhere *but* beware of being caught short in certain areas such as national parks, especially scenic

A word of caution

Most interstate freeways do not have motorway service areas as such (though there are exceptions as along parts of the New York Thruway and Florida Turnpike) so you must leave the freeway to get petrol – hence the enormous company logos looming up in the distance as you approach an exit ramp.

drives such as the Blue Ridge Parkway in North Carolina and Virginia. Some petrol stations do exist on such limited access tourist roads, but they are not well advertised, and you may have to leave the parkway to find petrol. Do *not* leave by the unmarked local access points or you will get hopelessly lost. Wait for the fully signposted exits (such as 'US220 to Roanoke').

■ Likewise out west distances can be so vast between places large enough to have a gas station that you must be careful not to run too low, so fill up before long desert or mountain crossings. Check water and oil too. Do not leave the main road looking for services. If there were any they would be alongside the roadway, or clearly signposted. Put up your bonnet (US hood), tie a handkerchief to the aerial and wait for assistance. Sections where tourists regularly break down or run out of petrol are well known, and usually state patrol cars will turn up (eventually). Traffic going the other way may well use CB (Citizens' Band) radio to alert 'Smokey the Bear' (police) that you need assistance as you may well be out of mobile phone range (another reason to stick to the interstates). Many an empty car has been found by rescue services, but with no sign of the driver, who is later found dead at some distance from the highway.

AAA ('Triple A') Petrol (Gas) Prices for North Carolina*
(Note how far some of these distances are *within* just this state)

Sample road trip ideas	Round trip mileage	Gallons used	Gas cost difference 2007–2008
Asheville to Raleigh	482	20.08	$22.31
Winston-Salem to Wilmington	420	17.50	$19.44
Greensboro to New Bern	384	16.00	$17.78
Durham to Charlotte	280	11.67	$12.96
Boone to Kitty Hawk	806	33.58	$37.31
Atlanta, GA to Asheville	416	17.33	$19.26
Norfolk, VA to Outer Banks	154	6.42	$7.13
Charleston, SC to Blowing Rock	588	24.50	$27.22
Columbia, SC to Raleigh	456	19.00	$21.11
Knoxville ,TN to Winston-Salem	516	21.50	$23.89
Washington DC to Nags Head	552	23.00	$25.55

*Source: AAA's Fuel Gauge Report with estimates based on gas prices as of 21 July 2008 and on passenger vehicle getting 24 mpg.

CAR INSURANCE

This is certainly essential, and mostly required these days. Rental companies will generally offer **collision** and **accident insurance** when you pick up the car. If staying for longer or buying your own car you really must obtain *adequate* cover. But be careful. Read *all* the small print, and ensure that you have bought the cover that you need, and that you have bought what you *think* you have bought.

> I found that my policy didn't cover the theft of the car engine on one occasion, nor on another occasion the theft of the car, presumably by 'joy-riders', with several hundreds of dollars' worth of damage on its return.

Check the arithmetic on your bill. If you have failed to pay the last dollar for whatever reason the company may well refuse to pay, and lawyers cost money to put the pressure on.

Insurance is very expensive, and it may be very tempting to obtain the minimum legal cover. Resist this temptation if at all possible.

Uninsured-driver liability insurance may seem a luxury against a very slight and unlikely risk, but given the number of uninsured drivers it isn't. In many states where insurance is required failure to have it still only produces a derisory fine, and may only be put into effect if the driver has committed a moving violation. Premiums are usually three times higher than in the UK. Even for those with a clean driving record and ten years behind the wheel comprehensive cover is very expensive. And if uninsured drivers are really poor you won't be able to sue them, so you do need to be insured against the uninsured.

LICENCES

Is a British driving licence valid?

Driving is a state responsibility, so the regulations change from place to place. A full British licence is valid for a year in most states, though if you take up residence you may be required to take a state test before that, say after three or six months. Usually there's a highway code test (sometimes automated, often multiple choice). Whether you then have to take a road test depends on the particular state. My Maryland test required the car merely to be parked neatly alongside the kerb, with little else beyond the highway code test and the fee!

Generally northern states have stricter requirements, the southern states more relaxed ones though most are now quite sophisticated compared to 25 years ago. You'll probably be asked to surrender your old British licence. If you do so you will have to tangle with the Swansea DVLC on your return. Avoid this inconvenience by saying you haven't got one to hand in.

What about the International Driving Licence?

This has a confirmation that your licence is in fact a licence, with a dozen translations, one being in Russian. As a British licence is in English it is usually okay on its own. Don't rely just upon the international one – all traffic cops and most rental clerks don't know what it is and don't intend to find out.

Date of birth

The snag with an old-style British licence was its lack of an obvious date of birth. All US licences have a date of birth (hence their use as ID to buy alcohol). New Euro-pink licences have a date of birth clearly visible (available from DVLC in Swansea).

Moving state

If you move home from one state to another you'll need to reapply for a new licence. Cars have to be re-registered too, replacing one state's plates (often called 'tags') with those of the new state. You may also have to remove windscreen stickers legal in a previous state but not in your new one. If you settle down you may still have to renew both from time to time. Sometimes this is automatic, sometimes upon application (plus fee, re-test of the eyes and the highway code).

Passing through

If you are just passing through your licence is valid if valid where issued even if, for instance, you are too young to get a licence in the state you are driving through. Reciprocity exists between not just adjacent states but cross the USA (but your behaviour still has to conform to local requirements even if you are passing through).

Passing the test

The good news is that getting a test is very easy. It may be necessary to book a test, or you may be able just to turn up on spec. Fees are nominal too. Most people pass.

If you can't drive in the USA you are looked upon as eccentric at best, suspicious at worst.

Other ID

Certain jurisdictions issue 'This is not a driver's permit' pieces of identification just so that people who don't drive for whatever reason can carry ID with their full date of birth and full name in a government issued format.

WORDS OF WARNING

Driving in the USA can be a relaxing activity in a large air-conditioned car along the interstate highway out in the countryside. But in cities, especially at rush hour, it can be a nightmare. The width of roads and parking spaces, the use of power steering, and the cheapness of the petrol can all make driving part of the holiday *but* in heavy traffic many US drivers are far from competent. It can also be quite intimidating to follow cars with guns on the back shelf and a bumper sticker proclaiming 'Jesus said it. I believe it. That settles it.' In such a worse case scenario just pull back slowly, and continue on carefully towards the Magic Kingdom.

Cars crowd together even more than in Britain, driving far too close to the car ahead in rush hour traffic. Overtaking takes place on all sides, which can be very alarming even to drivers used to heavy London traffic or the M6 through the West Midlands (Europe's heaviest traffic at rush hour). Drivers of large trucks often drive right up behind cars and intimidate them right out of the way.

After two weeks' leisurely driving across the South arriving in the Washington DC area can be a nightmare at almost any time of day: the traffic is likely to seem aggressive, fast and far too close together. The use of the metro (the underground railway) suddenly becomes very appealing.

And *always* drive defensively.

And *never ever* park within ten feet of a fire hydrant, or in front of a dropped kerb – you risk being towed away.

And *never* overtake a stationary (yellow) school bus. You risk being arrested.

TRAFFIC REGULATIONS AND ROAD SAFETY

Generally these are the same as those you are familiar with at home, though with some tricky variations to keep you on your toes. **Roundabouts** hardly exist, except in a few larger cities, and then only at the junction of large boulevards. If they are called anything it will be **rotaries** or **traffic circles**. Of course, traffic goes anticlockwise, often confusing to those of us who normally drive on the left and are used to giving directions clockwise.

Traffic lights are usually called **stop lights**. Their location can take some getting used to as they are generally on the far side of the intersection to which they refer. Draw up to them at your peril: you will soon find that your rear end is stuck blocking the intersection behind you. There are also a number of interesting complications:

- **Flashing red or orange** – beware! This means a four-way stop (see below) but with someone having the right of way. At night a main city avenue may well have flashing amber at every intersection. Go through with the right of way, but beware of crossing traffic. Flashing red means that someone else has the flashing orange right of way. Stop. Cross or turn only when safe to do so. Fortunately this system only operates when traffic is sparse, such as in the early hours of the morning.

- **No turn on red** means that when there is a red light traffic may not turn right. Though this may seem blindingly self-evident to a newly arrived visitor, it actually tells drivers that the normal rule is for traffic to turn right when there is a red light so long as they have come to a full halt and it is clear to do so. Most, but not all the states, have this rule. Beware of cities that have spread over state lines. Different rules may apply on either side of the state line, as around Washington DC.

- **Right lane must turn** is a delightful invitation to turn at right angles to the direction you have been going, and it is compulsory. If you have stayed in such a lane too long and try to go straight on you will find you get a ticket, at best, or a punch-up with irate drivers you block in when you find that by going straight ahead you've come up against no available lane. Even when the lane you want is blocked by roadworks you must obey the signs for your particular lane, or risk the consequences. I was once physically assaulted by a fellow commuter in just such a case.

- **Four-way stops** require *all* traffic to stop, but the driver there first *from whatever direction* has the right of way. In case of a dead heat give way to traffic coming from the right. See the opening sequence of *LA Story* for what can happen if you don't. Numerous local variations exist, which can be quite a trial for the outsider. For a **two-way stop** one road has the right of way, and on a **three-way stop** only one direction has the right of way, all others must come to a halt. The signs all look superficially much the same, and may not be placed in the most obvious position. Usually, though, these arrangements are only found in residential neighbourhoods away from the main roads.

Beware

Vital warning signs may disappear beneath summer growth or winter snowdrifts.

Road signs

As with so many directions in the USA, literacy is assumed. Only reluctantly have pictograms (such as are used in international signs) been introduced, even in tourist or immigrant areas.

State of the roads

Since the New Deal of the late 1930s paved roads have been built even in the most out of the way areas. Nevertheless vast areas of the West still have gravel or even dirt roads. Through-travellers will probably see little of this though. Motorways are generally well maintained, and at a far better standard than found in many cities.

The winter snows sweep much further south (occasionally even to the Gulf of Mexico) than you might expect. Traffic in the northern states usually adjusts fairly smoothly, but where snow is a novelty traffic can be crazy, with people driving either too fast or far too slowly. Snow-tyres are required in many states, both to avoid a ticket from the highway patrol, and simply to get about. Snow-chains may be essential in out of the way areas and in ski-resorts. To see how drivers adapt to vile winter weather watch the opening sequence of *Fargo*.

Speeding

Officially speed limits are set by each state, not the federal government. However, the federal government can withhold federal highway grants from states not agreeing to enforce federal standards on interstate highways (almost all of the motorway standard dual-carriageway). The 60 or increasingly 70 mph speed limit has thus become a national limit, but one rarely observed within metropolitan areas or in the vast distances out west. Buried traffic monitors record the proportion of traffic obeying the speed limit, and states lose highway grants if more than half of passing traffic is over the limit. Paying state patrolmen to slow the traffic down can become fiscally necessary given the expense of highway maintenance. So a guerilla war rumbles on between truckers and state patrol cars ('Smokey the Bear'). Western states periodically attempt to have the limits changed, or threaten to ignore the limit and take the consequences. In Montana the speed limit is whatever the traffic cop says is 'reasonable and prudent'. In effect speed all you like, but if you frighten anyone you just exceeded the speed limit.

In towns limits are usually 35–40 mph, but watch for local variations, often set to catch the unwary outsider who can then be required to pay a fine or post bail on the spot (which amounts to much the same). Obey all limits, at least until you have been in an area long enough to get a feel for how the traffic locally responds to them. At corners there are often advisory limits (on a yellow background). In the mountains, limits tend to be both realistically set and observed (drivers who don't observe them don't survive).

Traffic into cities such as Washington or Boston travels much faster in certain designated High-Occupancy Vehicle lanes. Signs indicate **HOV-2** for a minimum of two people, though **HOV-3** is more usual. Otherwise avoid this car pool/bus lane or collect a ticket.

Driving an automatic

Most rented cars have automatic gear boxes. If you haven't used one before, don't panic, after a few careful trips around the car park you will be able to master yet another American institution. Only fancy imports seem to have stick-shifts (gear levers) these days. Follow a few simple steps:

■ Forget about your left foot – there's nothing for it to do.

■ Keep your foot on the brake when stopped. Automatics tend to creep forward unless restrained.

■ On a steep hill put the gear shift (yes there is one, you just don't use it all the time) into **L** (Low) when the drive starts to feel underpowered. Don't forget to put it back into **D** (Drive) when you return to the level.

■ Use the **P** (Park) position before switching off the engine when parking.

■ Use a light touch on the steering wheel and on the brakes – most cars now have power-assisted steering and brakes.

■ Push a button next to the ignition to release the key if it won't come out.

■ You may have to depress the brake before you can shift into gear.

■ When you are ready to leave the car park depress the brake pedal before shifting out of Park (**P**) to avoid a jerky kangaroo hop forwards.

You may even begin to like this minimalist approach to driving, especially when you find there is a 'cruise control' which it is worth a few minutes learning how to set so you won't carelessly exceed the speed limit. Long eventless drives across country can easily involve the car gradually speeding up without the driver noticing, until you cross a state or county boundary when the cops appear out of nowhere and issue a speeding ticket. So set those controls, ease out of the car park onto the right hand side of the road, gently get up to speed, and let those miles roll by.

Parking

Parking downtown can be as bad as in central London. Fortunately, though, many downtown banks and stores have their own free or subsidised parking lots. Parking meters are often available, and feeding the meter is permitted if you dash out in time. Regular parking, though, can be very expensive, and is increasingly only available for all-day commuters using high-occupancy vehicles (HOVs). You can see cars being parked by attendants in the reverse order their owners can be expected to come and collect them at the end of the day.

Certain areas have surprisingly large parking areas available. Washington DC's central Mall, around which many sights and most of the museums cluster, has parking areas just for visitors, though in high season these will fill early on, and using the Metro may well be a better idea.

Safety tips

■ If you think you are being followed, drive to the nearest 24-hour convenience stores, hospital or police station.

■ If you are hit from behind in a minor collision, drive to a well-lit service station before stopping.

■ At a red light leave enough space to pull out quickly if someone approaches you.

■ Keep doors locked and windows shut.

■ Keep your petrol tank at least half-full to avoid searching for petrol, a vulnerable state to be in.

■ Keep car keys separate from house keys.

■ At rental pick-up ask for a map to reach main highways safely. If offered a free map take it and use it – it'll have ways to reach the freeway or the sights marked.

Driving in deserts

The western deserts stretch south from the interior of Washington and Oregon all the way to Mexico, becoming wider and more extreme the nearer the border you are. Beloved of generations of movie-goers is a series of quintessentially American landscapes (though many spaghetti westerns were filmed in Spain!). Explore and enjoy, but take care. These landscapes can be both beautiful and deadly. And if entering the Native American reservations please obey the posted regulations (such as not leaving the main transit roads).

An excellent series of guides are now available in the UK: Moon Handbooks. These exist for Arizona, Colorado, Nevada, Texas, Utah and Washington (which though wet around Seattle is very dry to the East) – from specialist shops such as Stanfords Map and Travel Bookshop, 12–14 Long Acre, Covent Garden, London WC2E 9LP. (*www.stanfords.co.uk*) or direct from the publishers (*www.moon.com*).

Points to ensure an embarrassment doesn't become a disaster:

■ Tell someone where and when you are going (and stick to it).

■ Check out the hire car's facilities *before* setting out.

■ Keep out of Death Valley (May–October).

■ If you must drive – keep to main roads
            – travel outside afternoon heat.

■ If you must go away from roads ('off-road')
            – minimum groups of two
            – keep to four-wheel-drive vehicles.

- Take lots of water, soft drinks, but NO alcohol.

- Take a first aid kit.

- Wear appropriate clothing (long sleeves, hat).

- Always stay close to your vehicle in case of breakdown.

- Light a fire (but beware of starting uncontrolled fires).

If you drive out into the desert to **hike**, heat stroke can soon be a real problem. The body's normal cooling mechanisms easily fail to cope, evident in an inability to sweat, high body temperatures and growing confusion. Not enough water is the usual problem, which can be complicated by a lack of salt (to replace that lost by sweating). Strenuous activity in the heat of the day can soon produce problems. Adults generally need two to three litres a day, but in strenuous conditions ten litres may well be necessary, which means people have to drink far beyond the quenching of any immediate thirst. In fact just like camels travellers need to suck up and store vast quantities of water, while avoiding alcohol, which only dehydrates the body. Just as important, though, is the need to wear loose-fitting, preferably white cotton, clothing and a wide-brimmed hat. As a desert hitch-hiker I used to use an umbrella when stuck by the roadside, more for the sun than for the sudden storms of rain. And who could drive on by an Englishman under an umbrella 'out in the midday sun'?

It is all too easy while on the great coast-to-coast trip to see the USA as either just a larger version of home or so exotic that something awful lurks behind every tree. Most of the time people's health is probably most at risk when they have broken down and are waiting for assistance in the emergency lane of a freeway. But from time to time you will hear or read about something that is truly exotic. Killer bees fall into this category, though you have more chance of winning a state lottery than ever coming across these particular creatures. Nevertheless it can be reassuring to know what might be involved, and how best to respond even though they may sound like a B-movie joke. They are not, and they are becoming an ever more familiar sight across the southern and western states. The results of some particularly injudicious breeding of African and European bees by scientists trying to improve honey production, the actual super bees tended to concentrate less upon honey and more upon migrating ever northwards, arriving in California in 1998, merely 30-odd years after the whole saga began down in Brazil. This hybrid bee is a killer, with what the scientists call an 'excessive level of colony defense', that is they are more prone to feeling under attack than regular swarms, and so tend to attack more readily. They particularly take offence against movement, especially when involving power tools, such as strimmers or outboard motors. So there you have it; if you hear an incessant hum that sounds like no air conditioning you've ever heard before keep as immobile as possible, especially, and this is the tricky bit, if they settle on you. If they detect panic they will sting, given half a chance. However long it takes, keep quiet and wait for them to leave. If you are on the water wait gently to float away. If you are in the car by the side of the road thank your lucky stars you aren't outside. But it also helps to know who is liable to go into shock. I was once attacked by a nasty swarm of the old fashioned kind while hiking in the Presidential range in New Hampshire and it helped greatly to know that if stung I wouldn't die, and that we had better make sure the allergic kid in front didn't get stung under any circumstances.

Maps

It is now possible to buy up-to-date city and state maps in the UK. Stanfords stock Rand McNally's folding maps. Don't expect free maps from gas stations these days (though state welcome centres still provide them). Prepare in the UK for long journeys with Rand McNally's *Road Atlas and Vacation Guide*, or *Hildebrand Road Atlas: the West* from large bookshops.

For those renting a car from an airport you can print out a map to your destination at Mapquest (*www.mapquest.com*) which comes with detailed step-by-step driving instructions. Or just ask for a map and directions at the rental desk.

Glossary of driving terms

American	*British*
beltway	ring road
block	distance from one street to another
Denver boot	wheel clamp
divided highway	dual carriageway
expressway	major urban roadway
fender	bumper
fender bender	collision involving only minor damage
flashlight	torch
freeway	motorway
gas(oline)	petrol
gridlock	traffic jammed in all directions

highway	main road
hood	bonnet
line	queue
muffler	silencer
no standing	no waiting
parking brake	hand brake
parkway	road surface
pulloff	lay-by
RV (recreational vehicle)	camper van
sidewalk	pavement
speed zone	speed limit area
stick shift	gear shift (manual)
trailer	caravan
trunk	boot
turnpike	toll road
windshield	windscreen
Winnebago	camper van
wrench	spanner

ALTERNATIVES TO DRIVING

Do visitors have to drive everywhere? Fortunately not, for alternatives do exist:

- buses, both long distance and local;
- underground systems;
- taxis;
- cycling;
- walking;
- flying;
- trains.

The most exotic of these is undoubtedly walking. *Time* (the US news magazine)once ran an article on how the British *of all ages* still actually do it for fun! Is there no end to British eccentricity?

Long-distance buses

The most well-known network is **Greyhound**. Unfortunately the number of towns served has declined substantially over the last few years as cross-route subsidies have been phased out, leaving the major cities well served, but unfashionable areas not served by either train or bus, though some local services do exist.

Though the 99 days for $99 are long since gone, fares are generally quite low, though the vast distances may disguise this. Bus stations are usually in the older parts of the town, so long bus trips can be a salutary reminder of the underside of US life. Rest stops may be at peculiar times of the day or night, often in out of the way fast-food strips in the middle of nowhere, a plot to make the British traveller suddenly start to appreciate motorway cafés back home!

Advantages:

- See a slice of the USA you might not otherwise come across, which includes a motley collection of passengers. Remember the opening and closing scenes in *Midnight Cowboy*?

- Comparatively cheap
  7 day pass $329   30 day pass $607
  15 day pass $483   60 day pass $750.

- Efficient, clean and tidy, with on-board WC.

- Good luggage facilities (far more than by plane, which may make the trip worthwhile by itself).

- Tickets available up to two hours before first journey if done in person at the Greyhound desk (locations listed at Greyhound website).

Disadvantages:

- Slow (comparatively).

- Can be very boring for cross-country travel.

- You may need to read about Greyhound on Wikipedia to fully appreciate how it is both iconic and yet confusing to deal with.

- The Greyhound web page seems initially straightforward until you try to make sense of actually buying a pass online. Do *not* expect to print off your tickets/pass. Online booking involves a three-week delivery just within the USA! Instead, buy through STA Travel at a university in the UK near you.

■ Too many bus stations have seen better days (and may be intimidating for women and children), though there are some newer ones.

Contact:

■ *www.greyhound.com*, which conveniently hides all reference to its Discovery Pass in the bottom right of the home page.

■ STA Travel (*www.statravel.co.uk*) seems to have cornered the market for Greyhound in the UK.

Greyhound's longstanding rival Trailways (*www.trailways.com*) has not completely disappeared. Unlike the Greyhound system, which specialises in transporting passengers from coast to coast. Trailways in a more regionally-based bus system involving privately owned and operated companies (franchisees) mostly serving passengers up and down the Eastern Seaboard, in the Southeast and Midwest, with localised scheduled service west of the Mississippi River in Texas, Montana, California, Washington and Oregon. Local operators operate within decentralised, regionally designated territories, which unfortunately means that the national Trailways website where visitors might reasonably expect to find details of routes, departure-arrival times, and, ticket prices, shows very few details at all. For these it is necessary to contact local Trailways operators at their specific websites or by telephone. See a hot list at *www.trailways.com/schedules.asp.*

Local buses

These exist in most large towns, but tend to focus on the downtown serving the rush-hour commuter traffic. Los Angeles has DASH (Downtown Area Short Hop) that serves the downtown and the main landmarks, with dedicated fast services to Beverly Hills, Hollywood and Pacific Palisades. New York City has a complex system including a reasonable frequently night-time service. A ride costs $2. In the daytime the subway is probably a better bet (out of the extremes of weather). Increasingly New Yorkers are using a Metro Card, similar to London's Oyster Card.

Underground trains (subways)

These exist in only a minority of US cities, and those that do exist vary enormously:

■ Bay Area Rapid Transit System (BART) is clean, reasonably priced, and an efficient way to cross the **San Francisco Bay** to cities such as Oakland and to certain suburbs, though many places are only linked in with feeder bus services.

■ **Los Angeles** has a new, highly contentious, subway that is increasingly difficult to miss. It may be worth a ride. The thriller *Collateral* was set on the section from downtown to Long Beach.

■ Washington Metro serves **Washington DC** with the surrounding suburban communities in northern Virginia and Maryland. Despite the rapid expansion of the suburban economy over the last 20 years this brand new system focuses upon the governmental city centre, and its radial routes serve only certain select communities, so cross-town travel remains difficult and certain parts of the city, and of the metropolis at large, remain inaccessible. But for all that it is cheap, very efficient, crime-, garbage- and smoke-free, and certainly on a par with Europe's better systems. Only the new Kiev system is supposedly better.

■ **New York City's** subway system is cheap ($2 any distance with free transfers), vast, quite scary at times, can be very dirty, and is an amazingly efficient way of travelling around to avoid the congested streets above. Over four million people use it every day. The 230 miles of track are the amalgamation of once separate systems, which can lead to quite complex interchange stations, especially between express and local trains. For travelling around Manhattan it is excellent as the buses get bogged down in the traffic. For Long Island the service is not so good, though there is an express route using modern trains to and from the station nearest to John F. Kennedy airport, with buses from the station to the terminal. The Michelin Guide has route maps designed to help visitors navigate the system. An interesting alternative is provided by the new water taxis on the Hudson and East rivers (see interactive map at *www.nywatertaxicom/map*). A recently introduced Metrocard gives visitors to New York City a day-long, unlimited card for travel on subways and buses for only $7.50. This 'Fun Pass' is available from sellers throughout the city, and from the new New York City Visitor Information Centre, 810 Seventh Ave at 53rd Street. For longer stays there is a seven-day 'Unlimited Ride' card for $47. The day pass costs $20 (but the two-day pass only $25).

Some systems are not underground at all, but as in **Boston** and **Chicago** elevated (as was the case in much of the New York network originally). The 'El' helped blight large areas around the downtown. To get some idea of what it must have been like having to live near such overhead systems, watch the John Belushi and Don Akroyd (1980) movie *Blues Brothers* set in downtown Chicago.

At some suburban stations you may see 'Kiss and Ride' signs, pull-in bays for drivers to let off commuting spouses. Park and ride facilities are also available at certain suburban stations.

Taxis

These are more likely to be of use in the more European cities of the east than in the more American cities of the west. In **New York City** it may be actually quicker to walk ten or even 15 blocks given the traffic, though a cab ride will ensure that you don't arrive wet through. Summers are long and very sticky. Winters are often very snowy. Taxis are metered, but don't expect cab drivers to be able to change large denomination notes. Many drivers may not speak English and may have little if any knowledge of anywhere outside the major destinations. In certain cities only certain cabs are allowed to drive over the city boundary, so check before the meter starts. In the national capital (**Washington DC**) a drive to most suburban communities involves crossing over into the next state, foreign territory to many inner-city drivers.

Long distance taxi rides are possible, but very expensive. It would usually be cheaper to hire a car and drive yourself. But in a domestic airline strike, for instance, such long-distance rides to another international airport that is open may turn out to be essential. Get a price *before* the trip starts, though.

Remember

Many cities are as large as London, and taxi rides across Los Angeles or New York City can be very expensive indeed.

Orlando International Airport is on the south side of the metropolitan area, with easy accessibility across to the hotels and time-share villas of International Drive near Disneyworld. BUT Sanford airport, often used by tour operators, is far to the north-east of the city, a $100 cab ride to the tourist area to the south side: an unpleasant financial surprise after a long flight.

You can arrange to take a vehicle that is half way between a cab and a bus – a limousine. These long huge cars may take half a dozen travellers plus baggage from out-of-town communities to the airport for bus-like fares for a taxi-like service. Check Yellow Pages, and book in advance.

Cycling

Cycling as a sport is increasingly popular, but commuting is only viable for a very few in places like college towns. States such as Florida are waymarking cycle routes, but they tend to be minor roads rather than traffic-free routes. Resorts have cycle hire. There are long-distance route guides: Vicky Spring, *Bicycling the Pacific Coast* (2005) and Donna Aitkenhead, *Bicycling Coast to Coast* (1996).

Walking

This is an art, one that has all but been given up except by a hardy few. Suburban neighbourhoods may well lack sidewalks altogether. Paths lead only from the house to the kerb! Certain neighbourhoods may be suspicious of any strangers, especially those on foot.

Some downtowns now encourage shoppers to use the shoppers' bus between the main shopping intersections. This encourages less walking per person, but probably helps raise the number of people walking along the streets. In hot and humid cities learn to walk down that side of the street giving some shade. Whatever the season work on the general assumption that car drivers cannot see you. Never assume a right of way, even at marked crossing areas (British style zebra or pelican crossings don't exist). But walking across as and where you will may result in a ticket for jay-walking (even in the deserted downtown on a Sunday morning if your luck has run out).

Overall walking is okay for young people, especially when combined with buses and subway trains. But it is not feasible for most families, if only for the extremes of heat and cold. Downtowns can be less than safe, and distances great. The central mall of Washington DC is deceptively laid out. Distances from monument to monument can be enormous, and with children impossible. The DC police patrols have been known to use bull horns to warn twilight pedestrians to leave the open spaces immediately for their own safety! And darkness comes much more swiftly than in northern countries such as Britain.

Flying

Flying is cheap per mile by European standards, but as distances are vast prices can still seem very expensive. Standby tickets are available, though around public holidays all seats will have been long since booked up. But given the sheer size of the USA flying is often the only way to travel any distance within the time available.

For an explanation of how standby tickets have changed from being the way airlines filled their remaining seats by offering waiting students or GIs a last-minute seat at a knockdown price to today where standby seems to be little more than a queue for any remaining spare seats sold at full price, see 'Flying Standby' (at *www.faqs.org/travel/air/handbook/part1/section-13.html*).

Traditionally the USA has had a network of international, regional and local companies, nested together to provide a service to most places within the USA. The cost of the overly cosy arrangement was seen as a lack of competition, higher than necessary prices, and an over-extended network necessarily subsidised by higher than desirable fares on the most popular routes.

Deregulation of routes has caused a major change in air travel. Popular routes attracted new services at lower fares, so forcing large companies to follow. Conversely many smaller places have lost their services altogether. Even large companies have gone bankrupt, been taken over, or have merged. The situation is still, and may well remain, in flux, not helped by the recent rise in fuel costs.

The implication for visitors is that whereas it has become cheaper and generally more convenient to fly into and out of large metropolitan areas (where, after all, most people live) it may be difficult to fly on to specific, smaller destinations. Relatives who could once have met you at Cullowhee airport North Carolina (a small college town in the Great Smoky Mountains) may now have to go to Ashville some 40 miles away across the mountains, though as a freeway has just opened on this route this is now no real hardship. They may even prefer to drive some hundreds of miles south to Atlanta for the novelty of meeting you at the international airport. Few Americans get any opportunity to meet arriving foreigners, so may be eager to travel to meet you.

Book from the UK whenever possible to take advantage of special rates not available once you are within the USA. These are often available via your transatlantic carrier (or its affiliated airlines within the USA). Various packages are periodically on offer, with a series of vouchers or an 'airpass' being purchased that can be exchanged for tickets, though if you know your schedule an inflexible series of flights can be booked from the UK. Transatlantic carriers often offer special internal flights to attract custom, and specific places can be visited by means of stopovers before an eventual destination.

■ Most people use Expedia, Ebookers or Kayak, but airline company websites will indicate flight connections and options more explicitly.

■ *www.flytecomm.com/cgi-bin/trackflight* can calculate times of arrival for flights leaving or arriving at North American airports – a boon for those meeting possibly delayed flights.

Fly-drive

With an 'open-jaw' ticket this enables you to fly into one city, drive to another, and fly home without having to drive all the way back: great for cross-country trips. Two weeks across country from New York City to Los Angeles, with a week in each place as well can be an ideal introduction to the USA. The extra drop-off charge at least means you don't have to dash back to New York City, and can instead spend a leisurely week in California before flying home.

Air-travel seasons

These are rooted as much in the calendar as in the weather. For travel purposes three unfamiliar seasons appear:

■ low   – off peak, especially term time;
■ high   – summer holidays;
■ shoulder – late November (Thanksgiving).

Summer is set by convention having almost the power of law. It opens with Memorial Day in late May and lasts until Labor Day in early September. To get, for instance, student rates after Labor Day may necessitate having convincing ID (identification papers) as all US students will then be back in school (or college).

Trains

Trains do travel the length and breadth of the USA, but services are less frequent and serve fewer places since motorways and flying have taken most of the long-distance passengers. Despite the poor state of repair of much of the remaining network, using the train has certain major advantages over flying or driving:

■ You will be seeing the country from an increasingly unfamiliar perspective that cannot possibly be provided by high-altitude flying.
■ It is relaxing not having to do the driving.
■ It is useful for travellers going from one downtown to another, such as tourists or certain business people.

Unfortunately only a railway enthusiast would want to do the whole cross-country journey, if only because of the timetable implications, not to mention the length of time involved. For details see John Pitt *US by Rail*, a 2005 guide with details of passes and long-distance routes (includes steam railways and museums). For an enthusiast's view see *The Great Trans American Train Ride*, (2005 DVD region 1) available from Amazon.

It is still worthwhile taking one of the more popular sections of the network, which is now run by **Amtrak**. This semi-nationalised passenger network tries to keep the passenger services going, but is restricted to using other companies' track, which is maintained to a variety of standards. Trains may have to crawl through certain areas to avoid track collapse, only to speed effortlessly away once back onto a commercially maintained freight network. Compared to the European system, the Amtrak network is very rudimentary. Only in the northeast's Boston to Washington DC corridor does it have anything like an Inter-City feel about it.

The US train system is an acquired taste, being a hodgepodge of what remains from the great days of steam. Only in **The Northeast Corridor** is there anything approaching a European system, being fully electrified to serve a densely populated string of cities from Washington DC, north-eastwards through Baltimore, Wilmington, Philadelphia, Trenton, Newark, New York, New Haven, and Providence to Boston. There are branches connecting Philadelphia with Harrisburg, Pennsylvania; New Haven with Hartford, Connecticut and Springfield, Massachusetts; New York City with Albany, New York, and several other commuter destinations. The busiest passenger rail station in the United States is Pennsylvania Station in New York, the north-east's central hub. The north-eastern line is immediately identified by the use of overhead wires and high-speed rolling stock. Mostly operated and owned by Amtrak, this has the only truly high-speed rail service anywhere in the country – the Acela Express – which runs alongside I95 for much of the way (as the M1 parallels the southern section of the west coast mainline in Britain).

The Empire Corridor refers to the 430-mile rail corridor between Buffalo and Albany, New York, including the cities of Rochester, Syracuse, Utica, and Schenectady. New York is, after all, 'The Empire State'. The Philadelphia to Harrisburg main line is a rail line owned and operated by Amtrak in Pennsylvania. The line runs from Philadelphia, on the Northeast Corridor, west to Harrisburg along the former Pennsylvania Railroad main line. It is part of the longer **Keystone Corridor**, which continues west to Pittsburgh. The **Cardinal** is a 1,147-mile route linking New York's Penn Station with Chicago's Union Station three days a week via Washington DC, Charlottesville, Virginia, Cincinnati, Ohio, Indianapolis, Indiana, Philadelphia, and Wilmington, Delaware. Travel time, end to end, is about 26½ hours. Four days a week there is also a service on the 196-mile section linking Indianapolis with Chicago. The **Piedmont** is a daily passenger train between Raleigh and Charlotte, North Carolina, while the **Carolinian** runs between Charlotte and New York City. The **Crescent** runs 1,377 miles daily from New York City to New Orleans. The **Palmetto** is an 829-mile service from New York City south to Savannah, Georgia. Its extension to Miami, Florida is called the **Silver Metro**. To the north, the **Vermonter** runs 606 miles almost to the Canadian border, one trip in each direction per day (with the worst delay rate in the USA).

This rather ad-hoc list suggests how undeveloped this system is these days, and how long journeys are, reflecting the long distances. If you want the speed and frequency of a European train service in the USA – take the plane not the train. If you can make a specific journey, it is great fun, but if you have to be somewhere at a precise time the trains are more of a gamble than any other kind of transport, apart from cross-town driving in the rush hour. It would be better to take the bus for most journeys. However, it is a piece of Americana to be experienced, even on the Washington DC to New York City tilting high-speed trains.

Changing trains and spending four days en route can enable the hardy traveller to reach the **West Coast** at a leisurely 40 mph. Once in Los Angeles there is a well-used service south to **San Diego**.

For travellers on the Atlantic seaboard bound for the **Pacific Northwest** it is probably better to go north to Montreal in Canada, take the trans-Canada system west to Vancouver, and then go south again into the USA. The service is good (though not so elegant as it once was) and the scenery is spectacular.

Amtrak's **Southwest Chief** runs from Chicago to Los Angeles (and back again). Speeds rarely reach 70 mph, but this enables riders to relax as the scenery rolls gently by. This route is something of a flagship for Amtrak's long-distance routes, with quite a high level of service, which includes films, leaflets on points of interest, and even speakers to talk about the areas being crossed. **On-board facilities** are appropriate for people used to travelling long distance by Greyhound, if not quite up to airline standards. Coaches are on two levels. The lower level has several airline-type toilets, changing rooms, luggage storage, and seating areas for those who find it difficult to negotiate the stairs to the upper deck. There is also a formal dining-car and a cafeteria, though as with captive markets everywhere prices are not cheap. One of the advantages of this particular journey is that a stopover at Flagstaff, Arizona, can be made. Take a hired car (I had to hitch-hike) north to the nearby **Grand Canyon**, truly one of the wonders of the world.

The **Zephyr** runs from Chicago via Salt Lake City to San Francisco.

For Californian journeys start with the 'Train and Thruway Service' map. There are three major routes: the **Capital Corridor**, the **San Joaquins**, and the **Pacific Surfliner** – plus a motorcoach network linking to the trains.

If you would like to get the feel of what it is like to arrive in a small western town by train, to step down onto the side of the tracks only to watch the train leave you standing in the middle of nowhere, read Malcolm Bradbury's novel *Stepping Westward* published in 1965, now an Arena paperback.

Go to the main Amtrak website and click on the International Visitors tab. This brings you to the route maps, accommodation details, and Rail Pass information. There is now a wonderfully interactive route atlas easily accessible (*www.tickets.amtrack.com*).

Practical train information

A complicated discount structure exists for foreign passport holders in the USA. You can book direct with Amtrak or via STA Travel in the UK.

USA Rail Pass fares

US-wide	15 day	off peak/£201	peak/£258
	30 day	off peak/£242	peak/£309
Northeast Region	15 day	off peak/£154	peak/£154
East Region	15 day	off peak/£170	peak/£190
	30 day	off peak/£185	peak/£237
West Region	15 day	off peak/£170	peak/£190
	30 day	off peak/£185	peak/£237

Off-peak period = 1 January to 31 May and 7 September to 31 December. Peak period = 1 June to 6 September.

Schedule and reservations: *www.amtrak.com*
Canadian links: *www.viarail.ca*

A valid passport is necessary to purchase the USA Rail Pass, to receive tickets to travel, and for identification while onboard. Unlike the situation in the UK, most long-distance journeys require advanced reservations and payment at all times. People do not generally just turn up and expect to travel (as they do on the long-distance buses).

Specimen single fares for 2008
New York City to Miami	$256
Seattle to San Francisco	$169
Los Angeles to Las Vegas	$163
New York City to Montreal	$162

■ For **disabled passenger information**, click tab 'Traveling with Amtrak' and then go to 'Special needs and accessibility' for further pages of appropriate information.

Camping tours

For independent travellers who don't want the hassle of travelling alone, try organised camping tours, all kit, driver and van included. This is only for those who don't mind sharing! From £450 for a west coast two weeks' tour up to £1,500 for a two-months' US-wide tour (all prices are plus food, and airfare to and from the USA).

■ Trek America (*www.trekamerica.com*);
■ Explore Adventure Holidays (*www.explore.co.uk*);
■ Cotswold (*www.cotswoldoutdoor.com*);
■ Blacks (*www.blacks.co.uk*).

For the completely independent camper try Camping USA for camping grounds, FAQs, and guides (*www.camping-usa.com*).

Packs

There are two main types: a conventional rucksack with an internal frame for serious hiking; and the travel model that transforms itself into a suitcase-like holdall. The convertible pack, in hiding its frame and fastenings, can be handled like a case in both airports and hotels where it may be advantageous to appear less the hippie and more the business traveller. For advice on getting a quart into a pint pot turn to the Internet (*onebag.com*).

TIME ZONES

North America stretches over eight-and-a-half time zones. When it's noon in Alaska it's 7.30 pm in Newfoundland. As you travel west you 'gain' time. If you drive from Pittsburg to Denver you may well leave at 10.00 am one day and arrive at 10.00 am the next, driving straight through. But the journey will have taken 26 hours. If you go from west to east you 'lose', so if you left Denver at 10.00 am and arrived at Pittsburg the following day at 10.00 am it would have taken you 22 hours (maybe you missed the traffic driving in this direction and saved a few hours!)

Most Americans, however, live with a four-zone world, from Atlantic to Pacific. Eastern Standard Time is five hours behind Greenwich, Central six hours, Mountain seven, and Pacific eight. So midday in London is 7.00 am in New York City, 6.00 am in Chicago, 5.00 am in Denver, and 4.00 am in Los Angeles. This is complicated by:

■ **Daylight Saving Time** which operates much the same as Summer Time in the UK. However, certain states refuse to use it, so watch out in Arizona, Hawaii and parts of Indiana. The switch-over is on the last Sunday in April, which is not usually the date(s) used in Europe.

A further complication is the refusal to use the 24-hour clock (except perhaps in the military). Timetables will only use the 12-hour clock, with bold type for times after noon. This has confused many overseas arrivals who think there are no trains, planes, buses in the afternoon on the very route they want to make! It makes you realise how even the 24-hour clock, like metric temperature, gradually catches up with even the most dyed-in-the-wool Brit.

TRAVELLING WITH THE KIDS

The USA is a wonderful place for families. From the moment you arrive you'll realise that it's still a more child-oriented society:

■ Most hire cars have rear seat-belts fitted as standard, and major agencies can provide safety seats for young children.

■ Most motels let children share their parents' room without extra charge (and most rooms have double-beds anyway as standard).

■ Restaurants keep high-chairs or booster-seats ready, and children's menus are common. Colouring books may emerge from folded children's menus too!

Don't despair! Children's food is not compulsory for adults. All-you-can-eat meals (a speciality in certain chains) have everything from sugar-puffs to spicy sausages at breakfast, via scrambled eggs, muffins and juices. Breakfasts are good value and usually provide something for everyone to feast upon.

Theme parks, whether Disneyworld and Seaworld in central Florida, or Dollywood in east Tennessee's Smoky Mountains, are for children of all ages; young children aren't ignored; and parents needn't feel like social outcasts for turning up with their offspring. Even more 'serious' places such as the science museums of Washington DC encourage children to touch, watch puppet shows, and generally behave like children. National Parks, such as the Rocky Mountains and Mesa Verde Parks in Colorado, have talks and activities especially for children. For toll-free reservations in the USA go to the US National Parks Service website (*www.nps.gov/findapark/ index.htm*). For family attractions close to cross-country motorways refer to the *Guide to Crossing America* by the National Geographic Society (£16).

Snags

It would be foolish to suggest travelling with children turns up no problems:

■ Summer heat can be so overwhelming that the car may become the only haven of air conditioning (and thus sanity) for all the family. But distances on cross-country trips can be extremely demoralising. A sufficiently large car is essential for all concerned.

■ Motels rarely have anywhere for children to play, nor are playmates available as would be possible staying with friends or in a country hotel.

Good news

Overall, most visitors would say the good outweighs the bad:

■ At least there's television (morning cartoons are everywhere, not just for an hour or so as in UK terrestrial channels). Most motels have a pool (check *before* booking to avoid disappointment). After being cooped up for long periods in the car a pool is usually very welcome by everyone.

■ Standards of hygiene are high throughout the USA; bathrooms with showers are standard in all motel rooms; disposable nappies (diapers) are at every drugstore; and the locals by and large speak English (for when the fanbelt breaks late at night as you are crossing the South).

■ Toys are excellent. Well, the range and price of toys is very good. In fact the range (and volume) of toys is as likely to startle you as the viciousness of the war toys. If you haven't seen a large toy shop in the UK for 30 years you'd probably get a shock! Use the Internet to find the nearby 'Toys R Us' toys-only supermarkets, giving both good value and great variety.

■ Children do enjoy the USA. Even young children will both cope with and enjoy it (though maybe no more or less than anywhere in Europe). Swimming together at the end of each day's travelling or exertions remains a fond memory for years after. Even surviving the ferocious summer heat becomes a well-earned battle scar. Also, for adults taking children can provide an open sesame to people and places you'd never otherwise visit.

Even if you do intend to take your family for an extended stay and wish first to try out living together in the USA it might be worth considering house-swapping rather than a touring holiday.

Tick those items you'd think would provide you good experience of what it would be like to live (rather than holiday) in the USA:

touring holiday	*house swapping*
on the move	*stay in one place*
motels	*house with garden*
eating out	*eating both out and in*
always together	*more flexibility*
strangers	*neighbours*
always something new	*return to base each day*

Books of advice

As there are more and more parents taking more and more children abroad there are ever more how-to-do-it guides. Those worth looking at include the following:

■ David Haslam, *Travelling with Children: A Survival Guide for Parents* (1987) has readable and authoritative sections on planning, safe car and air travel, strategies for journeys, eating and drinking, burns, bites and bugs. It's a useful introduction for anyone considering going abroad with children, for however long. Despite being over 20 years old its common sense approach still stands (and Amazon still sell it).

- William Grey, *Travel with Kids* (2007) is a worldwide guide, but full of practical ideas.

- Fawzia de Francisco, *The Rough Guide to Travel with Babies and Young Children* (2008). The British newspaper, *The Independent* said this was a 'must read' as a planning tool.

DISABLED VISITORS TO THE USA

The USA may well be the best country to visit if you are physically disabled and well able to afford such a distant trip. Though medical costs are very high and specialist medical cover is recommended, the action of 'physically challenged' groups in the USA has opened up most public buildings, the Washington DC subway system, and most if not all places of public accommodation (they don't get picketed).

For up-to-date information contact the following:

- *Discoverabroad.com* has a 'Disabled Visitors' page dealing with US airports.

- Chris Brown wrote an article for *The Times* (18 October 2007) 'A friendly face for disabled visitors to New York' available at Timesonline.

- Society for the Advancement of Travel for the Handicapped has a site with many links (*www.sath.org*).

- Mobility International/USA, based in Eugene, Oregon offers advice on low-cost options for travellers with disabilities (and offers information on exchanges, internships and work camps).

- *Smooth Ride Guide* gives details of hotels with appropriate facilities and accessible attractions for wheelchair users. There are now specifically US and Canadian editions. (*www.smoothrideguides.com*).

EMERGENCY PLANNING

There are an increasing number of websites that enable travellers to store information securely online. By all means take photocopies of vital documents, but they too can be stolen. Lonely Planet (*www.lonelyplanet.co.uk*) has a 'travel vault' service. Deposit your traveller's cheque numbers and credit card details, your passport and visa numbers, and anything crucial. If the originals go astray you only need find a cybercafé to retrieve your details (assuming you can remember your password). You can also prepay for calls back home, useful in an emergency. For your nearest cybercafé you can access *www.cybercafes.com* – but remember to do this before you leave home, downloading a listing of cybercafés in your destination while you can. Don't forget though that public libraries increasingly have excellent public access PCs if you get caught short anywhere in the USA. If you are still a registered student or member of staff back home you might be able to persuade a sympathetic university or community college to provide access to a PC even where they don't have public access as such. Say you need to access your home university and most educational institutions will help if they can. Of course it's always prudent to photocopy all your IDs, travel schedules, etickets, driving licence, passport, credit cards, traveller's cheque numbers, and so forth, just in case. Leave one copy back in the UK (preferably with relatives who are not going to be abroad just when you are!).

7

Finding Work

There are two major reasons for going to any foreign country:

- interest;
- job or career.

Of course you can make a holiday of a student summer camp job, and you may have taken up a job just to follow up your interest in the USA. But though all reasons are in some ways interconnected it helps to establish what your priorities are. Sort out in your own mind what the main reason is for wanting to stay in the USA. If it is a relaxing holiday then don't undermine that perfectly reasonable aim by being on the telephone all the time trying to set up useful business links! Checking email every hour does not help de-stress anyone.

Short-term options for young people will be dealt with later in Chapter 10. Let's look now at the various possibilities for those who don't have to be back for next semester or for a UK job.

STAYING IN THE USA FOR FUN

Many people find going abroad is something for the young, with few ties, between college and going to work. But consider the alternatives:

Staying in Britain	Going to the USA
Getting into a career	Getting experience of life
Getting into the housing market	Not being tied down by a mortgage
Having a family while fit and young	Being more flexible and able to take risks
Getting a job while one is still available	Expanding your horizons
Building up seniority in a firm	Gaining useful confidence
Becoming a sober, hard-working citizen	Changing job tracks

Now add your own counter arguments in the spaces provided! Once you've done that, choose which options are for you. If most are in the left-hand column:

- you could work hard at home but holiday in the USA;
- you could try for some US-based experience with your firm;
- you could house-swap for three or four weeks one year.

If most are in the right-hand column:

- consider taking a degree in the USA;
- take a long trip with casual work;
- consider what foreign experience would interest an employer when you got back.

Career advantages of a stint in the USA

The universities and colleges pour out new graduates each and every year, each waving their newly minted degrees. Three hundred applications for a single job is not an unusual situation. How can you stand out from the crowd?

Everyone wants someone with experience, but if no one will give you that initial chance it can all seem futile. But take heart: a new employer's interest may be raised by an applicant who has travelled, not aimlessly, but in relation to their field of interest. Political science students who've spent time at a college in Washington DC have something no amount of pulling pints in the students' union bar over the vacation can provide.

A three-month stint working in the USA offers an employer someone with just a suggestion of adaptability, initiative and a willingness to try something different, unafraid of trying something new. A stint in the USA may be the only thing separating you from the pack when a short-list is drawn up. And being a year or so older than the rest of the pack when you return may also be in your favour – you are just that bit more mature, that bit more self-reliant, and so should need just that bit less supervision. And employers like that.

Of course you may be looking to the USA for a more long-term job rather than a stint overseas to help you once back in Britain. Many British people do exceptionally well in the USA, from butlers to athletes, but don't expect the USA to provide increased career prospects, a better material standard of living, or just a good time by virtue of your arrival with a British accent. If you don't like hard work, long hours and a lot of knocks, the USA isn't going to do much for you except see your time and money slip away.

Working for fun

If you want to be able to return to the USA you need to be legal. See the section on visas in Chapter 4 for how this can be done. But the best laid schemes come adrift and you may find yourself out of money far from friends or the airport. Summer harvesting, working in bars, helping friends move or decorate, acting as a nanny: all can pay well, but the longer you remain within the black economy the more risky it'll become. If you do it only for a few weeks before moving on little risk will exist, but it's still illegal, and though it's possible to get the ever necessary ID (identification) via driving licences (US 'driver's license'), social security number and bank account it's an increasingly risky business.

The degree of paranoia this lifestyle can produce can be gauged by a certain non-event in New York City. The Immigration and Naturalization Service (INS) the pre-9/11 agency that used to deal with foreigners estimated that there were some 70,000 illegal Irish residents within this one city alone. An amnesty was declared: 'Make yourself known and you'll be allowed to "regularize" your status.' Two (yes, that's 2) people turned up at the INS. The source of this story has been checked with RTE (Irish Radio, 7 May 1987, Gay Byrne morning show).

Beware: if you think that the worst that can happen is for the immigration officials to catch you and deport you, remember:

■ The Internal Revenue Service (IRS) will first want their back tax before they'll let you leave the USA.

■ If you want to return to the USA you need a statement on your exit papers that you are not a tax delinquent, even if the IRS and USCIS will let you go this time.

> **Remember**
>
> *It was not the FBI that got Al Capone. It was the IRS who put him away for non-payment of taxes!*

THE BUSINESS CULTURE IN THE USA

> It is a sad fact of life that many people who go to work abroad, either on secondment to an overseas branch or subsidiary of a UK employer or on contract to a truly overseas company, give less thought to their circumstances than they would if they were simply to be going abroad on holiday for a few weeks.
>
> (Harry Brown in *Working Abroad?*, 1986)

Join another company, go to another school, or just change jobs and we're likely to find that many more things have changed besides our physical surroundings. Even if our job description remains much the same the way things work around us may change, sometimes so subtly that at first we don't notice what's going on. But soon we find people interpret rules slightly differently, a pleasant surprise when it's in our favour, but a bit of a shock when we seem to lose out. Expectations may be a bit different. How we bend the rules changes. In fact it's a little bit like being in another country. Those who study businesses say that each business has its own culture. How much more potentially confusing when the change of job is compounded with a change of country! Two cultures, one large, one small, change both at once, and we're expected to adjust without missing a step.

So it's easy to see why staying with the same company if you are moving countries can be a great advantage, particularly if the style of management remains the same. If you have been 'Americanised' during your time already with the company then moving to the USA will not be such a jump into the complete unknown.

If American companies pay well they do so because they expect quite a lot. This is a capitalist dog-eat-dog economy, which though not averse to protectionist barriers and government handouts still has a more raw edge to its business dealings than in Britain.

A word of warning

Don't be taken in by those firms that have a laid-back, casual air about them. These mainly new firms, especially in software and the media, can be just as efficient and hardnosed when they want to be, and if your presence turns out to be a waste of space they'll 'let you go' (fire you!). Read Crichton's novel Disclosure.

Being British means having certain immediate assumptions made about you. Your accent (whether Geordie, Liverpuddlian or Sloane, it matters not) will be seen as very formal, which will confirm their expectation of you as dour, a bit stand-offish, especially out west (where I have been taken for a Boston, Massachusetts, native, the distinction between England and New England being a little too subtle for certain laid-back West Coast residents!). Unless you really are pompous, colleagues are quite likely to tell you, say in the bar round the corner during Friday's happy hour, that you're not as stuffily formal as they'd expected. This will be a personal point, and will in no way change their belief that everyone else back in Britain is a stuffed shirt.

The greatest shock for most Britons starting work in the USA comes from the long hours and short holidays. The business culture demands it (and thinks it essential to continued prosperity even though those Germans in work tend to have five or six weeks' holidays and are at least as prosperous!)

Long hours

The minimum working week in the USA is often still 40 hours (not the 38 so popular in the UK), the eight hours per day meaning just that, with people expected to be at their seats working away bang on 9.00 am, and not leaving until precisely 5.00 pm. There's no five minutes grace, and certainly no couple of hours off for the dentist, unless sick-leave is first agreed.

This may be how your UK office was run, so it wouldn't be quite the surprise it is to some. What may be a surprise is that many people start earlier, at 8.00 am. Colleges usually schedule their first classes at 8 am, and having to discuss the finer points of a course so early can be quite a shock to the British visitor. Colleges too may schedule classes to start as late as 7.00 pm, so for some academics it can be a long day.

Holidays

The real surprise comes over holidays. In the first year employees may receive no vacation time except for the six public holidays required by law, a week if they are lucky, two weeks if very lucky indeed. Each year of employment raises the entitlement by a day, but it may take some years to gain a three-week break. Academics expecting an Easter vacation will find there isn't one, and the long summer vacation is often unpaid, so it's necessary and expected that you'll teach summer school, intensive courses for people in a hurry to graduate, trying to catch up or having to repeat a failed course.

Bad news time

US public holidays are not necessarily 'long weekends'. Only Memorial Day (the last Monday in May) and Labor Day (the first Monday in September) are always part of a weekend, and as the first and last days of the summer season these weekends are good days to avoid freeways, airports and resorts. Christmas Day, New Year's Day and Independence Day (4 July) obviously fall on any day of the week, and the days to the nearest weekend are not necessarily holidays. (Boxing Day is unheard of so expect to work the day after Christmas Day!) Service and retail employees will probably have to work most holidays (except Christmas and New Year's Day), albeit on overtime rates.

Sick leave

This is usually only gained after a probationary period with the firm, say three months. You'll be lucky to get five days a year for long service. When changing companies negotiate to keep your sick leave entitlement if at all possible. Remember too that sick leave involves any time off for medical reasons, not just being on your death bed.

The contract

The USA is a country where litigation is endemic. If things don't turn out how you expected it will be very difficult to play the litigation game to your advantage without the protection of a carefully prepared contract. If you came expecting full medical cover for yourself and for your family, plus a company car, first make certain it's all in the contract, and legally watertight. Fine words butter no parsnips, or as Sam Goldwyn (of MGM fame) warned: 'A verbal contract ain't worth the paper it's written on.'

Compassionate leave

Try to keep the length of your stay under your own control. If your family, particularly ageing relatives, are still in the UK you need to be able to leave your job and the USA for pressing reasons. If you are under contract with an over-the-odds salary you may not be allowed compassionate leave short of quitting and taking the consequences. Longstanding employees are more likely to be able to obtain emergency leave. Read your contract carefully. If a US company pays you over the odds (salary plus a moving allowance) they aren't going to be too happy about your leaving for any reason, especially for an open-ended period.

Smoking

Despite resistance from civil liberties groups and tobacco-growing states, US employers are increasingly banning workplace smoking, and for fear of costly health insurance and increased days lost through illness are trying to discourage out-of-hours smoking. Don't assume your smoking will be treated as a private matter, any more than it is in the UK these days. States are increasingly taking the onus from employers and banning workplace smoking, as in California (1994) and Florida (2002). Wikipedia has an intelligent entry on smoking bans.

WORK PROSPECTS IN THE US ECONOMY

Whether going to the United States for temporary or long-term work it is useful, if not essential, to know something about the US economy, particularly which skills the job market requires and, equally as vital, where these jobs can be found. The US economy is so large and the country so vast that without even the most rudimentary awareness of what is going on you will be like someone blindfold in a china shop.

The traditional view of the US economy saw a great industrial heartland from Boston south to Baltimore and west over the Appalachians to Chicago. Here lived most Americans once the US had been settled from coast to coast. After the Second World War the west coast, particularly California, became a major rival to the northeast, given its entertainment industries, defence industries and increasingly its aerospace industries. The south was seen as poor, rural and hostile to black people, Roman Catholics, and in fact most outsiders. The industrial midwest merged into the prairie and thinly settled mountains. Alaska far to the northwest remained a barren, frozen waste, and Hawaii a tropical paradise somewhere in mid-Pacific.

The effects of oil

Gradually this picture has changed as the global role of oil changed. As OPEC pushed up oil prices domestic suppliers in Texas, Oklahoma and Louisiana became very wealthy, able to invest in the further industrialisation of what came to be called the Sunbelt. Prosperity moved west to link up with southern California, and eastwards into Florida where tourism, aerospace and retirement developments forged a major rival to the once-dominant northeast.

The oil crisis that boosted the Sunbelt exposed the old decaying industrial bases of what came to be known as the Rustbelt, or Snowbelt: cars, shipbuilding, machine tools all collapsed as foreign competition took vast slices of the US market. Unemployment rose to levels unknown since the dark days of the Great Depression of the 1930s. This view of a prosperous southern rim and a decaying northeast is still widely held. But beware: just as it took its place in the public's 'mental map' of the US economy the map changed.

Bankruptcy for some

The 1980s and 1990s saw the farmers of the Mississippi valley plagued with over-production and falling prices. Like the heavy industrial cities of Appalachia and the Great Lakes before them they have hit bankruptcy, dispossession and decay. In contrast California still retains its prosperity, at least from Silicon Valley just south of San Francisco to Los Angeles, though even here individual communities can be hit by changes in the economy. The oil price decline of the mid-1980s has undermined the once-assured prosperity of Alaska, Oklahoma, Texas and Louisiana, where unemployment rose dramatically above average levels, and was especially high for those in exploration and drilling concerns. Present oil price rises may return some prosperity to such communities.

The US government policies that produced the economic boom of the early 1980s left a huge $200 billion national debt, slowing growth in certain areas to a barely perceptible level before the perilous mid-90s boom. Along the Atlantic coast growth persists, especially in the suburbs, but California lost 100,000 jobs as military contracts were cut back after the Cold War ended. For the impact upon men who thought they had a job for life see *Falling Down*.

The midwest, whether rural or once industrial, has for the first time replaced the south as the region with the lowest incomes. Agriculture, oil and declining heavy industry ('smokestack' industries in US journalism) have all lost ground, pulling the great Mississippi-Great Lakes heartland down. High-technology and service industries such as banking, insurance and advertising have enabled the coastal states to pull ahead. As food prices rise across the world mid-western farmers (and their bank managers) hold their breath in anticipation.

Job-seekers need to move

The importance of this for would-be job seekers can be gauged in the continuing small town migration of many Americans away from places such as Texas. Don't expect jobs to be available for the asking in Dallas, whatever memories the TV series would suggest. Don't even assume that investment in these areas will automatically hit pay dirt. Retrenchment of people's incomes puts often fatal pressure on small entrepreneurs.

Regional diversity

Awareness of regional diversity is essential. Central Florida may well have peaked – by 1994 even Disney had started to lay off workers (though only 100 out of a total workforce of 38,000). Las Vegas now has new casinos marketed towards families rather than just singles or adults. Central Florida is more prone to shifts in foreigners' confidence. Ten foreign visitors were killed in Florida during 1992: the following year visitors from Germany fell 37 per cent, from Italy 17 per cent. No wonder Florida spent much time and effort to ensure visitor safety, if only to sustain the job market so dependent upon out-of-state and foreign visitors.

Skills in demand

Fluctuations in demand for certain skills explains the US Citizenship and Immigration Service's rules requiring emigrants to have a specific job prior to the granting of immigrant status. A skill by itself might well not be sufficient, and might threaten the jobs of existing workers in a dwindling job market. With 40 per cent of all college teachers on part-time contracts (up from 20 per cent in the 1970s) foreign applicants for full-time posts would need to prove they were not taking a job from an existing resident.

Finding out about the US economy

On the next page are some magazines and newspapers (often available in public and university libraries and increasingly available online) that regularly carry articles on the US economy. How many of them do you read?

Look at the pattern of your answers. Do you think it would be useful to read the business section of more newspapers and news magazines?

What other sources are there for more detailed information on specific sectors of the US economy or even for individual corporations? You should be prepared to investigate:

■ trade magazines;
■ magazines of professional associations;
■ specific interest magazines.

To do this you need to explore not just the racks of magazines at the biggest W H Smith you can find, but also to seek out your local big city library, the reference room of your local college, and the periodicals section of your nearest university library. The range of professional and trade journals is almost limitless. You will be amazed to see computer journals from Australia, ceramic association newsletters from the USA, even Russian journals in translations.

		Often	Seldom	Never
The 'quality' press	*The Guardian* *The Times* *The Daily Telegraph* *The Independent* *The Scotsman*			
US papers available in Europe	*The Herald Tribune* *Christian Science Monitor* *US Today*			
US-based news magazines available in Europe	*Time Magazine* *Newsweek* *US News & World Report*			

For a wide-ranging grasp of modern changes see Alicia Duchak *A–Z of Modern America* (1999) available second-hand or as an e-book download from Amazon. For an excellent, speculative and highly personal view look at Dave Gorman, *America*

Unchained: A Freewheeling Roadtrip in Search of Non-Corporate America, 2009 (book or DVD).

WORK: PRELIMINARY CONSIDERATIONS

The whole complex issue of US entry visas has been dealt with in Chapter 4, but jobs and visas do need to be considered together. So here are a few facts to be going along with.

Which foreigners ('aliens') can take a US job?

Only those allowed to live in the USA for compassionate reasons, whether to reunite families or to obtain asylum are, generally speaking, allowed to take whatever job they can.

Everyone else must satisfy the US authorities that their reason for entering the USA is *not* to take a job. Only then will an entry visa be issued. Tourists, diplomats and transit travellers will have legitimate business within the country, but may not work within the US job market. If you aren't entering the USA on compassionate grounds and you intend to work then you need to provide proof that you should be considered an exception to the general rule, as provided for by the Immigration and Naturalization Act, Section 212(a)(14). Don't despair! Exceptions are many and are provided for. You just have to prove that you fit the criteria.

Making your case

Aliens (that's officialese for 'foreigners' not people from outer space) seeking permission to enter the USA to take up skilled (or unskilled) jobs need first to obtain a verification from the Department of Labor that there aren't sufficient US citizens (or permanent residents whom the US regards as trainee citizens) who are able, willing, qualified and available to do the work the alien proposes to do, and that if an alien takes such a job it won't adversely affect the working conditions of persons similarly employed within the USA already (that is, you're not there to break a legal strike or to force down contract rates of pay).

As you can imagine no single applicant can possibly do such a thing. However, companies actively recruiting overseas can make such a case to the US authorities on behalf of someone they want. If companies have made a conscientious effort to hire within the USA to no avail, then looking for someone overseas is not taking a job from an American, and may positively influence the job market by enabling other Americans to operate more effectively as vacancies are filled.

Now this all seems straightforward. However, if a US college, for instance, is trying to attract a specific person from overseas the job description might be so tightly drawn, tailor-made in fact, to fit no possible US applicant (eg 'must have engaged in at least ten years' full-time field work within the British Isles, speak and read English and Welsh, and have a proven track record in teaching Welsh medieval history'). It might be necessary to justify very carefully why such a specific set of criteria is deemed necessary, especially if the US Department of Labor knows there's actually a glut of good medieval history teachers and researchers already in the USA. But mostly US employers only headhunt overseas for specific skills to complement existing ones, or to bring in someone so prestigious no one is going to be able to object to a brain drain so obviously to the advantage of the USA. When the US economy seemed constrained by a lack of imaginative, highly trained, English-speaking software writers, US corporations actively recruited from Indian graduates in Bangalore willing and able to move to the USA in the knowledge that visas would be made available.

JOB HUNTING

Jobs as a result of specific advertisements have the advantage of someone in your corner to prepare the paperwork demanded by the US authorities. Removal expenses and help with finding a house and car may be available too (if only on a semi-informal basis).

Once the job's accepted, though, there's little or no choice as to which part of the country you'll have to live in. Having no job to go to does at least enable you to consider a wide range of possible places. Nevertheless a bird in the hand remains better than two in the bush.

Check out the travelling

An extended visit if you have no job arranged could enable you to see not just a particular city, but to check out feasible commuting. Freeways may imply swift movement between, say, downtown Washington DC and central Baltimore, but rush-hour traffic may in practice suggest otherwise. Riding the buses may show how slow public transport really is unless you can live and work near an express route (or a stop on the underground if you are considering one of the few cities to have one).

Checking out the area

An extended visit can be used to:

■ check out whether or not an area appeals;
■ check out whether housing costs are appropriate;
■ check out schools, public and private.

Think in terms of why you are considering the USA:

■ Can your love of the Rockies be met by living in Boston?
■ Could you afford to ski if you lived in New Orleans?
■ You may love New York City's television, but could you live with only three stations in the mountains of North Carolina?
■ You may relish the cultural diversity of the USA but what if you were to find yourself stuck in an almost all-white, Bible-belt town on the one hand or the racial battlefield of the South Bronx on the other?

It's very risky going to the USA for the first time *after* arranging a job. Ideally a month is needed to get the feel of the country, including at least a week at the proposed job location and a week in the surrounding area. A car is essential for getting about except perhaps in New York City, Washington DC and San Francisco. If you want to visit the suburbs away from public transport routes a car is still essential.

Beginning to job hunt

Job hunting is hard enough at the best of times. Trying to do it at a distance can be next to impossible.

■ A reconnaissance trip to start with can pay off handsomely if only to get you a toe in the water.

■ A *lot* of letters will have to be written. This is true in the UK, and it's going to involve a far higher failure rate doing it from overseas, so you'll need to send off that many more enquiries.

■ You'll need as large a source of names and addresses as possible. This book can only hope to start you off. You'll need to do considerable detective work in your own field to dig out more. You can always write any of the association names from the following pages into your favourite search engine (such as *www.dogpile.com*) and see what emerges. Though web page information is rarely as up to date as people expect, it is usually far more recent than anything in a printed directory.

■ For a useful overview of US business culture take a look at 'The Ten Commandments of American Culture' (*www.gmi.org/products/abcs_out_of_print.htm*). It's not critical of its list, but at least you have now been warned what to expect as the norm..

The rest of this section takes a look at some of the careers and fields of employment within the US economy today, with some general words of advice, and addresses. If you need to call, almost all websites will have the current number, if not boldly displayed, then in a small tab (top or bottom) labelled 'Contact'. Also useful:

■ *National Business Telephone Directory,* published by Gale Research Company of Detroit Michigan since 1956 (available in large city reference libraries).

■ *National Fax Directory* also by Gale (has addresses, faxes and phone numbers for 180,000 fax users across the USA). Published annually.

■ Useful places to find US employer information:

■ City Business Library, 1 Brewers Hall Garden, London EC2 (Tel: (020) 7638 8215 for opening times).

■ Price-Jamieson (*www.pricejam.com*) is an international recruitment agency (now part of Aquent) that uses a straightforward site gathering job opportunities into a dozen categories such as marketing, communications and the creative industries. You can create your own CV or Price-Jamieson can inform you of their latest vacancies matching your submitted details.

Self-employed business opportunities

The US can provide significant entrepreneurial advantages for the self-employed. But as at home it is going to be very hard work, probably more so:

■ US attitudes towards work mean people expect more of you.

■ You'll be operating in a new set of business and tax laws (often more demanding than in Britain, contrary perhaps to expectations).

- You'll need to adapt to a new and often bewildering set of commercial ethics, and there'll be a whole new set of trading conditions, expectations about delivery dates and lines of credit.

Will it be worth it? Only you can say so. If you make a go of it the profits can be very substantial. But the hectic race has its losers too, and the US has little in the way of a safety net.

A few addresses that may be of interest:

- National Self-employed Association (*www.nase.org*), PO Box 612067, DFW Airport, Texas 75261-2067.

- Insurance Information Institute (*www.iii.org*), 110 William Street, New York, NY 10038.

- National Association of Realtors (*www.realtor.org*), 430 N Michigan Ave, Chicago, Illinois 60611-4087.

> **Silver lining time**
>
> *Though failure is very harsh in the USA many would maintain that business failure is not necessarily terminal. Being bankrupt is not like having an anti-social disease. Many people start right over again, and are admired for it. Only those who once down are prepared to stay down are really deemed beyond the pale. The sin is not falling down, but staying down.*

Business and office jobs

As service industries continue to grow in importance and as computerisation seems to create even more jobs (though not usually for those losing the older jobs) periodic shortages of particular skills are often met by overseas recruitment. The quality press often carry advertisements from US firms, or on their behalf by UK-based recruiters. For those chosen the bureaucratic hassles will be minimised and company lawyers will smooth the way providing necessary supporting documentation for any visa application.

For more general information on recruitment it may be worthwhile writing to the following:

- National Society of Accountants (*www.nsacct.org*), 1010 N. Fairfax St, Alexandria, Virginia 22314.

- American Bankers' Association (*www.aba.com*), 1120 Connecticut Avenue NW, Washington DC 20036.

- American Institute of Certified Public Accountants (*www.aicpa.org*), 1211 Avenue of the Americas, New York NY 10036.

- National Association of Public Insurance Adjusters (*www.napla.com*), 21165 Whilfield Place #105, Potomac Falls, VA 20165.

- Insurance Information Institute (*www.iii.org*), 110 William Street, New York, NY 10038.

- International Association of Administrative Professionals, 10502 NW Ambassador Drive, PO Box 20404, Kansas City, MO 64195-0404.

- Institute of Internal Auditors (*www.theiia.org*), 247 Maitland Ave, Altamonte Springs, FL 32701-4201.

Media and the arts

Unless you are an artist of international renown able to obtain an H-1 visa it is very difficult to enter the USA to take part in its world famous communications industry. H-2 visas are only available for artists who will not be taking work from Americans. Artists visiting for concert tours need special arrangements with US Equity to ensure they come under reciprocal agreements arranged with British Equity. Visits and performance tours can and are arranged, not just by impresarios with legal departments to smooth the hassles but by various US agencies. The US Department of the Interior, for instance, arranges international festivals for traditional musicians from overseas.

Some skilled or gifted people enter this field by ways of placements as part of their postgraduate degrees in US colleges. Entrance to such courses is, however, competitive, especially where financial assistance is needed, and funds sufficient for the issuing of a non-immigrant student visa must be available *prior* to applying for a visa (see *www.fulbright.co.uk*).

Assuming that you are not wanting to be reunited with family already in the USA, that you are not an anti-communist refugee, that you don't have lots of money to invest, and that you aren't an artist of sufficient renown, you will need to be accepted by a US employer able to prove the post has been unsuccessfully advertised with the USA. This means in practice that only professional people already

well established in their careers will be recruited, and so eligible for entry to work.

If you consider that you are capable of getting the right entry and work permits here are some addresses you may find helpful:

- Society of Illustrators (*www.societyillustrators.org*), 128 East 63rd Street, New York, NY 10021.

- Professional Photographers of America Inc (*www.ppa.com*), 229 Peachtree St NE, Suite 2201, Atlanta, GA 30303.

- Photo Marketing Association International (*www.pmai.org*), 3000 Picture Pl, Jackson, Missouri 49201.

- Printing Industries of America (*www.gain.net*), 200 Deer Run Road, Sewickley, PA 15143.

- American Society of Interior Designers (*www.asid.org*), 608 Massachusetts Ave, NW, Washington DC 20002-6006.

- American Institute of Graphic Arts (*www.aiga.org*), 164 Fifth Avenue, New York, NY 10010.

- Graphic Artists Guild (*www.gag.org*), 32 Broadway, Suite 1114, New York, NY 10004.

- Industrial Designers Society of America (*www.idsa.org*), 45195 Business Court, Suite 250, Dulle, VA 20166-6717.

- Society for Technical Communications Inc (*www.stc.org*), 901 N Stuart Drive, Suite 904, Arlington, VA 22203.

- American Federation of Television & Radio Artists (*www.aftra.org*), 260 Madison Ave, New York, NY 10016-2401.

■ National Association of Broadcasters (*www.nab.org*), 1771 N Street NW, Washington DC 20036.

■ American Federation of Musicians (*www.afm.org*), 1560 Broadway, Suite 600, New York, NY 10036.

■ Software and Information Industry Association (*www.siia.net*), 1090 Vermont Avenue NW, 6th Floor Washington DC 20005-4095.

■ US Equity (Actors' Equity Association) (*www.actorsequity.org*), 165 West 46th Street, New York, NY 10036.

For those with electrical/electronic skills:

■ Communication Workers of America (*www.cwa-union.org*), 501 3rd Street NW, Washington DC 20001.

■ Institute of Electrical & Electronic Engineers (*www.ieee.org*), 3 Park Avenue, 17th Floor, New York, NY 10016-5997.

Education, caring and social services

A desire to get rich quickly will not propel you into this line of work. Also, such public jobs depend heavily upon government spending programmes as so many are directly tied to federal programmes (and so federal budgets). With money (outside the military budget) increasingly tight the job situation is not rosy. Furthermore many jobs will require US qualifications to work in the USA.

Many people from overseas will only enter these fields if eligible for residence on other grounds. Once within the US job market, however, foreign professionals may be able to gain credit for courses overseas, or must be prepared to enter related jobs, such as legal paraprofessionals, library technicians or teachers' aids.

Some useful addresses:

■ American Society for Information Science (*www.asis.org*), 1320 Fenwick Lane, Suite 510, Silver Spring, MD 20910.

■ American Library Association (*www.ala.org*), 50 East Huron Street, Chicago, IL 60611.

- National Recreation and Parks Association (*www.nrpa.org*), 2237 Belmont Ridge Road, Ashburn, VA 20148.

- National Education Association (*www.nea.org*), 1201 16th Street NW, Washington DC 20036-3290.

For enthusiastic youth workers who are seeking a career in social work and child welfare, aged between 21 and 30 and interested in an 18-month placement, The American Youth Work Center seeks experienced individuals and couples to work with disturbed adolescents in residential and wilderness settings. Placements may be available in various parts of the USA, particularly New England and Pennsylvania. Further information can be obtained from the AYWC, CVYS, Castle Community Rooms, 2 Tower Street, Leicester LE1 6WR enclosing a 9″ by 6″ SAE.

Engineering and science

Jobs are very competitive, so looking for a US job in these fields means looking for US firms that are actively recruiting overseas. Professional journals and magazines which carry such recruitment advertisements can be found in large public or university libraries – see their current acquisition section (ask at main desk, and don't worry: members of the general public are usually welcome to use such specialised materials).

US recruitment agencies will also pinpoint their efforts upon certain areas of the country. If an aerospace firm closes down, US firms hoping to attract away skilled labour will advertise locally, even open local recruitment offices. Of course it is the most modern skills they seek, held by people with at least 20 years' work left in them. The industrial cities of the USA already have far too many of their own approaching their fifties with skills no longer needed anywhere.

A few addresses that might be useful:

- American Institute of Aeronautics and Astronautics (*www.aiaa.org*), 1801 Alexander Bell Drive, Suite 50, Reston, VA 20191.

- American Society for Agricultural and Biological Engineers (*www.asabe.org*), 2950 Niles Road, PO Box 410, St. Joseph, Michigan 49085.

- National Aeronautic Association (*www.naa.aero*), Reagan Washington National Airport, Hungary Suite 202, Washington DC 20001.

- US Energy Department (*www.doc.gov*), 1000 Independence Ave NW, Washington DC 20585.

- American Institute of Biological Sciences (*www.aibs.org*), 1441 I Street St NW, Washington DC 20005.

- American Institute of Chemical Engineers (*www.aiche.org*), 3 Park Avenue, New York, NY 10016-5991.

- American Society of Civil Engineers (*www.asce.org*), 1801 Alexander Bell Drive, Reston, VA 20191-4400.

- Institute of Electrical and Electronic Engineers (*www.ieee.org*), 2001 L Street NW, Suite 700, Washington DC 20036-4910.

- Institute of Food Technologists (*www.ift.org*), 525 W. Van Buren, Suite 1000, Chicago, IL 60607.

- Society of American Foresters *(www.safnet.org)*, 5400 Grovenor Lane, Bethesda, MD 20814-2198.

- American Geological Institute (*www.agiweb.org*), 4220 King St, Alexandria, VA 22002-1502.

- American Institute of Industrial Engineers (*www.iienet.org*), 3577 Parkway Lane, Suite 200, Norcross, GA 30092.

- Instrumentation Society of America (*www.isa.org*), 67 Alexander Drive, Research Triangle Park, NC 27709.

- Marine Technology Society (*www.mtsociety.org*), 5565 Sterrett Place, Suite 108, Columbia, MD 21044.

- American Society of Mechanical Engineers (*www.amse.org*), 3 Park Avenue, New York, NY 10016-5990.

- American Meteorological Society (*www.ams.org*), 45 Beacon Street, Boston, Massachusetts 02108-3693.

- American Congress on Surveying and Mapping (*www.acsm.org*), 6 Montgomery Village Ave, Suite #403, Gathersburg, MD 20879.

- American Design Drafting Association (*www.adda.org*), 105 East Main Street, Newsbern, TN 38059.

Health care services

The shortage of doctors and nurses has significantly increased the need for technicians who can take over routine health care duties such as blood tests and dispensing medicines. The bureaucracy necessary to operate the complex private and public health care programmes, plus the growing number of older people, adds up to more health care jobs at many levels.

Once within the health care profession this is a career field that offers good salaries and good conditions. Health jobs offer steady work with few lay offs, as well as health care benefits, a most useful perk in a country where the high cost of health insurance can be a major drawback.

Most medical jobs require US training, but due to the pressures upon administrators to find suitably trained people it may be possible to gain significant credit for professional qualifications gained from recognised establishments overseas.

Nursing

To practise professional nursing in the USA you must pass a licensing exam in one of the states, or the District of Columbia. If you are already an SRN or SEN, passing an examination by the Commission on Graduates of Foreign Nursing Schools (CGFNS) is first necessary. In fact a CGFNS Certificate is required if you wish to secure a non-immigrant occupational preference visa (H-1), or to obtain an immigrant occupational (third) preference visa and a work permit from the US Labor Department regional office.

Information on taking the exam in the UK is available from:

■ Commission on Graduates of Foreign Nursing Schools (*www.cgfns.org*), 3624 Market Street, Philadelphia, Pennsylvania 19104-2651.

Addresses of state boards of nursing can be obtained from:

■ National Council of State Boards of Nursing (*www.ncsbn.org*),
    111 East Wacker Drive, Suite 2090, Chicago, Illinois 60601.

Expect higher pay and a higher social status in the USA, with more responsibility in emergency units if the doctor is not on the floor at the time. However, in less dramatic circumstances be prepared to refer to superiors even over nursing items, due to the fear of the institution being sued if improper treatment is given. Some aspects of nursing will be very different. British nurses can find obstetrics frustrating in the USA. US midwives have a shorter training than in Britain, and generally defer more to obstetricians, who do the actual deliveries rather than remain in the background unless a complication develops. Generally US nurses have less interaction with their patients. Doctors give instructions: nurses carry them out, and know their place. Likewise in geriatric medicine it is important to be aware of different medical ethics in operation. It is rare for the financially solvent but terminally ill, however aged, to be allowed to die without being first subject to levels of medical intervention most nurses would not want for themselves but which they are required by their employers to carry out to avoid malpractice suits by patients' relatives.

Some useful addresses:

■ American Chiropractic Association (*www.amerchiro.org*), 1701 Clarendon Boulevard, Arlington, VA 22209.

■ American Dental Assistants Association (*www.dentalassistant.org*), 36 East Wacker Drive, Suite 1730, Chicago, Illinois 60611-2211.

■ American Dental Association (*www.ada.org*), 211 E Chicago Avenue, Chicago, Illinois 60611-2678.

■ American Dental Hygienists Association (*www.adha.org*), 444 North Michigan Ave, Suite 3400, Chicago, Illinois 60611.

■ American Hospitals Association (*www.aha.org*), 1 North Franklin, Chicago, Illinois 60606-3421.

■ American Pharmaceutical Association (*www.aphanet.org*), 1100 15th Street NW, Washington DC 20005-1707.

■ American Association of Medical Assistants (*www.aama-ntl.org*), 20 N. Wacker Drive, Suite 1575, Chicago, Illinois 60606.

■ American Society for Clinical Laboratory Science (*www.ascls.org*), 6701 Democracy Boulevard, Bethesda, MC 20817.

■ American Medical Informatics Association (*www.amia.org*), 4915 St Elmo Avenue, Suite 401, Bethesda, MD 20814.
Chicago, Illinois 60611.

- National Association for Practical Nurse Education & Service (*www.napnes.org*), 1940 Duke St, Suite 200, Alexandra, VA 22314.

- American Nurses' Association (*www.nursingworld.org*), 8515 Georgia Avenue, Suite 400, Silver Spring, MD 20910-3492.

- American Occupational Therapy Association (*www.aota.org*), 4720 Montgomery Lane, PO Box 31220, Bethesda, MD 20824-1220.

- Association of Surgical Technologists (*www.ast.org*), West Day Creek Circle, Suite 202, Littleton, Colorado 80120.

- Association of Perioperative Registered Nurses (*www.aorn.org*), 2170 S. Parker Rd., Ste. 300, Denver, COL 80231-5711.

- National Academy of Opticianry (*www.nao.org*), 8401 Corporate Drive, Suite 605, Landover, MD 20785.

- American Optometric Association (*www.aoa.org*), 243 N Lindbergh Boulevard, St. Louis, Missouri 63141.

- American Physical Therapy Association (*www.apta.org*), 1111 N. Fairfax Street, Alexandria, Virginia 22314-1488.

- American Society of Radiologic Technologists (*www.asrt.org*), 15000 Central Ave. SE, Albuquerque, NM 87123-3909.

- American Association for Respiratory Care (*www.aarc.org*), 9425 N. MacArthur Blvd, Suite 100, Irving, TX 75063-4706.

- American Association of Orthodontists (*www.aaomembers.org*), 401 North Lindbergh Boulevard, St Louis, Missouri 63141-7816.

- American Osteopathic Association (*www.osteopatric.org*), 142 E. Ontario St., Chicago, Illinois 60611-1773.

Recruitment drives are held from time to time in the UK, and can be accompanied by considerable media interest, so opportunities may present themselves to anyone ready and willing to relocate. But beware: US salaries may seem very high, but if you couldn't afford to move from Birmingham to London because of the high cost of living in the south-east you may not be able to afford housing in New York City either. But a move from London to rural Minnesota might be very profitable (though the winters are a tad harsh).

Any move by a single person to the USA (if only for a year or so) may be worthwhile just for the experience. And of course many single people going over to work in the USA also marry an American, whatever their original plans.

UK-based recruitment agencies include:

■ British Nursing Association International (020) 7629 9030 (*www.whe.co.uk*)
■ Grafton International 01827 280280 (*www.grafton.co.uk*)
■ Medic International 0800 731 9758 (*www.medicint.co.uk*)

For carers for the elderly placements:

■ Private Care Association (*www.privatecare.org*), 5505 Connecticut Avenue NW, # 169, Washington DC 20015-2601.

■ Association of Homes for the Aging (*www.aahsa.org*), 2519 Connecticut Avenue NW, Washington DC 20008-1520.

Service industries

As people have more money and more leisure time, service industries, particularly those dealing directly with the general public, grow and grow in number and importance. Many service jobs, though, are poorly paid, recruiting non-unionised teenagers, as in fast-food outlets. These jobs may be available on a casual basis, but are not career jobs, nor are such jobs available for foreigners without resident status. However, some services do require specialist skills, such as the rescue and police services. Unfortunately such public services are often geared to government spending levels. In certain parts of New York City public services have long been subject to 'planned shrinkage'! If you have already served in the fire service contact:

■ International Association of Firefighters (*www.iaff.org*), 1750 New York Avenue NW, Washington DC 20006.

For information on police opportunities write to the state police department of any state you are interested in, which will probably be located in the state capital (eg Albany for New York, Tallahassee for Florida, or Sacramento for California). There is no federal police force (unlike the Mounties in Canada) as law and order is very much a state responsibility (as it remains for each country in the European Union, with which the USA should perhaps be more properly compared). Alan Whicker presented a British police officer's view of both the service and his Los Angeles 'beat' on his 1986 television series (see *Whicker's New World*, once a Book Club choice now turning up in second-hand bookshops and on the second section of its Amazon entry).

Transport

Employment is expected to increase for highway and air jobs, but continues to decline for railway work. Sales and reservation jobs are now much like any other job that deals directly with the general public within catering or tourism. Most jobs are therefore only available for those already US residents. Aircraft mechanics need a licence from a Federal Aviation Administration (FAA) approved school, plus considerable experience, usually gained in the US military. Except for overseas applicants with highly unusual skills this field is essentially closed to people who don't already have US residency.

> **A note of warning**
>
> *If you are thinking of investing money, time or effort in any commercial trucking enterprise, please get professional advice. Moving furniture in a VW bus for friends or acquaintances is one thing, but getting into long-haul trucking may soon bring you up against the International Teamsters (at best) or the Mafia (at worst). Neither organisation tends to encourage people moving onto their turf.*

Contract work

Contract work is advertised in the UK press primarily as available for engineering and electronics persons, ranging from a few months to a couple of years. Employment is on US terms (with minimal holidays) but at very good rates of pay even by US standards. Fixed terms are usually necessary for immigration regulation purposes. Beyond the end of the contract there is no security, and you will have to have one eye always on the next contract opportunity, which may mar the travel time between contracts. It'll play havoc with family life.

Good news:
■ good pay;
■ experience of USA;
■ formalities undertaken by employer;
■ fares paid;
■ nomadic;
■ travel between contracts.

Bad news:

- fixed term;
- you may not be able to stay on;
- can't change employer;
- can't visit beforehand;
- hard on family life;
- you may be reluctant to spend money if no further job is in sight.

APPLYING FOR A JOB

Applying for any job, especially one overseas, demands great care. You are presenting yourself, so take your time. You only get one bite of the apple. Show your draft copy to someone, whether a careers adviser, a relative in business, or just a friend. Their comments may be all the feedback you'll get, and so may be invaluable.

How well you fill in an application form is generally crucial: it is usually the first contact with an employer. The overall impression created by a completed form will precede you to any further interview. In the competitive job market today, the importance of well presented and well thought out applications *cannot be over-emphasised.*

The job hunter's perspective

From the job seeker's perspective application forms are a huge hurdle: you generally have to complete a great many just to get one interview; it can be very time consuming; and they often ask the most awkward and difficult questions. But there is no escape from them if you hope to find a job.

Think of applications as a challenge – a means of presenting as positive and interesting (but truthful) picture of yourself as you can. Make sure the employer will want to find out more about you.

The employer's perspective

From the employer's point of view application forms are vital selection documents. Most employers cannot interview all applicants, so half or more are usually eliminated through this initial screening. Application forms provide an economical basis for deciding which candidates are most likely to meet their criteria. Their decisions will be based not only on what you write, but also on *how you present it.*

Presenting your application form

The effectiveness of your application will depend largely upon your prior preparation. You cannot expect to sit down 'cold' with any application form and do justice to yourself there and then. Prior work is essential.

Assess yourself

Many questions will focus on you as a person:

- What have you gained from your education/training/career so far?
- Why do you think you would make a useful member of their firm?
- What are your main strengths and weaknesses?

Thorough self-analysis and relating your skills, interests and background to the demands of the job are vital steps in the application process, enabling you to present a convincing case for yourself.

Research

Research the job and the particular employer before filling in the forms. You need to find out as much as you can about both the organisation and the job. Lack of such homework is almost always evident and a common basis for rejection at this stage.

Types of questions

Although forms vary, and range from one side of foolscap (Americans don't use A4) concentrating on factual information, to booklets requiring almost a total life history, they usually ask for the following information.

Personal details and educational background

Make sure all the information is accurate and nothing relevant has been omitted. It is usually best not to list failures unless specifically asked to do so or unless they indicate a gap in your life that cannot otherwise be accounted for. Try, however, to be positive wherever possible. If you feel you must say how far you fell make sure they know how soon you came back up to try again and to succeed.

Interests, extra-curricular activities and positions of responsibility

Selectors will deduce quite a lot from what you do (or do not do) with your spare time. They will be particularly interested in positions of responsibility and evidence of initiatives. This is particularly crucial when applying for your first ever job (when you cannot offer practical experience). Do you seem to be an active, social type or more of a loner? Are you a single-minded specialist or an all rounder? Is there evidence of leadership abilities, of being able to work well in a team? The main thing is to try and write positively about your activities – whatever they may be.

Work experience/previous jobs

Employers are interested in any work experience you have had. When describing your employment include a brief description of the duties involved. Try to demonstrate what you gained from this experience, such as working under pressure, with the general public, out of doors, shift work, etc. Particularly if you are applying for your first job do not leave anything out. Anything and everything can count as useful experience.

If you are further along with your career you can be more choosey. Even here, though, vacation work 20 years ago might be worth mentioning, if for instance it was in the USA (and so the company knows that early on you showed initiative, and that you have already had some experience of living in the USA).

Job choice/career aspirations

Almost all application forms will have some questions aimed at drawing out your motivation for the particular job, and for determining your longer-term career aspirations. It is vital that you communicate interest in the job and the organisation, backed up by whatever concrete evidence you can use.

Knowing precisely what the company has to offer is crucial (you must read the recruitment literature carefully). Relate your needs, interests and aspirations to what they say they need. Indicate what specific factors have influenced your career choice and why you think your combination of experience, qualifications and personal attributes is appropriate for the job in question.

Open-ended questions

These can include:

- What have been your main achievements in life?
- What initiatives have you taken and what have you been able to accomplish?
- What difficulties and disappointments have you met and how have you tackled them?

Such questions may seem very intimidating at first, particularly since most of us have had relatively ordinary careers, unpunctuated by momentous accomplishments, events or turning points. However difficult such questions may seem, try to see them as an opportunity to portray something interesting and positive about yourself and to demonstrate your ability to communicate clearly and concisely.

Employers are generally more concerned with what an experience meant to you personally, how you dealt with it, or what you gained from it, than the actual event itself. Thus, persevering with months of boring assembly line work rather than going on the dole could be more relevant than going to climb Mt Everest (if, for example, you were killing time and raising money before going to take a business management course).

It is useful to think about what the employer is trying to get at by asking such questions. There is no standard or correct answer. You need to write about your own experiences!

Additional information

Many forms have a space for anything additional you feel you could usefully tell them. There may be something you thought they would want to know but don't seem to have asked for. Perhaps you could mention foreign travel, expeditions, or special qualifications that might suggest the sort of person you are. Maybe you could use this opportunity to explain why you were made redundant. You may be able to write something distinctive that will make you stand out from the general run-of-the-mill applicant. If your area of responsibility was increasingly profitable but was undermined by an asset-stripping take-over then say so. You may get no other chance to explain why you are looking for work.

Questions to be raised at interview

This gives the interviewer advance notice of questions you might want to ask and gives the selector a further opportunity to assess the quality of your thinking about the job. Never leave this section blank. And never ask just about salary and holiday matters. Think carefully about what you have read in the company literature. Are there gaps in what they have said about the company? Perhaps you still feel you need to know about the range of training they will provide? The likeliness of career progression? Do not be afraid to ask challenging questions.

Referees

If you have recently completed formal education one of these should be an academic referee. The second should be a previous employer or someone (not a relative) who knows your career well, and can comment upon your performance, particularly if it is not possible to ask your present employer for a reference (if you don't want it to be known that you are applying for jobs elsewhere). Always consult referees before naming them, and make sure that they have a good idea about what you are applying for.

General guidelines

- Try to approach the firm as *positively* as possible. It is important to be truthful, but you will have to **sell yourself** and convince the employer that you really want the job and have the ability and potential to succeed at it. Don't make claims you cannot substantiate, but remember, no points are given for modesty.

- Do all the necessary preparation – **assess** yourself, **research** the job and the company and **relate** your attributes and aspirations to the demands of the job.

- Before writing anything, **read the form carefully** to get the feel of what to put where and how much space you have.

- Follow all the **instructions** carefully – mistakes will be interpreted as an indication of carelessness.

- **Make a draft version of what you intend to write.** If you download the form just download two copies or photocopy the application form if it is a hard copy. It is particularly important to draft out answers to open-ended questions and, ideally, to put the draft away for a day or so before returning to it with a fresh eye.

- Use **black ink** (many photocopies may have to be taken), typing where possible.

- Pay particular attention to **neatness** and **spelling**. Selectors will not be well disposed to applications that are untidy, difficult to read or filled with spelling errors. Type, unless specifically asked to write in your own hand.

- Make sure the **layout** is clear and attractive. First impressions are important.

- Do not leave any unexplained chronological **gaps**.

- Answer **all the questions**, unless not applicable (and indicate N/A).

- Relate what you write to the precise **requirements** of the job.

- Always keep a **photocopy** or screen shot of completed applications. They will be necessary at the interview stage (you'll need to see what you told them beforehand!).

- Many of the questions asked at **interviews** will be based on answers you have provided on the form. Before an interview it is vital to think about how your response might be further developed.

- If you need **help**, ask a friend or colleague. They can help you think through the difficult questions and can advise on the overall impact your application makes.

Curriculum vitae (CV)

Some very detailed application forms (similar to those for university entrance) do not require a separate CV, but with most applications you should send one along. Known as a **résumé** in the USA it is a personal, one-page statement of:

– who you are;
– what you have done already;
– what qualifications you have;
– what you have to offer.

- It should be set out in a generally acceptable format, must be typed, and should be carefully spaced so that the layout draws the reader's attention to essential information in a methodical and logical fashion. The usual British format is as follows:

Personal   Nationality, age, date of birth (spelled out in full), marital status, address, telephone numbers (work and home), relevant extra information (hobbies, association memberships). However, US laws to combat discrimination restrict the types of information that can be included in applications (date of birth, marital status and driving licence record) so do not include details that will render your application invalid.

Work experience Names and addresses of past employers, dates of employment, positions and responsibilities held, with reason for leaving. Don't distinguish between paid and unpaid work experience.

Education Dates and schools, colleges, universities attended, examinations passed (with dates and grades), with any other qualifications. Mention any awards, honours or scholarships.

■ It's usual to set out present positions first and then work back. If a column for dates is kept clearly visible on the left this should be quite clear to any reader.

■ If you have little or no employment to record (if straight from college) place the education section before the employment section.

■ If you are sending out multiple applications use the best copier you can afford. It may be worthwhile to visit a copyshop rather than rely on doing it yourself in a coin-in-the-slot machine. For isolated applications send an original rather than a copy.

> **Remember**
>
> *US students have long typed all their work so the quality of your competition's CV will be very high. If in doubt pay for your CV to be professionally typed and copied. At the very least use a template from a Desktop Publishing (DTP) or word processing package such as Microsoft's Office (try Word or Publisher).*

Sending off applications

■ **Type** your covering letter on good quality A4 paper, and send it in an appropriately sized envelope with your CV, unless required to submit it online (increasingly the case). Neatly type the envelope using the correct zip code. It is usual in the USA to place your address in the upper left hand corner of the addressed side of the envelope. Use the correct value stamp and an airmail sticker. The use of a commemorative stamp on a well-produced envelope may well catch someone's eye in a pile of applications.

■ If you wish for confirmation of receipt of your application, or further information to be forwarded, say so, providing a suitable email address.

For more information see Appendix E (Job Applications) in Roger Jones, *Getting A Job in America*, 7th edition, How To Books, 2003 for suggestions on tailoring applications to US guidelines.

Offered a job?

Before accepting any job abroad make absolutely certain you are aware of all relevant factors:

■ Are your professional qualifications acceptable in their existing form in the USA?

■ Who will be responsible for getting the appropriate papers, yourself or the employer?

■ What is the length of the contract? Is there a probationary period?

■ What is the salary and when will the first payment be made, and in what form?

■ Who is responsible for deductions?

■ What vacation entitlements are there in the first year?

■ What relocation help is available? If so, when and how much?

■ What accommodation arrangements are there, for how long and at what cost?

■ Will commuting be necessary? Is public transport feasible?

■ What sickness provision is there for self and for family? When does it take effect?

■ What pre-conditions exist? Will you be asked to sit any in-house examinations, undergo medical tests?

If you are offered a job it may well be necessary to accept or reject it quite quickly. The more versed you are in the problems of moving the easier it will be to concentrate on the essential factors upon which you'll make your decision.

COMMUTING AS AN OPTION

Rather than change countries it may be easier to commute between Britain and the USA. Academics, journalists and certain businesspeople may find living in both countries feasible.

Points to consider may include:

- costs of maintaining two bases;
- costs of air fares;
- time involved in travelling;
- tax liability;
- immigration standing.

All these points need careful consideration, else you could find yourself committed to far more travel and far greater costs than initially anticipated.

Two bases

There are several options worth thinking about:

- *Home in the UK and staying with US friends*
  You can't stay too long, or you'll outlive your welcome. Paying for a spare room may solve this problem. You'll avoid US local taxes and the problem of leaving your UK base unoccupied (and thus vulnerable) for long periods.

- *Home in the UK and own place in US*
  If this involves owning in the UK and renting in the USA you may get tax advantages from having your rented US flat as a business expense. This is easier than the other way around, as it leaves a Briton with an existing relationship with HMRC. Avoid starting any relationship with the more strict Internal Revenue Service in the USA. Better the devil you know...

- *Base in the UK, with long-stay hotel accommodation in the USA*
  This could be right for you, but only if you intend to stay put, say in New York City or Los Angeles. Otherwise you'll be humping stuff around the USA. But for a month or so long-stay rates can be attractive, being much lower than daily rates. At worst you could try staying at a basic level at the YMCA or YWCA, though security for business materials while you're out at work might be worrying. A half-way solution might be to rent an efficiency room from a motel, which would include a kitchen besides the usual facilities.

Cost of air fares

If you are self-employed these costs can start to eat into profits, even if you are able to claim them as business expenses for tax purposes.

You may well not want to be going online all the time for cheaper seats, nor can you travel to and fro wedged into a tourist seat too frequently. Eventually you'll need to travel at some expense if only to get some sleep and to minimise jet lag. Concorde back from Washington DC or New York City was ideal, but pricey, but is no more.

Other costs would include:

- getting to and from the airport;
- long-stay car parks;
- shipping over goods and materials.

Travel times

Few will live in the lee of Heathrow or Gatwick nor will a US base necessarily be near to JFK or Newark. The journey from Birmingham to Heathrow is tortuous with luggage, though easy by motorway. What do you do with the car at the airport? Flying down from Birmingham International may be more convenient, but may raise your travel costs by 20 per cent. British Airways now fly directly from Birmingham to JFK from which connections can be made, especially convenient if by USAir, BA's partner in the USA.

Do you want to have a three-hour motorway drive home after arriving at Heathrow from New York City?

Tax liability

Though US-UK treaties ensure that you'll only be taxed on the same income once, each country will want it to be in their system. The rule of thumb is that you'll be taxed in the country where you spend most of your time. The United States IRS uses a complicated formula to calculate a notional definition of where you live, or as bureaucrats prefer to put it: where you have a 'substantial preference'!

You'll need an accountant or financial adviser at the very least to secure your best tax deal.

If there's any doubt where you live then both bureaucracies will read their own regulations to their own fiscal advantage (wouldn't you?), may change the rules from year to year, and may redefine what is meant by a permanent base, the indicator of where you intend to be taxed.

If at all possible keep your residency status the same from year to year, so that you only have to deal with one pack of wolves at a time (remember the military nightmare of a war on two fronts).

For the US view of tax details and so forth see the IRS booklet No. 518 *Foreign Workers, Scholars and Exchange Visitors*. Unfortunately this does not seem to be online, but a useful array of similar advice points is made at UCAR's website in Boulder Colorado (*www.fin.ucar.edu/hr/visitors/manual/taxinfo1.html*).

Immigration standing

US regulations assume that you are either a visitor or an immigrant. Exceptions get very messy and confused. Many people, afraid of falling between two stools, hire a lawyer specialising in immigration matters, though this can be expensive, and is no guarantee of a satisfactory outcome, especially if the lawyer is mainly used to dealing with people who want to get permanent residency status. Most people would get by with the normal commercial non-resident B1 visa. Academics, for instance, usually get the B1-2 visa valid for multiple entry that would allow visits and commercial trips. This is because they would be working for UK-based employers (colleges and publishers).

If you want to work for a US-based employer you will need an employment visa or residency status (the famous so-called Green Card). This is much harder to get, of course, unless you can arrange to be hired by, and paid by, the UK subsidiary (or even a UK parent company). Do *not* use the movie *Green Card* as your how-to-manual.

INVESTING IN THE USA

For people with more than their lives and families to invest in the USA investment may or may not involve actually moving to the USA. Either way it needs expert advice. Selling your thriving fish and chip shop here, packing the money into a suitcase and going through US customs and immigration as a tourist (it's been done) is not advisable. There are too many tales of people coming sadly and very badly unstuck, investing in motels that then go bust as the new freeway opens and takes all the passing trade elsewhere (haven't they seen *Psycho* or *The Postman Always Rings Twice?*). Don't buy a bar just as the state's liquor laws change. Too many small investors end up washing floors, dishes and windows, one-step ahead of the US Citizenship & Immigration Service, not to mention the Teamsters or the Mafia if they think you are muscling in on their patch.

Finding out information

For more specific and detailed information see the appropriate *Daily Telegraph Guide* by Peter Farrell, *How to Buy a Business* (second edition available on Amazon). Though certain specifics may age the general approach necessary to such a major transaction surely doesn't.

If property investment is proposed an essential work of reference is Nigel A. Eastway and David Young's *The Allied Dunbar Expatriate Tax and Investment Guide* (2000). Besides dealing with the joys of double taxation, capital gains and capital transfer taxes, this otherwise general source of information specifically presents a section tailored to the needs of those people with an eye on the United States.

Penetrating the US market

The behaviour of UK firms well illustrates how difficult it is to penetrate the US market. UK retailers have been badly mauled by trying to impose British retailing formats and techniques upon US consumers. Laura Ashley's costly investment in the USA almost destroyed the company. It had to close its 150-store US chain just to survive. American shoppers just didn't go for the English look. Marks and Spencer took over Brook Brothers in the late 1980s, but in a complex deal that involved access to specific shopping malls found that their long-term interest in gaining access to the convenience food market was fraught with difficulties. Not all malls are modern with access to the market niche desired. Learning the hard way can be an expensive option. Dixons, likewise, found its US subsidiary a money pit. Sock Shop found collapse followed initially massive expansion. If such enterprises cannot read the US market, with all their support services, what chance has a small business going it alone?

The fear of massive initial cost will, of course, exclude most UK companies from even considering going it alone. Other options do exist:

- the brochure blitz;
- the phone call campaign;
- the personal contact;
- the transatlantic trip;
- buying in skills from local colleges and universities;
- co-operation with bodies actively promoting US investment in the UK, such as **Business Link** (*www.businesslink.gov.uk* – where there is a tab for 'International Trade');

- co-operation with agencies promoting British exports in the USA, such as the **Department of Trade and Industry** on (020) 7215 5000 in London or (0121) 212 5000 for the West Midlands.

WORK AND THE INFORMATION HIGHWAY

The research for this book has involved not just working in the USA but searching out directories in many libraries, turning pages in search of that illusive piece of information. Increasingly, though, such data searches will start and finish at my desk: an information revolution has taken place. I already contact US colleagues more by computer than by phone or fax. Public libraries provide public access to the electronic highway, the Internet. Most university students already log onto a network computer to research their papers and write their dissertations. But this revolution is more than just efficient ways of accessing books or writing essays. The revolution allows us to search for information anywhere in the world. I can already access the US Library of Congress, the US National Archives and even the CIA from home. Most public agencies make databases available for all of us, if not for free then at a price the market will bear. Books such as this already focus more on how to find out about living and working in the USA than actually on how to live and work. If you seriously want to be part of the USA you will have to join the information highway to find the necessary information. Once you are connected people and institutions will actually come and find you; already the daily White House press release arrives in my electronic mailbox, whether I like it or not: electronic junk mail has already arrived, with daily summaries from *The New York Times* and *The Washington Star*.

Further reading

There is a regular small business column in the financial section of the *Guardian*. General business climate and conditions in the USA are increasingly important in the weekly *Economist* (as an ever large proportion of its readership is American). There is always, of course, *The Financial Times*. Knowing your way around the *FT* makes going through back copies much easier for large parts can safely be ignored so long as relevant sections are carefully monitored. Also search out:

- *Hoover's Handbook of American Business*, William Snyder, annually (*www. hoovers.com* has a 'look inside' pdf feature if you open the 'Books' tab).

- *The American Almanac of Jobs and Salaries* has links to some 15 job-related books worth looking at (available second-hand from Amazon).

Some contact numbers:

- US International Marketing Center (020) 7629 4304. See Commercial Service (US Embassy) at *www.buyusa.gov/uk/en*.

- US Embassy Information Resource Center (*www.usembassy.org.uk*) (020) 7894 0925.

- British-American Business Council (*www.babc.org*) (020) 7290 9888.

- For a more detailed guide to practical job-hunting in the USA consult another book in this series, *Getting a Job in America* by Roger Jones (How To Books, 2005), which contains useful copies of immigration and taxation forms (forewarned is forearmed).

Financial health warning

Investing overseas is fraught with danger and may only be for those who can afford to lose everything. Most foreign investors just do not appreciate the cultural difference between home and the USA. US consumers are particularly price and brand sensitive, while insisting upon regular changes in the products offered ('this year's line'). Unless you can address brand recognition costs you really shouldn't approach the US market. It takes successful companies decades sometimes to get a substantial return on their investment, and they can be caught out by serious exchange rate fluctuations.

8

Money Matters

Payment is made with cash far more widely than in the UK, despite the widespread use of credit cards, chargecards, personal cheques (checks) and traveller's cheques. The return of troubled times is likely to encourage even more people to stay with cash.

CASH

Beware:

- All US banknotes (bills) are **green**, the same size, and have similar layouts (though a different president's face appears on each denomination). Watch though for the new forge-proof $100 bills.

- You may come across the following sign: 'Legal tender not accepted.' It means just what it says. Payment is to be prepaid token or by card (credit or charge). It's all part of the war against crime: no cash means there's nothing to steal.

PERSONAL CHEQUES

Personal cheques are far less convenient than they are in the UK. They are subject to more scrutiny and more delay than you have ever met before. Personal cheques can usually only be used locally within the area served by your bank. Unfortunately your bank may well turn out to be far more local than you might have expected from its name as 'First National Bank of...'.

To use a cheque it must be overprinted with your name, address, telephone number, account number, and in some places your driver's licence number. *And* you'll need local identification (ID). And to write $11.60 write eleven and $\frac{60}{100}$ dollars. No wonder more and more people use cards to make payment.

What's ID?

This usually means a driving licence at the very least. It'll be asked for whenever you use any form of cheque, even traveller's cheques! Don't bother trying to explain to the clerk that traveller's cheques are as good as cash if signed at time of use. You'll be shown the sign that hangs everywhere 'all checks must have local ID'.

Once, in the Smithsonian Institute bookshop in Washington DC, my American Express dollar traveller's cheque was refused by a clerk who wanted local identification. The cheque wasn't accepted until a five-year-old, almost expired, US government ID was produced (a relic of a previous spell working in the capital).

Of course most shops and restaurants will be all too happy to take your *dollar* traveller's cheques, just beware of someone who has never been on the till before.

The reason cheques cause so much hassle is quite simple. Cheque theft is endemic. Furthermore, if you leave a retailer with a cheque that bounces (and there are no guarantee cards to ensure payment up to a certain level) they'll want to find you to cover the value of the cheque, plus their administrative costs, plus the penalty payment the bank charged them. You may see signs warning you that a bounced cheque will cost you $10. As current accounts cannot go into the red the possibilities of going into cheque bouncing territory is high if you'd been used to the more casual situation in Britain. When, in 1992, a hundred members of Congress were found to have bounced cheques a national scandal ensued!

Overdrafts are generally frowned upon. In some states you are guilty of a felony if you write a cheque for more than you have in your account: you are trying to spend money that is the bank's not yours. Overdraft protection is available whereby an account likely to go into the red is topped up automatically (from another account or from a credit card).

Trying to go overdrawn on a debit card is equally heinous (a word far more popular in the US than over here).

CREDIT CARDS

Credit cards are more widely used than in Germany, but, surprisingly not as widely as in the UK. Most stores and petrol stations will accept VISA or Mastercard but there are still enough places that won't accept either card to make things tricky if you run out of petrol or need accommodation in out of the way places. Check beforehand if you can. Also, you may have to pay a surcharge for using a credit card.

Creditworthiness

Creditworthiness is different from what you're used to. It is *illegal* in many states to go unexpectedly overdrawn. If the bank were to honour your cheque or debit instruction or debit card it would be giving you its own money, so you would have spent what doesn't belong to you. If, on the other hand, the bank won't honour your cheque you have just attempted to defraud the retailer. Either way you are deemed to be beyond the pale. And your creditworthiness will disappear, which may hurt you when it comes to buying a car, or just trying to obtain a credit card.

Credit card companies require an indication you won't do a bunk and disappear after a shopping spree, so they may check your bank, your employer and commercially available bad-debts lists. If you are self-employed and live in a trailer then credit won't be available.

DEBIT CARDS

A short trip, up to a semester long for students paying fees in other ways, may call for a debit card withdrawing cash as required from Automated Teller Machines (ATMs) which, as at home, are now everywhere. Beware of withdrawing small amounts as each withdrawal involves a 1.5 per cent handling fee (and depends upon having money in your UK account). It may well make more sense to keep a UK account and ensure it keeps being topped up. Use the Nationwide Building Society to avoid overseas withdrawal fees.

BANKS

Banks are organised somewhat differently than in Britain, and this affects how they operate and the services they provide. Don't deposit any money in an uninsured bank. Many lived to regret doing just that in the 1930s Great Depression. The federal government set up the Federal Deposit Insurance Corporation (FDIC) to guarantee deposits (and so minimising the chance that there would ever be a dangerous loss of confidence in the financial system among small to medium savers). The maximum insured individual deposit continuously rises. By the mid-2000s it had reached $100,000 (more than most of us will ever have in the bank!).

There are web-based ATM locators, particularly useful at airports (*www.visa.com/pd/atm/main.html,* and *www.mastercard.co.latml*). Check these out *before* you set off for foreign parts.

SAVINGS AND LOAN ASSOCIATIONS ('THRIFTS')

Savings and loan associations are the nearest equivalent to British building societies. Loans have traditionally been fixed interest (good if you finance a property when the rates are low, not so good if they were very high), though loans are often refinanced if rates change substantially, or if house prices rise so high you are undermortgaged and so find you can raise more money on the property (say for an extension, a pool or even to go back to college). Since the 1990s, half all new loans have been on a flexible rate. If depositing make sure the association is insured by the savings and loan version of the FDIC, the Federal Savings and Loan Insurance Corporation (FSLIC), known as 'Freddie Mac' or the Federal National Mortgage Association (FNMA) 'Fanny Mae'. You will have noticed by now that the US and UK experiences have converged over the last few years.

MORTGAGES

American-style mortgages differ from traditional British ones in that the loan is linked with the property rather than with the borrower. That is, US mortgage levels are more directly based upon the collateral value of the property than is the case in the UK where the lender is more interested in the borrower's ability to repay almost irrespective of the potential of the property. American concern for the collateral value of the real estate explains why mortgages can be passed on to the next purchaser, providing some with a more efficient way of entering the housing market than starting a huge new mortgage that will be front loaded with interest payments rather than reducing the principal. Americans do not share the widespread British assumption that all mortgages must be as long as possible. Indeed the standard British 25-year mortgage reflects merely a long-standing concern for interest rate cycles among building societies. The downside is that US lenders, like new British banks, are more directly geared to seeking out profitable business with minimal risk, so they tend not to be very sympathetic to borrowers in financial trouble.

Borrowers who run into trouble with their US savings and loan can easily lose their home, but unlike in the UK the lender will not pursue them through the courts for any shortfall between the value of the property and the outstanding mortgage debts. US lenders only lend what they can realise from the collateral view of the property, and if they misjudge its redeemable value that's their problem not the borrower's. It makes lenders more circumspect, though, about giving loans in the first place. The losers are those with lower incomes and jobs with poor security wanting mortgages on property they can afford but for which they cannot get a loan: Catch 22. When lenders did find a way of providing mortgages to almost everyone, the infamous sub-prime crisis soon developed.

PENSION PLANS

Pension plans depend upon how long you intend to stay in the USA. If you are going to return home in a year or so you may just have to accept that all your required pension payments will be for nought. If your company can transfer them all well and good. If you leave the USA with all taxes paid you may be able to claim your US social security payments back, but only if you can show that you have taken no deductions, have paid tax at the flat rate, and will not be returning to the US to live. Students on an F visa may be able to do this, but it may well be cheaper for long-term visitors to pay as little tax as possible and to pay their social security knowing they'll get nothing for it. Students on a teaching assistantship or stipend should consult their foreign student office at their university (usually known as the 'international office').

For those more affluent visitors who pay both tax and social security a tax accountant may be needed to get the best deal. And if you hear Americans talk about how rapidly support for the IRA is growing remember that in all probability they are referring to **individual retirement accounts** which involve tax-free savings earmarked for retirement somewhat like British ISAs. Such accounts enable people to move between jobs with no pension loss (so long as they can keep making the payments).

HEALTH INSURANCE

Health insurance may well be a major fringe benefit of a job offer. Few companies, however, offer full coverage for the employee and the rest of the family. You need to know precisely what the cover includes. Pre-existing conditions will, of course, be excluded, but beware of ceilings on payments for treatment. Cover will often only be for 90 per cent of costs up to say $10,000 and 100 per cent over that. Pregnancy may not be included, nor will dental and optical charges. Check when the cover comes into force – it might not be until six months into the job. Ask:

- When does the cover start?
- Who's covered?
- What's included?

It is essential to know what the situation is beforehand so that you can arrange bridging cover before you leave Britain. And you had better get those details in writing in case there's any dispute when push comes to shove. Illness can be emotionally devastating. In the USA it can also destroy the financial security of a family, and often does. Catastrophic illness can destroy the family just as much as the patient. At least be insured!

Medicare

The USA is the only G8 country with no basic medical insurance for all even though pre-election polls in 2008 suggested over 80 per cent wanted some form of national health service. Instead private schemes compete with a jerry-built structure of private, state and federal systems – some overlap, others leave gaping, unbridgeable holes for the working poor.

Medicare is the nearest thing the USA has to Britain's National Health Service, but it applies only to the aged (not to be confused with **Medicaid**, a joint federal and state health care programme for the poor). Medicare pays hospital bills less certain deductibles for the first 60 days only. Then the patient typically pay on a sliding scale.

Over 30 million patients rely on Medicare each year (of whom over 800,000 pay over $2,500 for Medicare during treatment). Life-savings are threatened by any catastrophic illness, or just the need to be in a nursing-home, which costs about $5,000 per person per month (of which only about 2 per cent has been covered by private insurance).

It is not unheard of for surviving partners to be left with $100,000 worth of debt upon the death of a loved one. This is paid off like a mortgage (say $100 per month,

Warning

Extras to the above include outpatient drugs, extra physicians' charges, eye glasses, and dental costs.

with, if lucky, the balance due at the death of the surviving partner from whatever is left in the estate).

Health care is increasingly costly. A family of two adults and three children paying $2,500 a year at the end of the 1980s would be paying, by the end of the 1990s, over $7,500 for Blue Cross Insurance cover and over $9,000 in the mid-2000s. Not surprisingly, most Americans with adequate cover obtain this through work. Even less surprising is that about 47 million Americans have no health insurance at all but are nevertheless not poor enough to qualify for Medicaid.

TAXATION

A necessary summary of a necessary evil:

Is there a US version of PAYE?

Yes, but it is calculated in a way quite different from that traditionally used in the UK. The system goes something like this:

- You estimate what your allowances will be for the coming year.

- A proportion of your salary is excluded from tax on this basis and the rest is taxed at a variable rate plus a flat fee according to income.

- At the end of each tax year you fill in the tax form with the actual (not estimated) allowances. Tax actually due is compared with tax actually paid, and either you pay them or they pay you.

Any good news?

At least the tax year is the calendar year, though the infamous 1040 tax form doesn't have to be submitted until April, to give time for information to be collated.

If this sounds a complicated routine, in practice it's actually worse, as the allowances actually allowable are open to dispute.

Any useful short cuts?

- There is a short form for those lucky people with no complications (for instance, no deductions for things like mortgage interest).

■ Most people find it pays to use the long form, which means getting professional help or spending at least 17 hours filling it in (officially it should take less than three hours). You'll see tax accountants as often as car exhaust and tyre companies on the edge of shopping malls. The major chain (H & R Block) is as well known as any fast-food firm.

Will it get any simpler?

Reagan's popularity with ordinary voters was partly based upon his promise to simplify government, which for most people means easing not just their tax burden but the burden of doing their taxes. Reagan also promised to do something about national debt. He did – he enlarged it as never before.

Needless to say tax reform has not materialised, though there is a W-4 form designed to help calculate withholding levels. Paradoxically this form is four pages long, twice the size of what it replaced!

What can I as a foreigner do to simplify my tax?

The criminal justice system never got to nail Al Capone. The tax people did, though, and sent him away for a long time for not paying tax on his illegal income. It makes you think. No wonder Americans are often heard saying only two things are certain in life: death and taxes (though not necessarily in that order!).

The IRS **audit** taxpayers. Audit is a word that conjures up fear and loathing across the USA. The IRS can ask for all written evidence to support your claim for tax allowances for the previous seven years.

Most taxpayers' returns are not scrutinised – the volume of returns wouldn't allow it. *But* the IRS do undertake *random* examinations of tax returns, and if anything untoward turns up then an audit may result. Many Americans liken this to shooting hostages, but mostly tax returns are so honestly completed only people pulling a fast one will suffer from an audit.

Does the IRS deal with all income taxes?

The IRS is the *federal* tax gatherer. Each state is entitled to tax as it sees fit. Most, but not all, do. This means that you have to fill out state *as well* as federal tax forms, though the state forms are usually simpler, shorter and information from the federal form can often be reused (and may be cross-checked if there's a feeling you are trying to defraud the system).

Any other taxes?

For the first three years working in the USA you can continue to pay UK National Insurance Contributions. After that you are liable under the Federal Insurance Contributions Act to contribute to the old-age pension fund and to Medicare (generally for those over 65, or disabled veterans). Reckon on about 8 to 10 per cent of salary for these deductions. You must have paid for 40 quarters to be eligible. Many payments from these funds can be made available anywhere, and some people retire back to Ireland or to Poland to get the most from their pensions.

Individual states may have their own social welfare taxes, such as a disability insurance scheme taking off another 2 per cent or 3 per cent from salary.

And, of course, while your overall tax burden may well be lower than in the UK, even when you've added federal and state payments, you'll still have to pay for your private health and pension plans. The total outgoings from your salary may end up being very familiar to those from Britain (though less than from such countries as Sweden or the Irish Republic). The good news, of course, is that with an initially higher income you hope to be ahead at the end of the day.

In short: if at all possible avoid being liable for US taxes by continuing to pay UK taxes. Though UK taxes are somewhat higher it's worth the extra to avoid entanglements with the US Internal Revenue Service, whose penalties are greater if you fall foul. Remember Al Capone...

Just because you live in the USA does not necessarily mean that you can avoid a tax liability in the UK. If you are within the UK for 183 days in any one tax year the HM Revenue & Customs (the old Inland Revenue) will consider you liable for UK tax. Furthermore, if, over a three-year period, you spend an average of 90 days a year within the UK you will be deemed liable. And as we go to press these guidelines are being tightened up so get professional advice. Unless you have a full-time job outside the UK you could also become liable if you have and use 'available accommodation' here in the UK. Of course, if your property is let out and you have no access to it during a return to see the family that doesn't count. But if a non-working spouse comes home s/he could be considered a resident for tax purposes if using a residence that can be used at any time, such as a 'granny-flat'.

US tax economists now believe that the effective income tax rate stands at 30.8 per cent. This means that everyone who works a full year has to work until 23 April each year to pay off their tax burden. But that is just direct taxation: don't forget that there is considerable taxation (as in the UK) by other means, such as user fees to have permits issued. The authorities say you have to have a passport to leave the country but then charge people for the privilege. It hardly surprising then that they make foreigners wanting to come in pay user charges for handing visas. The same economists have worked out that in the USA these days the citizen has to keep working all the way to 25 June to pay these fees. Yes, in the land of the free, despite its overseas images of small government and low taxes, Americans spend almost half of each year working for the government. No wonder tax relief bills are so popular with politicians: the average taxpayer works longer to pay for the government than they do for basic necessities such as food, clothing and shelter combined. For more, albeit somewhat partisan information on this all too familiar and deeply depressing topic contact: Americans for Tax Reform, 1320 18th Street, NW, Suite 200, Washington DC 20036 (*http://www.atr.org*).

Taxation at a glance

Figure 2 shows all compulsory payments to federal, state and local governments for six countries during 2008. After the Reagan revolution and a generation of post-Woodstock conservatism it was perhaps surprising the US tax load wasn't lower.

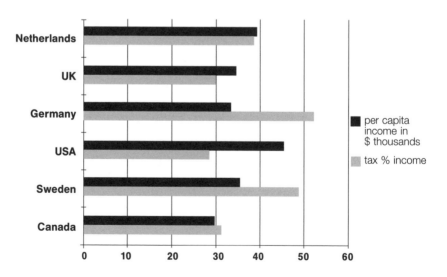

Fig. 2 Comparative tax rates (Source: *The World Fact Book*, 2008)

These figures should however be interpreted with some caution. Sweden and Canada may have had higher tax rates than either Britain or the USA, but the Swedes were probably materially the most well off, with the least poverty, so beware of assuming that tax rates are the only factor to consider. If you are sick the USA may well help you become the fastest bankrupt, if inventive the richest success story. Bill Gates after all is not Swedish. But Saab is.

But federal taxes are compounded by state taxes, which vary greatly. A useful site to read in small bites (*www.retirementliving.com/RLtaxes/htm*l) demonstrates how complex any federal system with 50 self-governing states can be.

Where can I read more on this?

The Allied Dunbar Expatriate Tax and Investment Guide, though due for updating, remains useful.

There are also magazines for expatriates which may be of interest:

- *Nexus*, Expat Network Ltd, Advertiser House, 19 Bartlett Street, Croydon CR2 6TB. Email: expats@expatsnetwork.com (*www.expatnetwork.com*).

- *British-Expat Magazine* has a useful website (*www.britexpat.com/USA.402/0.html*) with links to various tax sites and a discussion form.

9

The Children and Their Education

...It is often the children who truly lead their elders to America, the sons who take their fathers to their first baseball game or shepherd them to their first rock concert to give them a real sense that they have a stake in America's future.

Henry Grunwald, editor-in-chief, *Time Magazine*
(born in Austria, arrived in the USA aged 17)

Many if not all people emigrate for their children. Safe within their family children are amazingly resilient. They'll pick up the language in weeks not years. They'll play with any child who'll play with them. They'll accept wherever they are as normal. They seem to possess a secret weapon unavailable to their parents.

Parents may be as ambivalent towards the USA as Americans are about them. Parents may keep one eye open towards the old country, following its progress, watching for it on television and in the papers. Their children, however, will not. They live in and for the present, which is now the USA. Where parents need gumption, courage and ambition plus the will to make it, their children will have all that and more besides, with no homesickness, no sense of alienation from things American and no feelings of exile. So great may be this feeling of moving forward that parents too may get left behind, seen as old-worldly, accent-ridden, out of touch. A national spelling contest was once won by a 13-year-old Tamil student!

Placing a child in the US educational system will be one of the major implications of moving to the USA with a family. Even if you can afford and want to place your children in the private sector there will be remarkable contrasts both with what you remember from your own days at school and from what is going on in Britain today. You may find surprisingly little difference if you are moving from a stable middle-class school to one in an equivalent part of the USA, but if you are moving a child from a small rural British primary to a large suburban American school the culture shock experienced (not least by yourself) may be immense, just over this aspect of the move. Prepare your child, and thus yourself for the move.

- Talk it though with your child.

- Get to talk with the teacher responsible for your child's pastoral care (who may or may not actually teach them).

- Make sure the school knows the background, educational and otherwise, that your child has experienced to date.

- Take as active an interest in things like the Parent-Teachers' Association (PTA) as you can to keep track of what's going on in the school. This may be particularly necessary if you are not a church-goer (where many parents will meet, discuss their children and generally keep in touch).

- Don't expect your child's schooling to be like yours was. It wouldn't have been even if you were still back in the UK!

- Don't despair: your child could still return to the UK for third level education if necessary (though this would place a different and perhaps even more unanticipated pressure upon the family, and not necessarily a financial one at that).

THE US EDUCATION SYSTEM

The USA actually has two parallel education systems: one private and one public. In the public sector, which involves about 90 per cent of all pupils and students, control has traditionally been vested in state and local authorities under the general supervision of State Boards of Education, usually appointed by the Governor, though sometimes elected. Each state is divided into school districts, over 16,000 throughout the whole USA, each administered by school boards either elected or appointed locally.

Education is therefore far more locally controlled even than it used to be in Britain. This means that by and large rich areas run well-funded schools, poor districts poorly-funded schools. However, a widespread concern for civil rights and the belief in the need for a high minimum level of general education has led to the provision of federal funds for the improvement of educational facilities, though not always in the most needy of areas.

Regional variations

Education is by far the greatest item of expenditure for state and local governments, averaging about a third of total spending, being generally lowest in those states where average earnings are depressed. Though southern states have, with some reluctance, come to regard the provision of high quality public schooling for all children regardless of race as an urgent social necessity their generally lower incomes mean that they cannot always afford to improve their educational system.

In rural America, particularly in the West, the level of expenditure is partly dictated by the scattered nature of settlement, making educational costs quite high. Cultural characteristics are also quite important. Minnesota's liberal German and Scandinavian traditions have included considerable support for the adequate funding of education. In the Dakotas, by contrast, a decrease in general levels of prosperity has been reflected in a serious decline in proportionate support for education.

Racial integration

After the Civil War, southern whites were unable to accept the social, economic and political implications of the freeing of the slaves. They were supported by the US Supreme Court which declared that segregation was permissible, provided that facilities for black people were equal to those for whites (though they rarely were so). In 1954, though, the Supreme Court reversed this 'separate but equal' doctrine, declaring that separation was itself a form of inequality. Federal action followed to integrate the education system. After the 1964 Civil Rights Act Congress cut off funds to any school district that failed to provide fully integrated education.

Between 1966 and 1967 the once racially segregated public school system of the South was turned around, most dramatically in those states initially most segregated. In the northern states the problem has been focused within the huge cities where segregation, though it surely existed, had not been backed by the force of law.

However, concern with the changing official position has obscured two very important trends: within much of the South white children are now sent to privately funded and segregated schools, often called 'academies', leaving the officially desegregated public schools to the black children, thus defeating the object of federal policies; and across the North the movement of much of the white population to the suburbs has left officially unsegregated but often totally black schools in the inner cities of huge conurbations. Here the only way to achieve integration has been to bus children from one school district to another, a policy much at odds with the established tradition of neighbourhood schools.

Though the practice of **'bussing'** black children away from their local schools to preserve segregation had long been established the introduction of bussing to integrate schools came as a rude awakening to many white parents, particularly in those areas that thought the new standard applied only to the South. Widespread resistance followed, and still smoulders. Black students trying to enter once all-white schools have been subjected to verbal abuse and even to physical violence, with law and order only being restored with the arrival of the National Guard.

This kind of lawlessness should not, however, be permitted to over-shadow the amount of social change that has come about, especially in the South. The segregation of so many black children in poor, inner city schools remains, however, a much more intractable issue for American society.

A BEGINNER'S GUIDE TO US SCHOOLS

As if the practical issues of getting a child into school aren't enough, going to school in the USA may turn out to be quite different from the equivalent experience in Britain. There is no national curriculum as at home. Furthermore the history, geography and literature taught may well change quite dramatically. Religious instruction and prayers are actually forbidden in the public, tax-supported, system. Other ceremonies like the pledge of allegiance will incorporate your child from day one, and there's little that you can or should do about it.

Children start school at age six, and pass through 12 grades, finally 'graduating' at 18. The term 'K-12' is often used. It means kindergarten through high school. After that there are community colleges (usually a further two years) or universities (four years). All institutions of learning at whatever level are commonly called 'school'. And *public* schools are just that, schools run for the general public from the public purse.

The groupings of years together in the same school varies from district to district as in Britain (as anyone who has moved into or out of a middle-school district will realise), but the following routine would be widely recognised (a couple of variants are compared to one English norm in Figure 3).

Two US variants				British variant	
	kindergarten		kindergarten	infants year 1	
1 2 3 4 5 6	elementary school	grade school	1 2 3 4 5 6 7 8	primary juniors	2 3 4 5 6
				year 7	8 9
7 8	junior high				
9 10 11 12	high school	freshman sophomore junior senior		lower sixth (12) upper sixth (13)	10 11
1 2 3 4	university freshman sophomore junior senior	two year community college		first second	
		move over to state university for degree		final postgraduate	

Fig. 3. School years compared.

Grade or elementary schools (grades 1 to 6 or 8) are for those aged six to ten or 13, and usually resemble their British primary equivalent (though without the uniforms so beloved of middle class schools in the UK).

The real contrast will come in both **Junior High** (grades 7 through 8, ages 10 to 13) and **Senior High** (grades 9 through 12, ages 14 to 18) where an amazing lack of discipline and petty rules so prevalent in Britain will be both exciting and frightening, especially for the British pupil making the transition halfway through the system. Younger children will take it more in their stride. For older pupils the lack of discipline will resemble that of going to college, with all its opportunities for individual discovery and the pitfalls of having to work it all out for themselves.

Academic grades

These appear straightforward:

A – very good worth   4 points
B – good   3
C – average   2
D – poor   1
F – fail   0

Grades such as these are given for every essay (paper), exam and course taken, and the grade points average (GPA) calculated (hence 'he's a genius, got a straight four-oh in his senior year'). All grades are internal, and are in comparison to the appropriate peer group. They cannot be compared to GCSE exam results at all. Most grades are from continuous assessment, including marked exercises and short tests rather than lengthy final examinations.

Graduation from high school may be all that's technically required for a place (self-financed though) at the local state-funded college. For entrance to a private college further assessments will probably be required, plus recommendations from teachers, culminating in an interview.

A few choice words on maths standards

Government studies continue to show US school students ranking low among the 20 or so nations considered in mathematical skills (even though US-based standardised scores have actually risen since 1980). This is especially so in geometry and calculus. Only 20 per cent of college-bound US students have ever taken any calculus, deemed essential in applying for any maths degree course elsewhere.

Why such a poor US showing?

■ Most Americans see maths (US = math) ability as innate rather than learned, so if it seems difficult it is because the student is pushing against a locked and bolted door and no amount of teaching or time will ever change anything, so it's best to shift attention to something else. Asian immigrant parents do not share such prejudices and their children tend to outperform all other children in mathematical skills.

- US schools generally stress broader, more 'creative' skills such as reading and writing rather than the maths skills emphasised in other countries, and encouraged by Asian immigrant parents.

- The use of 'tracking' (assigning students to ability levels) tends to reinforce both good and bad evaluation, with the poorer student giving up completely.

- 'Spiralling' in the curriculum has failed to provide an adequate system for developing advanced skills; spiralling involves an initially light introduction to maths, returning later to the same concepts at supposedly increasingly sophisticated levels. But in practice it has students revisiting the same material again and again, covering much the same ground at about the same level, with boredom setting in all around.

- Teachers, especially at early grades, are generally generalists rather than well-trained maths specialists.

- Geometry and algebra are only introduced after students are more than halfway through the 12-year programme, whereas elsewhere the ideas have already been introduced, if only very generally, much earlier.

If you are from much of Britain, this may seem uncomfortably all too familiar.

Girls v. boys

Programmes over the last 20 years to undermine the gender stereotypes as to who is supposed to be good at maths and science seem to have started to raise everyone's standards.

A 1998 study clearly shows that girls had at last caught up with boys in maths achievement, a goal long sought after by educational reformers.

Who runs the schools?

The decentralised administrative system of the USA deeply influences the public schools. They are run not by counties but by specially constituted **school boards**, which have to raise money locally from taxes.

By and large school boards in well-to-do areas have the money to maintain the schools, pay attractive salaries, and suitably equip the libraries and laboratories. In poor areas the converse happens. Government grants are available in target areas (say if a school is next to an airforce base which influences the student intake and may overburden the local tax base).

Federal monies may be available for remedial programmes, but by and large schools reflect the local tax base. As this shifts so does the quality of the schools.

General points worth considering

■ *Size*
Often much bigger than (traditionally at least) in Britain. A graduating year may reach 1,000. Hence the number of yellow school buses out on the roads!

■ *Assembly*
In British 1944 Education Act sense assemblies don't exist in the USA. The US Constitution requires the separation of State and religion, so religious observances far from being required are forbidden (and would be deemed divisive).

■ *Sport*
Low key, which may be a surprise given the high profile nature of much school competitive sport. Most effort has traditionally gone into the school teams, so 'jocks' used to get most of the attention. Women now participate in a wider range of sports than ever before, which may help explain the success of school soccer (and it's less expensive and less dangerous than American football!).

■ *Uniform*
Unheard of in all but a very few select private schools pretending to be British prep schools or else pseudo-military academies (like most of continental Europe), though periodically proposed by politicians seeking a quick fix.

PRIVATE EDUCATION

Across the whole range, from kindergarten to graduate school, private education parallels the public system. This is based upon two things:

Money

The first factor is the desire to *buy* a better education for the children. As in Britain a bought education is not necessarily better than what is publicly available, but so long as people are looking for conspicuous consumption *and* an edge over other people the private schools will continue to have a social cachet if nothing else.

The east coast tends to have two main variations:

- the military, usually but not always, southern-based school where military style uniforms, discipline and hygiene are imposed upon a chosen few;
- 'prep' schools, preparing students for college, usually prestigious 'Ivy League' ones (hence the term 'preppy' for an American Sloane Ranger).

Both types are rare out west, being seen as too European, and thus more suited to a supposedly decadent east.

Religious principles

Since religion is excluded from the public schools by the US Constitution, private schools based on religious principles have developed, with 'Parochial' schools like you'd find in the UK, through to fundamentalist academies which might be a little too vigorous for British tastes, even for those of a religious persuasion themselves.

Unfortunately too many parochial schools, especially in the South, are merely attempts to create all-white schools given that the public schools have been racially integrated.

There are other schools, such as those run on experimental lines for usually well-to-do liberal progressive parents with lots of money to spend.

GROWING UP IN THE USA

In the whole range of everyday activities things won't be quite the way they were back home. Moreover, your children will not be yours for very much longer. This would be equally true if you had stayed where you were. But taking them to the USA and immersing them in American society means that it may well seem all that much more dramatic. The values, habits and expectations they pick up will be from people who do not necessarily share the same cultural background, even more so than had you stayed at home. Rather the children will come back to you ever more American as each day passes. And while there will be good things about this, aspects of which you will approve, there will also be things of which you may strongly disapprove.

Getting a job

It has long been taken for granted that middle-class children get some kind of job as early as possible, if only around their own yard (that is, the garden). Children are after all in training for an adulthood of getting and spending.

Babysitting is often a daughter's first experience with the great world of work. If you have young children you'll find that local junior high school students will expect to babysit for you (as they will expect you to buy Girl Scout cookies from them in due season). The babysitter may well bring her young sibling along with her (so doing two jobs at once). These even younger would-be earners may well return in due course ready and eager to haggle with you over garden chores you might have been expecting that you or your children would do as a matter of course. Watering the lawn and flower beds is a great favourite for those too young to babysit but not too young to spend. Television assures an intimate knowledge of every possible product aimed at children whether clothes, foods, drinks or toys. If you live in a condominium apartment complex where the children may not be able to offer gardening services they will still find ways of earning money, if only watering the plants and feeding the cat when you are away.

By high school mere babysitting will have been supplemented by working in the local ice-cream parlour, fast-food outlets, dog-walking, bagging-up or even cashiering in local stores. It is all good preparation for 'working your way through college', and through life come to that.

US children seem to grow up quickly. In this they are generally encouraged by families, neighbours and friends. If you believe that everything should be in its due season you may be seen as sheltering your children from the harsh facts of life. Children are introduced very early to that most American of claims: 'there is no free lunch.'

How to respond?

- Talk things through with your children. They may actually prefer to get paid for mowing the lawn (like their friends) rather than have a set amount of pocket money come what may. The children have to live with their friends, just as you have to live with new colleagues and neighbours. Though no-strings pocket money may sound great it may not be as good as doing what everyone else at that age does.

- Your children will want to be exactly like their US friends, rather than like you. They will say the pledge of allegiance along with everyone else even if you are only in the US for a fixed period. After all, as grown-ups you wouldn't want to be excluded from the Fourth of July party just because you are foreigners!

What can I read about US education?

There's not a lot available outside the USA. You may be able to order the following couple of critical exposes, both by a (not the) David Owen, *High School*, Viking, New York 1981 and *None of the Above* (the title echoing the last choice of a multiple-choice test), Houghton Mifflin, New York 1985. For an extremely jaundiced view of being an American student see Allying Bloom's *The Closing of the American Mind*, Simon & Schuster, 1987. For a work of more careful scholarship try Amy Gutman, *Democratic Education*, Princeton University Press 1987.

For an extremely detailed, place by place, outline of America's school districts see the Education section of David Savageau and Richard Boyer, *Places Rated Almanac*, Prentice Hall, New York, annually. For a most useful introduction see David Hampshire's *Living and Working in America: A Survival Handbook*, 1995.

GOING TO COLLEGE

Where once upon a time 12 years of schooling was supposed to be enough to give the immigrant and native alike a sufficient leg-up to do well in the US job market, and thus in life, a further four years of college is a minimum prerequisite these days. A further two years of postgraduate work are also highly desirable. This is due to the growing sophistication of the job market and the corollary that 12 years of schooling prepares people for very little these days. Compared to British sixth-formers most American high school seniors are a couple of years behind academically. By the time they received their degrees this difference has disappeared.

Student optimism

Middle-class American students display a far greater sense of optimism than their British equivalent. They may seem to talk about ozone depletion, the greenhouse effect and AIDS, but their unselfconscious optimism seems to surround them with a protective shield. For them their good will defeat anyone else's evil. They may be publicly cynical about the 'system', but they will never doubt that this century also belongs to the USA. They are on the winning side, the side of democracy, even while buying ever more Japanese goods.

Such myopic optimism may seem little more than the positive thinking of a prosperous society, but it also comes from the kind of education they receive. Debate as understood in the UK is quite rare for school children. The political system that they learn about in Civic classes, and which they follow through the congressional hearings on television (Watergate to the most recent scandal), is quite different from that in Britain.

Congress's role is to act as a check upon the executive. On the floor of the House of Representatives members do not argue, that is debate by a series of arguments laid out to sustain an internally consistent line of thought. Rather members make speeches that will get into the papers, or if they are lucky, get onto the TV news back in their home state. Students themselves don't debate as such but hold arguments that are often little more than rows, people talking past each other. Try following any web forum for how participants all too often shout past each other.

'Really educated people'

By the time high school students have moved on to college they often come over as amazingly erudite. Talk to them and you feel you are talking to really educated people, even if you can't quite put your finger upon what it is they have been educated in. But they are amazingly aware, interested, studious even (if there's a test due). They have courses in subjects that British high-fliers have only heard of: nutrition, family dynamics, even 'world history'. And their more traditional courses seem so well focused upon the 'now' of it all: feminism in George Eliot, Stonehenge as a proto-computer, or Chinese history (especially if the terracotta army is on tour across the USA). Everything comes to be channelled towards tomorrow's big chance. It's all very professional. No knowledge for knowledge's sake, or even as a hobby (leave that for retirement). All are being educated for the job market whether coming to it from the humanities, the social sciences or the natural sciences. On the other hand colleges run courses that would seem bizarre elsewhere, such as bagpiping as part of a BA at Pittsburgh's Carnegie-Mellon University (in association with the university pipeband, a legacy of Carnegie's Scottish roots).

College entrance tests

There is no US equivalents to the German Abitur, the French Baccalaureate or British A levels or Highers. Students' high school grades are averaged out to produce a grade point average (GPA) – the origins of the cry 'I got a 4 Oh' – straight As. The SAT Reasoning Test (formerly Scholastic Aptitude Test) is a standardised test lasting about four hours and costing overseas applicants $71. Possible scores ranged from 600 to 2,400 combing test results from the three 800-point sections (maths, critical reading, and writing). The tests supposedly measure critical-thinking skills needed for academic success. Usually taken by high school students in their final or penultimate year SATs, when used intelligently along with school GPA, supposedly provide a better indicator of success in college than school grades alone. There is a rival scheme, ACT (originally American College Testing), more popular in the South and Midwest.

Having no common nationwide school-leaving exam, SATs provide a common baseline against which college admissions departments can judge students coming from very different school systems. SATs supposedly recognise that GPAs are highly dependent upon the quality of the school, and so aim to measure the more fundamental skills that may not be reflected in GPAs (which may result from a lot of rote learning rather than the development of analytical skills).

As mentioned above, SATs consist of three major sections: mathematics (US = 'math'), critical reading, and writing. Each section receives a score on the scale of 200–800. Frequently, applicants are required to chose between a series of possible answers, rather than provide the correct answer themselves. British students may find this is their first major engagement with the kind of multiple-choice questions with which American have long been familiar, and so may seek assistance from books promising to provide easy familiarity with SATs, such as *The GRE Test for Dummies.*

The GRE (Graduate Record Examination) is a standardised test that is an admissions requirement for many US graduate schools. Created and administered by the Educational Testing Service, the exam is primarily focused on testing abstract-thinking skills in the areas of maths, vocabulary, and analytical writing. The GRE is typically a computer-based three-hour exam that is administered by select qualified testing centres (including overseas) for a fee of $115. However, the level of emphasis that is placed upon GRE scores varies widely between schools and even departments within the same university. Sometimes a GRE score can be merely an admissions formality where admissions tutors feel that the exam format is so rigid that it tests little more than how well a student can do the tests. See *www.gre.org* for more details or, better still, start with the advice offered at *www.fullbright.org.*

Standards

The traditional British put-down of the American high school graduate and the self-satisfied observation that their first two years at college raise Americans to about A-level standard should not blind the British arrival to the fact that US graduates, those who complete the four years at college, are at least as competent as their British equivalents, or put another way:

■ it's easier to get into college in the USA,
■ but just as hard to get out.

In most states publicly-funded colleges admit state residents who have graduated from high school. This means that first-year undergraduate classes are *huge* (200–300 per lecture, 30–40 per 'discussion group' where the lecture and this week's chapter and exercises are gone over in more detail). Exams are set so that vast numbers of students (usually a pre-set percentage) will fail.

Electing a major

Those who survive this in-house selection of the first couple of years 'elect a major', that is declare to the college which subject they want to specialise and so graduate in. They then proceed to choose from the college catalogue those courses that when added together constitute a degree programme. Each course is usually self-contained, with tests and exercises most weeks, with a longer term paper (essay) plus a final, written exam at the very end of the course. Each course successfully completed provides credit plus grades, markers on the way to graduation.

Graduating

At the end of the programme, which is supposed to last four years (but can last as long as the money and stamina remain available for weaker or poorer students), those with the highest grade point averages may graduate *Summa cum Laude* (excellent), *Magna cum Laude* (very good), or on the *Dean's List* (good).

College terms

Terms are generally called **semesters**, of which there are two, Fall and Spring, each lasting about 15 weeks, with some places having a break about midway. At the time of 'spring break' thousands of students swarm south to the beaches. The papers go wild with talk of 'sex and drugs and rock'n'roll' in places like Fort Lauderdale, Florida.

Semesters run from late August to Christmas, and January to May. For those who missed or failed a course and wish to catch up, shorter, more intensive eight-week courses are offered between two semesters in **summer school**, when staff, often on auto-pilot, teach again at great speed what they've just taught earlier in the year, but for extra money.

Some colleges (US = 'schools') have three quarters, like the old British term system. The fourth quarter is summer school.

Fees

Publicly financed state universities and community colleges charge reduced tuition fees for people from within that state. All others pay 'out of state fees', which can be hefty. This naturally encourages students to stay within their own state.

But remember that most states are the size of countries elsewhere, so many still have to leave home to go to college. Even with cheap tuition there are still 'nominal' registration fees, health centre fees, sports centre fees, all of which must be paid at the beginning of the semester (and don't forget that parking lot fee too!).

And of course if you want to live on campus in a dormitory (hall of residence) you will have to pay a residence fee for accommodation, and these are not grant-aided. Over four years even a 'cheap' college education can be expensive. How, then, do students manage it?

■ Living at home may be necessary just to survive. For parents this means supporting an adult until they are at least 22! Does this seem familiar?

■ Part-time work, which can mean anything, just to raise cash for books, clothes, etc, even where parents provide the accommodation. In college towns most menial and service jobs, such as in fast-food outlets, are held by students.

■ Work-study, where government or the college provides students with menial work for low pay.

■ Loans, repayable upon graduation, whether governmental or commercial.

■ Many go to local two-year 'community colleges', transferring to the more expensive universities for only the last two years of study.

Financing a college education

Ronald Reagan once starred in *She's Working Her Way Through College* in which a burlesque star tries to better herself by going to college, promoting the US ideal that students should be both willing and able to work their way through college, so becoming free of both parents and the State. The reality today, however, tends to be otherwise. Less than 4 per cent of the average student's financial package comes from work as against just under 45 per cent grants and almost 52 per cent loans. The soaring costs of college and diminishing federal support means that commercial loans are becoming ever more necessary.

Work-study programmes provide help with fees in exchange for working in the college itself. Almost a million students nationwide work on federally funded work-study programmes, but the maximum is 12 hours per week during term time, the pay is the legal hourly minimum, and as it involves mostly washing floors, dishes and serving food hardly amounts to vocational training.

Some universities hire their own students to do the menial work. Each year, for instance, the University of Minnesota hires 17,000 of its students for up to 29 hours each, with a yearly pay bill of about $70 million. But with financial pressures bearing down upon college budgets at least as hard as upon individual students there's always the temptation to cut down upon financial support except for those in dire need or for those sporting or high-flying students likely to bring credit to the college. Everywhere the need for student loans seems on the rise.

Loans are becoming even more necessary. The best are at fixed low-interest rates not repayable until after graduation. In the past these have tended to be governmental, or underwritten by government, but so many people disappeared after graduation and never paid up that the authorities have tried to end these altogether. **Commercial loans**, preferably based upon parental collateral, are ever more important. By the late 1990s students and their parents already borrowed over $10,000 million. This all places graduating students under great pressure to get good well-paid jobs as soon as possible, with many socially necessary but not so well-paid jobs (including college teaching!) being far less attractive than well-paid legal and commercial jobs. This skewing of the job market is getting quite serious in places.

Tuition costs $6–15,000 per nine-month academic year plus a further $8–15,000 per academic year for living costs.

Private colleges

Many world famous US universities are private foundations, but be sure to distinguish between those of social status and those with high academic standing. The most prestigious universities in popular standing are the **Ivy League** (Brown, Cornell, Dartmouth, University of Pennsylvania, Princeton, Columbia, Yale and Harvard), so called because of their 'ancient', ivy-on-the-wall, standing. Together with once all-girls colleges such as Vassar and Smith these form a self-sustaining first division, though for many this rests upon high social-standing as much as upon world renown.

The Massachusetts Institute of Technology outside Boston is at least as world renowned as Harvard, but like other institutions such as Stanford on the West Coast, has a 'boffin' image. There are also a large number of often quite small, once experimental, colleges right across the country, such as Reed in Oregon or Swarthmore in Pennsylvania.

All tend to be expensive. 'If you need to ask the cost you can't afford them' is a pretty good rule of thumb. Expect to pay $8–20,000 per nine-month academic year (plus $7–12,000 living costs per year).

Community colleges

These are two-year post-secondary, mostly vocational colleges funded out of the public purse, attended by almost half the 18–22 age group. Good grades can be translated into a transfer to the state university system. Community colleges are the unsung work-horses of US further education.

How to choose a college?

If you decide to send your offspring to a US college, rather than fly them back to the UK for a British education (which may be cheaper and possibly better if you choose well) it is very much a question of detective work, asking other parents of college-age children, scanning websites, reading prospectuses (**catalogs**) and if possible visiting the campus and appropriate departments. Do you really want your 18-year-old to go to a state university, living at home, commuting every day (along with maybe 10,000 other drivers) onto a campus of 35,000 students, where classes will be in vast lecture rooms seating 300 at one go, being taught in classes of about 35 students a time by overworked and underpaid and often foreign postgraduates (**teaching assistants**)? The same university might be just the place for postgraduate work after graduation elsewhere. Graduate classes will be of about a dozen, with sustained personal contact with senior staff over several years, with access to facilities only a vast state university library and laboratories could offer.

'It's all Greek to me'

The film **Animal House** may have introduced the notion of **fraternities** (for men) and **sororities** (for women) to a British audience. Fear not, such excesses as portrayed there are as likely as the school rebellion in the British film *If.* Nevertheless, it's useful to know something about these institutions, if only to know what to avoid:

■ **Greeks** – members of societies so called because of their use of three Greek letters, such as Delta Beta Phi.

■ **Frat house** – houses owned by Greek societies, usually on the edge of campus, providing room and board for members.

■ **Rushes** – recruitment of new members, which can involve recruits passing through initiation rites (often masonic by way of Monty Python).

■ **Honor societies** – undergraduate societies that recruit students with excellent grade averages for social and academic functions (rather like subject-based societies at British universities, but nationally based, as with the Geographers' Gamma Theta Upsilon).

■ **Greek week** – a week for 'fun' activities run by fraternities and sororities (resembling a rag week in the exuberance, high-jinks and potential for mayhem).

10

Opportunities for Young People and Teachers

There are many easily found packages for those with money to spend: visit any good travel agent or just go online. For those who need to work their way across there are basically two routes:

- Work over here and spend over there — take a look at www.summerjobs.co.uk or at a range of similar sites (a Google moment).

- Work overseas and spend time and money in the USA.

SHORT-TERM OPPORTUNITIES

The most usual and still highly popular jobs in the USA are:

- summer camps;
- au pairing;
- bar work;
- resort work.

It is quite possible to arrange jobs unaided by specialists, but it's likely to be more convoluted, time-consuming and risky. You can find information on US summer jobs in:

- US newspapers;
- US magazines;
- via US contacts;
- by writing to US branches of groups you may deal with over here, such as the YMCA, YHA, Scouts.

If you do get a job this way you'll have to pay your own ticket (which might be a financial blow) but you'll get to keep your final pay: it'll be yours, which wouldn't be the case if you've used a broker (like BUNAC or Camp America). You may be able to negotiate a better deal than you'll get if you go through an agency. But you may be ripped off, exploited, sacked or worse. You take the risk (and it may well pay off).

If you've little room for manoeuvre you may have to go through an intermediary. At least that way your papers will certainly be in order.

SUMMER CAMPS

If you are a student, a teacher or a nurse and are over 18 then Camp America or BUNAC may be able to help you arrange a nine-week job in the USA teaching sports, arts and crafts, or camping and other outdoor skills in US summer camps. Jobs in camp maintenance are also available.

Being a camp counsellor

This is a demanding job, but for the right people summer camps can be both challenging and fun, an incredibly rewarding way to experience a slice of American life. Specialist counsellors need specific qualifications and experience in a particular field or activity, such as swimming or archery. General counsellors need experience with children in a leadership role. Counsellors are assigned to a cabin of about six children and, along with other counsellors, take responsibility for their welfare. The camp will expect counsellors to set a good example, ensuring that the children keep themselves and their cabin (or tent) clean, that they follow the camp routine and have a great but safe time. The children may experience homesickness or other personal problems and the camp counsellor needs to be a mature friend (like a big brother or sister) as well as an impartial adviser. Earning their respect can be difficult, so it is vital counsellors are sure of their own strengths and weaknesses beforehand. Applicants need to be flexible, adaptable and positive enough to adapt to living and working abroad, which may include working in camps isolated from the rest of the world, with a limited social life given there will be few evenings off; plus rules and regulations to be kept (curfews and no alcohol), dealing with difficult children, coming to terms with the 'rah-rah' atmosphere of many camps and the mosquitos and other creepy-crawlies. You may also find that not only is the setting a little more isolated than you thought, but the job involves doing over and beyond what was initially expected.

Applications

Applicants must be in full-time study or training doing a degree level, tertiary (HND, two-year BTEC, NVQ4/5) or postgraduate course.

Benefits include the right paperwork for US the Citizenship and Immigration Service, free or cheap return flight, board and lodgings, insurance cover, pocket money and free time for your own travel plans at the end of the job before flying back home. This is an excellent way to spend time in America, but, even though you don't have to pay upfront for your airfare you do have to spend about £400 before going (fees, insurance, visa), so it helps to have worked one summer to invest in the next. I worked in a variety of seaside hotel jobs (night watchman, waiting table, pulling pints, fast-food) to invest in one great summer in New York. Contact:

- **Camp America** (*www.campamerica.co.uk*) which has a long-standing reputation for sending thousands to work in the USA. Do not confuse it with the US-based organisation with a particular take on prayers and American patriotism.

- **BUNAC** (*www.bunac.org*). Members have access to special summer employment lists, summer camp jobs, and the necessary J-1 visas through three authorised programmes. Gap year students with a confirmed university place will be considered (especially for Canada). As an example let's look at BUNAC's 'Work America' scheme.

This is a very popular programme, but it is *only* available to students. This is because it is part of an agreement between the UK and the US to enable UK students to pay their way while visiting such a large and complex country, and most students have to be home for the next year of study, so ensuring that they do leave the USA as the programme requires them to do. Most work is going to be seasonal, whether pulling pints, guarding beaches or cleaning tables. It's an experience in itself, and then you have time to travel afterwards with the money you have just earned. And the longer the hours worked the less time there is to spend money, and the more left to spend at the end on travelling.

Complete a Work America application form (download from the website) and send to BUNAC with the registration fee of £259 and, if you are not a current member, the £5 BUNAC membership fee.

BUNAC then confirms your place on the programme and sends you an acceptance pack which includes information regarding flights and insurance. Such convoluted arrangements are necessary to ensure the programme conforms with official US requirements.

A completed insurance booking form with payment, along with SEVIS (see page 260) payment and proof of study status, then has to be sent in. Once sent a BUNAC notification of a confirmed job offer or paid for the BUNAC Travel Package, the DS-2910 (the official document which allows you to apply for the visa) is requested by BUNAC as your sponsor on your behalf. At that point information on how to apply for the J-1 visa is sent out. Further information on the application process is available on the Work American Application Form itself. The **costs** involved are:

– $259 registration fee (£215 for those who were on the programme the previous year);
– £5 BUNAC membership;
– £133 insurance;
– £75 US Embassy visa processing fee (this could change);
– £23 US government SEVIS fee;
– £499 BUNAC Travel Package (if applicable).

Don't forget: applicants are also required to take a minimum of $400 in support funds with them, $800 if working in a commission-based sales job or not job hunting until arrival in the US.

You will need a **US visa** and the US government requires participants to attend the US Embassy in London in person in order to obtain the J-1 visa. BUNAC will provide full instructions regarding this with your visa application pack. At this stage, the visa application fee (currently £55) is payable to the US Embassy by all applicants.

When should I apply? Applications are accepted until 23 May, but the process always takes longer than people expect so apply as early as possible, with a minimum of six months.

How do I apply? Apply online, download an application form, or request to have one sent to you.

Do I need a job to apply? You do not need to have already found a job before you apply, though it is best to start looking early. If you plan on taking the independent flyer option, you will need to have a job arranged before the visa application process begins.

How can I find a job? BUNAC's Job Directory lists hundreds of employers across the USA who have hired before and are keen to do so again. The directory also provides practical advice on working and living over there.

Can I wait until I arrive before looking for a job? Yes, but you have to take the BUNAC Travel Package and attend the arrival orientation in New York and will have to demonstrate that you will have $800 at the port of entry.

How much can I earn? It varies according to where you work and what you do, but the average wage is around $8 per hour, though you may find that if you have a resident job, such as at a summer camp, you will be paid a lump sum at the end (so it can be useful to have spending money with you already, though some employers will provide a sub before the final payout).

How do I find accommodation? One of the main advantages of residential work is that you don't have to worry about this (though you may find that your camp expects you to live in a tent or cabin). Many employers used to hiring foreign young people will have options already set up (ask them!). You can also try:
– local newspapers (many are available online);
– university accommodation (this may be basic as college students usually rent practically unfurnished, getting only a bed and mattress, and bringing everything else themselves);
– accommodation websites such as *craiglist.com*.

How much will it cost? Expect to pay somewhere between $50 and $100 per week (though this can be for something very basic).

How long is the visa valid? Your visa is valid for a continuous period of up to four months between 15 May and 10 October. This will be more than you need if you have a new semester starting in late September. Only those students taking a year out will need to make sure they move on by the end of their time.

What if I have to come home early in an emergency? Call the New York Office of BUNAC for their advice. If you took their Travel Package they may be able to organise transferring your flight date.

How long can I travel around after I finish working? The four-month validity period of your visa may be split up between working and/or travelling as you wish. Once your visa expires, you have an additional one month's 'grace period' during which you may travel but not work, a great advantage for those taking a year off who don't have to be home for the end of September.

What is IENA? The International Exchange of North America (IENA) is the US-based programme sponsor who issues your DS-2019 and is ultimately responsible for you in America.

What is a J-1 visa? As you will be working in the USA (where the ground rule is that foreigners cannot work) you need the paperwork to show that you are allowed to work. You are not on the Visa Waiver Program because you are not, initially at least, on holiday.

What is a DS-2019? Everybody needs an official certificate of eligibility, the DS-2019, in order to apply for a J-1 visa. Such certifications have to be obtained through authorised and vetted organisations, such as BUNAC.

What is SEVIS? This is a US State Department system which tracks holders of J-1 visas while they are in the USA. You will need to validate your record upon arrival and keep it updated if you change jobs or move into new accommodation. With the fear of imported terrorism, the USA is very hot on keeping tabs on all incoming foreign students. Don't forget: it was foreign students who attacked them on 9/11, so they are entitled to be more than careful.

- **International Counselor Exchange Program (ICEP)** has been sponsoring exchanges for over 50 years (*www.icep-usa.org*).

- **YMCA International Camp Counselor Program** (*www.internationalymca.org/ ICCP/Participant/Parthome.htm*) has a useful array of information, much of it general and so of interest to anyone looking to have a working summer in the USA. There is also information about the jobs they offer to overseas applicants.

When?

The US summer is somewhat earlier than that in the UK so you'd need to plan accordingly. Summer starts when school gets out, which can be as early as the third week in May. Summer camps are well underway by the end of June, so you should be able to leave Britain no later than the middle of June. As summer formally ends with the first Monday of September (Labor Day) summer camps end by about mid-August. Then you'll have time to travel until you're due back in Britain.

How can I find out what it's like?

- Ask around at college.

- Contact **Camp America/BUNAC/YMCA.**

- Attend various **Recruitment Interview and Orientation** meetings (representatives visit colleges).

- Contact the US Educational Advisory Service, the Fulbright Commission, 62 Doughty Street, London WC1N 2LS. The best initial contact is via their website: (*www.fulbright.co.uk*).

Are gap year students eligible?

Those of you with an unconditional offer of a university/college place are eligible during the summer preceding your first year studies not during the gap year itself. Canada may accept gap year students from the February before starting higher education (see BUNAC's *Work Canada* page *www.bunac.org.uk*).

AU PAIRING

British au pairs have traditionally been in great demand in the USA, even where cheaper local or Mexican help is readily available. This has something to do with the snob value of having someone from Europe, someone a little bit exotic but who speaks English. Any British accent is deemed upper class and so desirable (at least among the class of people who want and can afford to hire au pairs). Applicants must have childcare experience (NNEB an advantage), non-smoker, full driving licence, aged 18–25. Expect a couple of hundred dollars per week pocket money plus flight plus two weeks' holiday and medical insurance. Since the Woodward case be prepared for considerably more conscientious vetting of credentials by agencies, sponsors, families and US Citizenship and Immigration officials, which given that there are now well over 10,000 applications every year, will take time.

How do I find out what's it all about?

■ **EIL (Experiment in International Living) Ltd** runs a similar programme called Au Pair Homestay for 18–26 year olds. The aim is to facilitate 'an extended homestay immersion'.

■ Au Pairs in America Agency also provides au pair jobs in the USA (*www.aupairamerica.co.uk*).

Can I do it without such help?

■ The US authorities are tightening up their response to US residents hiring people who lack the necessary papers to work in the USA. In practical terms it's unlikely that people staying on after a holiday would ever be found out, but you would have to be prepared to live in something of a limbo, and if you do get caught you may find that deportation will mean you won't be allowed to re-enter the USA again (which later might have career or family implications).

■ Camp America and EIL provide a fully legal service based upon over 30 years of dealing with the appropriate US paperwork.

■ They also have the contacts built up over the years.

■ You might be able to find a suitable employer from this distance, but even if you made contact you are taking a far greater risk than when going through an agency that in effect acts as a vetting process, for both employer, employee and for the US authorities.

■ If you organise everything yourself and things don't work out who can you turn to? Recognised agencies know the ropes.

■ If you do everything for yourself and it works well you will of course stand to make more money: your employer won't have any agency fees to pay.

What do I need to apply?

■ A willingness to give it a go.

■ A character reference.

■ A curriculum vitae (CV) setting out what you've done, what skills and qualifications you have.

- Any sporting, teaching or professional certificates you have to support your application.

- A willingness to go carefully. Do smaller agencies explain the complexities of US paperwork sufficiently? Compare what they offer with what large well established agencies, such as the YMCA, provide.

Alternatives?

- **Winant Clayton Volunteers Association** (*www.winantclayton.com*) organises three-month programmes (June–September), including three weeks for travel before returning home, for volunteers in community work programmes in New York City, Boston and Washington DC. Once in place volunteers receive room and board and pocket money. Expect to pay the airfare and have a further £800 available. UK residents only, minimum age 19. Interviews are held in late January and early February.

- **New York Internship** is run by the Mountbatten Institute (*www.mountbatten.org/ mipweb.nsf/pages/ny_about_US*). In 2006 there were 277 internships in and around New York City. Interviews are held May/June for September and in October/November for March. The Institute arranges the placements, which are always for 12 months and are for participants to experience 'high-powered business environments'.

STUDENT INTERNSHIPS

Many students benefit from work experience during their academic studies. Enquire from schools liaison officers at higher education fairs, open days for applicants, or at interview as to opportunities that exist for work in the USA during your course of study. There are several schemes:

- **The International Association for Exchange of Students for Technical Expertise** (IAESTE). Internships provide practical experience in agriculture, architecture, commerce, engineering, science and technology (but NOT medicine) during the long vacation (or exceptionally as part of a sandwich course). Student applicants must be from institutions which are already affiliated to the scheme, and applications should initially be focused through the college's appointed representative. Work experience in the USA is over-subscribed, but any application that can offer an equivalent UK traineeship will be enhanced. The UK side is co-ordinated by the British Council (email: United_Kingdom@iaeste.org).

■ **The International Association of Students in Economics and Business Management** (*www.aiesec.co.uk*) co-ordinates international management training for students of economics and management with at least two years of full-time study already completed. Applications are initially through a local representative, details from your local careers service. Applicants only prepared to go to the USA rather than also consider an alternative venue may not be considered, though a preference for the USA may be expressed. All expenses are paid for by the student.

■ **The Mountbatten Institute** provides internships with multinational corporations, advertising, legal and financial institutions for *graduates* in secretarial studies, management, accountancy or business studies (*www.mountbatten.org*).

■ **Bunac OPT** (Overseas Practical Training) offers those over 18 an opportunity to spend from three to 18 months in the USA as an intern or trainee. The snag is that you have to arrange your own placement (education, social sciences, library science, counselling and social service, management, business, commerce, finance or health-related occupations). Bunac provide the screening, help, and access to the necessary J-1 Exchange Visitor Visa.

You may also find the following of interest:

■ *Working Holidays* published annually by the Central Bureau for Educational Visits and Exchanges, 10 Spring Gardens, London SW1 2BN. Tel: (020) 7389 4004.

■ *2000 Internships*, Writer's Digest Books, F&W Publications Inc, 9933 Alliance Road, Cincinnati Ohio 45242.

■ *Directory of International Internships*, Office of Overseas Programs, Michigan State University, East Lansing, Michigan 48824.

■ *Advisory List of International Educational Travel and Exchange Programs*, Council on Standards for International Education Travel, 1906 Association Drive, Reston, Virginia 22091.

There are three organisations that can help with the necessary paperwork, though they do not themselves arrange traineeships, placements, or internships.

■ **The Council on International Educational Exchange** (CIEE) (*www.ciee.org*) is the major supplier of the necessary authorisations for those undertaking placements arranged as part of the course requirements for British degrees. Students must return to the UK upon finishing their placements, and so should take the US experience mid-course not after graduation or as a gap year activity. Students usually deal indirectly with CIEE, a link between UK colleges and the US hosts and US authorities.

- **The Central Bureau for Educational Visits and Exchanges** is involved with the UK/US Careers Development Programme which allows UK nationals aged 19–35 to work in the USA for up to 18 months. Participants must secure their own placements and have a couple of years' experience or appropriate professional qualifications. The Hotel and Culinary Exchange is an equivalent system geared to those who have completed, or are presently studying, a hotel or catering course with suitable work experience. Job placement assistance is available, but would slow down any application considerably. An application and a substantial processing fee will be charged to successful applicants and/or the US employer.

- **The US Educational Advisory Service, the Fulbright Commission,** 62 Doughty Street, London WC1N 2LS Tel: (020) 7404 6994 (open to the public 10.30 am– 1.00 pm and 2.00 pm–4.30 pm Monday–Friday). Provides information through an excellent website (*www.fulbright.co.uk*) with most documents you could need, and a Frequently Asked Questions (FAQs) section. Almost all the information you could need about being a student in the USA is available here.

WORKING IN WASHINGTON DC

Thousands of young Americans regularly work in the offices of the US Congress. An estimated 19,000 more swell the staff of political think-tanks, lobby groups, media and business institutions, or work in the State Department, the White House, or elsewhere in the administration. These high-fliers enjoy positions of prestige that will place them on the road to further privilege. The bad news is that these **interns**, as they are known, are paid little if anything. The pay-off comes in the experience, the connections and their enhanced CV (or resumé as they'd say). It is an investment in their future whether or not they envisage a future in politics or public administration.

Increasingly students are placed in **programmed internships** by their own college working through college representatives permanently stationed in the capital. Students get course credit towards their degrees in exchange for writing a report on their experience. The best programmes are carefully scrutinised by academics knowledgeable in the ways of Washington politics to ensure that interns are more than office dogsbodies. With the local University of Maryland alone providing 600 interns per year there is demand and supply far exceeding anything found in British local government or even Westminster. Congress alone employs about 5,000 interns per year, who gain first-hand experience of the legislative process, lobbying and wheeler-dealing.

The American University in Washington DC organises intern programmes for about 500 students per semester, of which about 10 per cent come direct from foreign universities. For each semester the total cost is about $9,500 (including $3,500 for tuition and $3,500 for board and lodging), the availability of which must be proved on the F1 student visa application. If you wish to transfer your course credit to your British degree programme there is a further $5,000 fee! The good news is that the programme provides three days of tuition per week and two days of internship in a wide range of public or private agencies and businesses associated with the capital's main activity: government (lobbying, reporting and legislating). For details contact The Washington Semester Program at the American University website (*www.washingtonsemester.american.edu*). There is a shortened summer programme, details also on the website.

Competition for political internships is fierce. There are over 200 applications for each place in a senator's office. Preference is given to people from the home constituency, particularly those already known to the senator or representative in the election campaign that brought them into office.

Interns answer the telephone, answer constituents' mail (using word processors for letters and machines that 'sign' outgoing constituency mail), may attend meetings of Congress to prepare memos and report on matters of concern, and may get to draft position papers based upon library research.

Non-governmental options go through a clearing house: **The Washington Center**, (*www.twc.edu/*) which ensures a quality placement, laying on courses and seminars for over 600 colleges. It ensures that no more than 20 per cent of the intern's time is spent on mundane clerical work. The think-tanks are privately sponsored research and policy monitoring institutions such as the conservative **Heritage Foundation** (*www.heritage.org*) has 17 summer programme places or the (liberal) **Institute for Policy Studies** (*www.ips-dc.org*) for those who think *West Wing* was a documentary not a soap opera. Another avenue would be the *Student Guide to Mass Media Internships* published by the School of Journalism, Boulder, Colorado (*www.colorado.edu/journalism/*) which lists 2,000 different internships in the

USA (newspapers, magazines, television, radio, and publishing). Hands-on experience prior to a formal job-search would be good for the old CV.

Few British students participate, but doing an exchange year in the USA may make it possible via your US college's own programme, particularly at the state level. Some British students with family connections in the USA have worked 'on the Hill' as it's called, but without remuneration. British students in the USA as 'resident aliens' may be able to work in the office of their local representative as part of a US-based degree course. If still interested in working on Capitol Hill contact:

■ The Intern Program Director, US Congress, Washington DC 20515.

For the nearest thing to a comprehensive listing of governmental internships take a look at the 'US Government Info' web page (*http://usgovinfo.about.com/b/internships.htm*)

APPLYING FOR SUMMER JOBS

Before an employer can employ a foreigner s/he must be willing to obtain, fill out and submit all the necessary US government forms. Remember the basic rule is that foreigners cannot take jobs in the USA. The paperwork makes a case for exceptions to this general rule. It means time and effort for the employer, for little if any immediate gain if people already in the USA could be readily hired. But as a student there are special arrangements to provide temporary permission to work – so the employer doesn't have to worry so long as the foreign student has the right visa.

Dealing with such organisations as BUNAC, Camp America, or the YMCA can help with the paperwork as:

■ they are familiar with what's needed;

■ they deal with US contacts also familiar with the problems;

■ US authorities will only issue work visas through authorised organisations such as these.

Even if you arrange something on your own it may help to obtain the kind of advice available only through groups such as BUNAC.

It helps to understand what is involved. As a general rule there are only three types of visas suitable for foreign students who will be returning home after their summer employment:

H-2 'Temporary Worker'

This requires a US employer to obtain a 'labor certificate' from the local state employment service. The US Department of Labor requires evidence that:

- a real job exists;
- reasonable effort has already been made to fill the job from within the USA;
- no qualified US resident has applied.

> **Example**
>
> *Camp Manhattan takes a lot of Canadian children for whom a French-speaking canoe instructor is always hired. This year though, despite advertising in college newspapers since October, no suitable applicant has applied. Then a British canoeist who's just spent a year at a French college applies. The camp wants to hire him, and is prepared to do the paperwork. Certification would be granted as a legitimate case has been made.*

For a neat summary of the visa's intent take a look *http://en.wikipedia.org/wiki/H-2A_visa* or the equivalent page for other visas.

H-3 'Industrial Trainee'

Here no labor certification is required, but any application must include:

- a detailed training plan;
- a training/on-the-job breakdown;
- an explanation as to why this training cannot be obtained in the applicant's home country.

> **Example**
>
> *Camp Manhattan prides itself on the quality of its management, and especially its own camp counsellor in-house training programme. A British student who's worked in a British day camp writes asking if she can join their programme for residential experience. The Camp organisers could submit the necessary details for an H-3 visa, but it might well be rejected if USCIS believe it's just a fiddle to get someone's British girlfriend into the USA for a paid summer job.*

J-1 'Exchange Visitor'

These visas are *only* available for applicants participating in educational programmes specifically approved by the US government. Approved **Exchange Visitor Programs** are granted only to US sponsoring organisations such as US government agencies, colleges, hospitals and private educational organisations, who in turn only work with established UK organisations (such as BUNAC).

J-1 authorisation for a summer 'work-travel' programme permits students to work on any job they can find (though not to undertake practical training such as medical internships). No extensions or visa changes are permitted. Details of this Work and Travel USA (WAT USA) Programme are available via their excellent website *www.ciee.org*, which has specific details on summer job availability. Most British students find that which visa type they apply for is specified by the agency they are going with (again, such as BUNAC).

J-1 summer camp placements are authorised for the International Camp Counselor Program of the YMCA (*www.icep-use.org*), with an eight-week limit, and must involve counselling or skills instruction rather than kitchen or office jobs.

Paid practical training is organised via a number of sponsors who have J-1 programmes such as the International Association of Students in Economics and Business Management (AIESEC) (*www.aiesec.co.uk*) and the International Association for Exchange of Students for Technical Experience (IAESTE) Trainee Programme (*www.iaeste.org*) The maximum length of practical training time for any one person is 18 months.

What happens now?

- H-2 and H-3 visa applications, if successful, will lead to the US Embassy being so informed, where the visa will be issued to the student presenting a valid passport plus a handling/processing fee.

- J-1 applications, if successful, lead to sponsoring organisations issuing a 'Certificate of Eligibility' (DS-2019) to be taken, plus passport and processing fee, to the US Embassy.

- Upon entering the USA the immigration inspector will issue form 1-94 upon which the visa type and maximum stay date are recorded.

How difficult is it?

The process takes time. Securing a visa can take up to six months, so start early, at the beginning of the academic year. When contacting prospective employers let them know which visa you are seeking, which sponsoring organisation (if any), and which forms they would need to submit, if any.

A word of warning

The summer officially ends on Labor Day (first Monday in September). Colleges and schools start back in the last week of August. If you don't intend to return to Britain before the end of September (say for a British university term or semester) you may have difficulty persuading US officials that intending to return that late in the year isn't incompatible with being a student. You'll need to explain when term starts (particularly if your term didn't end until early July rather than late May).

FURTHER OPPORTUNITIES FOR STUDENTS

Undergraduate study in the United States

Colleges vary in quality of education provided, prestige, location and costs. There are two major systems, the private and the public. The former are deemed more prestigious, cost considerably more, and claim to offer a better education. In Maryland, for instance, the private John Hopkins University fees stand at over $16,000 per nine-month academic year, whereas the public state university charges 'only' about $8,000. Out of state students (and that includes those from abroad) are charged a special 'out of state' rate, a surcharge ranging from 25 to 400 per cent. Understandably very few British students attend college for their whole under-graduate programme. Most British undergraduates attending colleges in the USA do so as part of the British degree programme. Just as language students have to spend time abroad so students taking American Studies degree programmes offer, some even require, their British students to spend a year or a semester (half a year) in the USA. Such programmes involve two sets of costs:

- Fees – these continue to be paid for by your British local educational authority (LEA) and the student (normally over £3,000 year) if the modules taken abroad count towards your British degree. Many UK institutions arrange exchanges, balancing their outgoing British students with incoming US ones, so that the LEAs continue to pay UK fees even while you are in the USA and the student pays their home institution as if they had not gone abroad.

■ Travel – discretionary, and so at the whim of cash-strapped LEAs. You will probably have to pay this yourself (just as if you lived in Inverness but went to Exeter University). But if you don't ask…

You need to explore who will pay for health insurance and emergency repatriation, though such matters are often part of the package negotiated between participating colleges. Expect to pay about £200 for a semester. For advice on insuring your belongings, particularly computer equipment or musical instruments, contact Endsleigh which has long specialised in covering students (*www.endsleigh.co.uk*).

When applying for details of American Studies degrees in the UK ask whether there is a required semester in the USA. Increasingly other degree programmes offer study time in North America. Keele students, for instance, can apply to go to Maryland if they are political scientists (the campus is 12 miles from the White House), or Texas if musicians or Ball State if they are historians or Texas if musicians. For a highly informative leaflet on one university's offerings contact the North America officer at Lancaster University (*www.lancaster.ac.uk*).

For a scholarly exploration of the college experience see:

■ Ernest L. Boyer, *College: the Undergraduate Experience*, Harper, New York, 1988.

For two vast over-views of admissions, enrolment, costs and financial aid at 2,000 accredited colleges and universities see:

■ *The College Handbook* available from College Board Publications via Amazon (but also in most university careers libraries).

■ *The Princeton Review America's Best Value Colleges*, annually, from Princeton Review via Amazon.

However, the best source of US information in the UK is probably:

■ The US Educational Advisory Service, The Fulbright Commission, 62 Doughty Street, London WC1N 2JZ. Tel: (020) 7404 6880 (*www.fulbright.co.uk*).

Most colleges and universities have a careers library that should stock a wide range of continuously updated published materials on studying in the USA, with assistance in tracing appropriate websites.

Student visa holders

Visa regulations now allow foreign students who have successfully completed their first year of study to take off-campus jobs for up to 20 hours per week during term time (previous regulations had insisted all jobs must be on-campus). Out of term time the hours restriction is lifted. To ensure that such a job does not undercut US workers' wages any employer offering foreign students employment must attest that the position has already been offered to US workers for at least 60 days, and that foreign students and US workers are being offered the same wages for the same work. If the Department of Labor decided that these conditions are not being met the employer will be barred from employing foreign students.

> **A note of warning**
>
> *The present arrangements only remain in force as long as US authorities continue to believe the regulations are enabling foreign students to graduate. Any suggestions that they are being used as a way around the immigration regulations and they will be allowed to lapse.*

POSTGRADUATE DEGREES

In the US the word postgraduate is always shortened to just graduate. Large universities usually offer both Master's and Doctoral pro-grammes, though smaller institutions might only offer graduate courses to the Master's level. If you would like to carry straight through at the same institution you need to check up on this very early in the process.

Master of Arts (MA)

MA programmes are designed primarily for students who wish to acquire a further degree but who also wish primarily to make their career within the world beyond education, whether in business or government. Courses generally last one year for full-time students, a minimum of two years for part-timers. Programmes are by taught courses followed by either a thesis or at least two publishable research papers. The programme provides a firm theoretical and methodological foundation for either moving on to the doctoral level like the British Master of Research (MRes), or for a move out into the wider job market, which increasingly requires an MA rather than a BA, as more and more people complete the first degree.

Doctor of Philosophy (PhD)

PhD programmes are more complicated than in Britain, usually requiring considerable high-level taught courses (which might be in statistics, computing, languages or philosophy irrespective of the main field) before progressing to the preparation of a lengthy research dissertation. It is usual for the PhD stage to take at least three years after the two years spent on the master's degree, a total of at least five years, with the writing up often taking a further couple of years. As most people will be in employment in order to pay the bills by this time it can be very difficult to complete, especially if work takes you away from your university to live elsewhere, and if growing career and family demands gradually ease the PhD to one side. Beware: completion must be within a pre-set timetable, and unlike the UK situation cannot be extended almost indefinitely.

For a useful introduction read 'The American doctoral programme' in E. M. Phillips & D. S. Pugh, *How to Get a PhD*, OU Press (2000).

How to apply

If you wish to apply for (post)graduate work in the USA you should first write to the **heads of departments** you might be interested in asking for general details. Technically you should contact the Director of Graduate Studies at each institution asking for forms and additional information, but procedures seem to be more relaxed for foreign applicants.

Be prepared to write to a wide range of universities, and don't be bothered by the vast number who never even reply. A dozen letters for two or three replies might not be unusual. Twenty initial enquiries is not unusual. Those that do reply are usually taking your application seriously.

In theory you should be prepared to supply:

- Three letters of recommendation.

- Graduate Record Exam (GRE) scores (1,000 minimum). For details contact US Educational Advisory Service, 62 Doughty Street, London WC1N 2LS. Tel: (020) 7404 6880. The Fulbright Commission website (*www.fulbright.co.uk*) has considerable details on GRE-specific matters.

- College records ('transcripts') of all previous academic work showing a grade point average of at least 3.0 or equivalent (B+ for coursework, plus 2.1 degree).

■ Proof of proficiency in English, usually waived for applicants from English-speaking countries.

■ Proof of sufficient funds to pay all fees and expenses for at least one year. This is vital. If you don't have such funds you must make it clear that your taking up a place is contingent upon being awarded some kind of assistantship, fellowship or stipend. You may, however, be expected to fund your initial year (fees plus living expenses).

Universities that deal regularly with certain foreign countries' applicants may waive the need to take a GRE exam and may automatically assume you will need to apply for financial aid both to get the visa and of course to stay alive.

For anyone wishing to be considered for financial aid all applications, letters of recommendation, etc, *must* be received by the US institution by 1 February (for entry the following August) and preferably earlier. Most university career advice centres should be able to discuss opportunities and ways of approaching US institutions, and may well have copies of US catalogues (prospectuses). The available guides include:

■ The Association of Graduate Careers Advisory Services (*www.agcas.org.uk*) provides careers advisers with country-specific advice on post-graduate study, so ask in your own careers service on campus.

■ The US Educational Advisory Service through the Fulbright Commission, 62 Doughty Street, London WC1N 2LS. Tel: (020) 7404 6880 provides the best source of specifically US information for UK applicants. Most items are available on *www.fulbright.co.uk* pages.

Most students wishing to further their studies in the USA will probably start with their own institution's careers service who should have the above guides, and may well have others such as:

■ *Peterson's Guides to Graduate Study* (six volumes) published annually by Peterson's Guides, Princeton, NJ.

■ *Graduate Study in the United States: A Guide for Prospective International Graduate Students* is published by the Council of Graduate Schools, Washington DC (*www.cgs.org*).

- Take a look at the website *www.gradschools.com* which has one of the most comprehensive arrays of information with dropdown menus that help you find the material relevant to your particular interests.

Often the initial response to seeing this volume of information is growing dismay. Fortunately the *US Educational Advisory Service* has recognised this and now provides ways through the problems of information overload:

- Placing its files on its website.

- Talks to prospective students. These may be given as part of the annual 'milkround'. Watch careers service notice boards (or ask!).

- Listings on graduate study in particular fields.

- A schedule for applying.

- A summary of tuition costs across the US.

- A summary of awards for postgraduate study and research in the United States.

- An outline of the application procedures

- Information on moving to the USA.

- A pre-departure orientation in late June.

The US EAS has traditionally encouraged attending their London office in person, Monday and Wednesdays 1.30 am–7.00 pm and Fridays 1.30 pm–5.00 pm. Forms can be picked up and videos watched, plus advice given in person. Much of their material is supplied annually to British university careers service libraries where it should be on file, so avoiding a London visit. But always start with a visit to the excellent website (*www.fulbright.co.uk*).

FUNDING GRADUATE STUDY IN THE USA

Costs

State universities offer graduate education for fees that are considered 'moderate' compared to those of private, ivy-league ('Oxbridge'-style) universities. Typically residents of that state pay about $3,000 per semester (two 14-week semesters). Non-residents (US or foreign) pay considerably more, anything up to 400 per cent in some institutions. Academic fees alone may well then be prohibitive for the self-financing foreign student, never mind the need to have some $15,000 for living expenses to get an entry visa. For a useful tuition calculator take a look at the University of South Alabama's Office of Admissions 'Tuition Estimator' (*www.southalabama.edu/admissions*).

Working your way through college

Americans expect to work their way through college, but as an outsider you will be expected to pay your way with funds from overseas, at least for the first year. New visa regulations now permit students in good standing to work from their second year on to graduation on or off campus. Most foreign students who are not independently wealthy or bringing with them a UK scholarship will need to consider an assistantship, that is, teaching undergraduates on campus.

Assistantships

The good news is that most universities offer their graduate applicants assistantships, foreign applicants included. As a graduate assistant you will be paid a regular ten-month stipend each year, plus a waiver of fees (which may double its value). You may have to be frugal to live off such a stipend. Be prepared to share a flat, perhaps even a room, and don't expect to be able to run a car at least initially. For that you will have to teach extra courses during the summer vacation, or given the new visa regulations, find off-campus work. The stipend though has to be earned: it is no sinecure. You will have to teach first year undergraduates in large introductory classes, under the supervision of a professor, assemble reading lists, grade papers, invigilate exams, conduct lab classes and help out on field courses if appropriate, plus act as the professor's research assistant (or dog's body) for no more than 20 hours per week, all alongside your own studies. It is a very busy life, but it pays the rent, avoids paying fees, and is sufficient proof accepted by the US Citizenship and Immigration (USCIS) that you have the necessary wherewithal to support yourself, so enabling the visa to be issued with a minimum of fuss. About one third of foreign MA students have some form of assistantship, two /thirds of foreign doctoral students.

In the long run assistantships provide an excellent academic apprenticeship, each year involving ever more responsibility. Doctoral students may well take full responsibility for a course they have previously helped teach under the careful supervision of a senior member of staff, for which they will be paid at the top of the assistant salary scale.

Colleges vary in quality of education provided, prestige and crucially location: a California stipend may be almost twice that of somewhere in the Midwest but may provide only the same material standard of living. For some people Los Angeles might be intolerable at any price. For a lone British postgraduate, without friends and family for support, Los Angeles without a car might be far less satisfying than a Midwestern college town with less money, where you could walk to work, save up for a car, and visit the big cities with new college friends as and when chances present themselves. And what is the cost of living anyway? Do you expect to have your own flat immediately upon arrival or would you share? But would you share a room with a fellow student? Would you walk or hitch-hike to work? Are you on your own, or with a spouse not allowed to work by visa regulations?

■ Location of research materials or study area may mean a high stipend college is not where you want to be.

■ Computer connections mean for certain resources you can be almost anywhere and still gain access to your research material.

If you are single, able-bodied, and prepared to be flexible upon your arrival, getting a graduate stipend should solve not just your visa problems but keep a roof over your head. And if that doesn't always work out many graduates have made long-standing (though supposedly temporary) nests in their office on campus – while intending to look for somewhere else of course! For a married student survival is possible, but can be financially very tight and demoralising for the non-working partner.

The advice of experience is: **go**, if at all possible. It's worth it for the experience. And with an academic department as your base, a place to live in, people to share with, old cars to borrow or even to buy, things always turn up via the grapevine. Americans are proverbially hospitable, and no more so than when they hear of someone at the office sleeping in a bag on the floor or walking to work from an unfurnished apartment. For further funding information see:

■ *Funding US Study: An IEE Directory*, Institute of International Education (www.fundingusstudy.org). There is a hard copy version available from the website too.

■ Frequently Asked Questions about graduate admissions (*www.fulbright.co.uk*) particularly 'what are my chances of getting financial aid?' and 'what are my chances of being fully funded by a university?'

POSTGRADUATE SCHOLARSHIPS

There are several well-known UK scholarships specially available to British postgraduate students wishing to study in the USA: **Fulbright, Thouron** and **Kennedy**.

Fulbright scholarships

These are available for travel and maintenance for British UK-based postgraduates for 'a year of advanced research in the United States'. Applications must be submitted by late October each year. Details and application forms available from July each year.

■ Fulbright Commission, 62 Doughty Street, London WC1N 2JZ. Tel: (020) 7404 6880. *www.fulbright.co.uk* is an excellent and essential site for any prospective postgraduate student considering the USA.

Thouron awards

The Thouron-University of Pennsylvania for British-American Student Exchange offers five awards covering maintenance and fees for study at the University of Pennsylvania (in Philadelphia). Closing date is early November each year. Details can be obtained from the Thouron Awards website (*www.thouronaward.org*).

Kennedy scholarships

These are for postgraduate study at Harvard or the Massachusetts Institute of Technology. Twelve scholarships exist to cover tuition, health care, travel and maintenance. Prospectus and application forms from the Kennedy Memorial Trust website (*www.kentrust.demon.co.uk*).

Closing date for applications is mid October.

Post-doctoral awards

Awards for scholars already holding a doctoral degree or of similar standing are listed at the Fulbright Commission website: *www.fulbright.co.uk*.

Harkness fellowships

These are for UK-educated professionals dealing with health provision, education or urban management, approximately 21–40 years old on 1 September of the year of application, which must be made by 5 September for interviewing the following February. For full application materials contact the Harkness Fellowships via the Commonwealth Fund website (*www.commonwealthfund.org/fellowships*). Please note there is a 'video brochure' on their site.

For a list of *Awards for Postgraduate Study & Research in the US* see the information pack produced annually by the US Educational Advisory Service, 62 Doughty Street, London WC1N 2JZ which contains details of some further 14 award schemes available to UK citizens or look up their excellent web page (*www.fulbright.co.uk*).

OPPORTUNITIES FOR TEACHERS

Teachers wishing to spend time in the USA might like to consider a scholarship specially geared to their needs, or a post-to-post exchange with someone. For a general introduction see:

- Roger Jones, *Teaching Abroad*, How to Books, 3rd edition, 1998. Though only available second-hand it has useful general points and is *very* cheap on Amazon.

Teacher scholarships

These are organised by the English-Speaking Union (*www.esu.org*) to enable participants to explore their field of study within the USA and to become more broadly acquainted with American life. There are two main sets of scholarships:

- the Walter Hines Page Scholarship for eight-week term-time visits (October to May);

- Chautauqua Institution Scholarships for a nine-week summer school-based tour.

Other Page scholarships for shorter (four-week) visits are sponsored by teaching unions and associations such as NASWT and NUT.

Applications usually have to be submitted by the end of November for the following year, and short-listed candidates are interviewed in February. Hospitality in the USA is provided by the US branch of the ESU, though successful applicants will be expected to contribute a top-up amount (dependent upon the dollar–pound exchange rate).

Post-to-post exchanges

These are organised by the **British Council's Central Bureau for Educational Visits and Exchanges** (*www.britishcouncil.org*), a UK government agency responsible to the various British departments of education. Their aim is to develop contacts, co-operation and exchanges between British teachers and teachers overseas.

The scheme is open to all qualified British teachers from nursery schools through to universities with five or more years' experience, of which the final two years must have been with the same school or college. Posts can be exchanged for a full year, or for a term. Applications for a year's exchange have to be completed by early December, or by the end of June for spring term visits.

Exchanges are organised centrally. If a high school geography teacher from North Dakota applies to the US organisers just as another such geography teacher from Inverness applies, the Central Bureau would try to arrange for them to swap jobs, perhaps even accommodation, subject to both teachers being accepted as suitable. As this might be a very hit and miss way of getting an exchange it has been suggested informally that teachers *already* in contact (say after a holiday trip or via friends and relatives) might like to submit a statement to both sets of organisers saying a link has already been established. This is the way university teachers usually swap jobs on similar schemes.

Teachers return to their post upon returning home. They are seconded to full salary with all rights safeguarded. The visit counts as service for all purposes, including incremental credit. Grants from central government also cover return travel and any necessary extra cost of living allowance (a British salary will not go very far in the USA, especially not if the exchange is for central New York City!).

In addition the US authorities give each teacher a free insurance policy for sickness and accident during the period of the exchange (as the US visiting teacher in Britain would be eligible for NHS treatment).

Teachers (and others) interested in meeting a wide cross-section of Americans might usefully contact the US wing of **Servas**. The name is Esperanto for 'we serve'. Contact US Servas via their website (*www.usservas.org*).

School exchanges

For those teachers hardened by years of school trips, camps, outward bound and field trips the ultimate organisational experience might now be available: a UK/US school exchange. After matching, school pupils from the UK live in the homes of their US partners and attend the link school for four weeks. The US pupils return the visit either in the summer or in the autumn terms. It is hoped that once established links would continue between the two communities, a form of educational twinning almost.

Contact the various Central Bureau through the British Council website (*www.britishcouncil.org*).

School visits

School and college groups are increasingly going to the USA just as earlier generations once made their first trip across the English Channel. Usually one leader will go free for every 20 fee-paying students. A week in New York City or Washington DC will cost each student about £500 for flight and accommodation.

For details:

- **UK Connection** (*www.ukconnection.co.uk*) are specialists in UK student travel to the USA.

- **Euro Study Tours** (*www.euro-study-tours.co.uk*) provide expert tailor-made student tours of New York.

Higher education exchanges

Full-time academics may also be eligible for Fulbright grants for head-for-head exchanges lasting a full academic year. Travel and subsistence expenses may be approved for those initiating exchanges of younger staff. Closing date is usually 1 November. Information and application forms are available from either:

- **The British Council (Higher Education Division)**, 10 Spring Gardens, London SW1A 2BN. Tel: (020) 7930 8466.

- **The US/UK Education Commission**, 62 Doughty Street, London WC1N 2JZ. Tel: (020) 7404 6880.

For information on a scheme which recruits teachers for inner-city programmes from the ranks of the newly graduated without any previous teacher training, contact **Teach for America** (*www.teachforAmerica.org*).

GAP YEAR OPPORTUNITIES

A break before college has become increasingly popular, and if spent usefully can be highly advantageous: students arrive back more confident and mature. But for the US the gap year can be a problem. Most visa regulations require student applicants to be mid-course. A place on a course a year hence may not be sufficient. After all, you have no investment you wish to complete by returning to the UK as would a student approaching their final year.

If you are going to college and wish to consider a gap year off it can be a worthwhile investment to visit the college to talk to the recruitment officers and course tutors. Don't rely on being able to talk in any great detail with any of these people on an advertised Open Day. Thousands of would-be students attend these occasions and you may never find a specific person, with the best will in the world. But particularly if you intend to take a gap year visit the college where you intend to study upon your return, if only to give yourself a mental image of what you would be missing if you start reconsidering the wisdom of returning to college at all. And when you do visit phone or email ahead so that the college can arrange for specific people to be available to talk about the implications of a gap year. Let the college know precisely what you want to talk about so they can be prepared to brief the right people. And of course a gap year in the USA may be much more attractive to certain departments than others.

For general information:

- *The Gap Year Book*, Lonely Planet (2003).
- *The Gap-Year Guidebook 2008*, Catt (2007).
- *A Year Off...A Year On?*, Lifetime Careers (2002).
- *Planning a Gap Year*, How To Books (2005).
- *Work Your Way Around the World*, Vacation Work (2005).

11

Staying or Returning

Most visitors to the USA, whether long or short stay, will at some point consider the possibility of staying on permanently, making the USA home, if only in the medium term. You'll need to consider:

- career implications;
- family reactions;
- implications for health care and retirement;
- possible status — resident or citizen.

REMAINING IN THE USA

Career implications

Only you can judge how good an idea staying on could be for your career prospects. It is possible to get locked into your US-based career structure without giving adequate consideration to moving sideways back into the UK. Who wants to get off a moving staircase if it's going steadily upwards? But remember: career implications are only one reason for staying or returning, even if they seem the most obvious.

Family reunions

These need careful consideration, both for the immediate family, presumably with you in the USA, and those back home such as ageing parents. Whereas the side of the family back in Britain will probably be stoical (they may have assumed you'd gone for good when you set off originally) your family in the USA will react in terms of their immediate needs, fears and expectations. Most children will have settled down quite quickly and will not want to move anywhere, certainly not back to a country they hardly remember. But remember, they would not want to move to the next town if they were still back in Britain, so you need to consider how much weight the grown-ups should give the views of the children. But do let them have their say, and explain why you intend to overrule them if necessary.

Perhaps more critically you'll need to ask certain questions about the family staying on:

- What are their US-based career prospects?
- Will college be an affordable option in the USA?
- Will you want them to become US citizens?
- Should you give them the option to return home at, say, 18 to make up their own minds?
- What if they return to the UK and stay on?

Health care and retirement

You'll probably just continue with your existing health plan, but what of retirement? The US social security system is getting very fragile, with no prospects of improvements as more and more people reach retirement age and the US budget deficit grows ever larger. The pensionable age is being gradually raised, but with economic restructuring pressure on people to retire earlier and earlier continues. The US military has helped promote the belief that after 20 years' service, at whatever age, it's time to retire, or at least take a pension *and* start another career. Ever more people are opening an Individual Retirement Account (IRA). This will allow you to supplement any government pension, but if you attempt to use the money before the agreed term you'll lose most if not all of the tax benefits. As IRAs proliferate the information about them grows. See a trusted accountant!

A word of warning

Your health plan was for a limited stay (with a return to the UK always a possibility if things got dire). Is your health plan now adequate if you want to stay on a different basis? It's essential you check it out. Ask other people who've stayed on whether they changed their health care plan, or if not, do they wish they had.

Citizen status

Though the Green Card no longer exists, permanent status does. If you want to change your status consult a lawyer specialising in this field. Marrying a US citizen is the most popular reason for staying on in the USA, and it's the way that certainly makes the paperwork easiest if you arrived on a non-immigrant visa. And you won't necessarily have to return home before applying! Failing that you'll need to gain status as set out earlier in this book. Your employer will probably be the most important factor, emphasising skills needed for the US economy, and that the job won't deprive an American of a job.

Should you adopt citizenship?

For many people publicly disavowing their country of birth is one step too far. Whereas it was presumably easy for Germans fleeing the Nazis in the 1930s, for those not in exile it's probably a much more difficult decision. Fortunately taking US citizenship doesn't cancel British citizenship, except as far as the USA is concerned. British law accepts dual citizenship. US law doesn't. And if you think this is a lawyer's quibble it's worth recalling that the 1812 war between Britain and the USA was over just this point (Britain press-ganged US citizens on US vessels on the high-seas saying they were still British and there was a war on against France, etc).

If you do take US citizenship and lose your British passport for an American one you could still re-enter the UK and settle down back home again. You'll forfeit US citizenship if you take out a British passport or run for office outside the USA (as would *any* US citizen).

There might still be a joker in the pack that you've not considered when considering permanent residency and citizenship: **military service**. Once legally settled into the US all men over 18 must register (see notices on how to do this at your local US Post Office). Once the Vietnam War ended, the draft (conscription) ended. The USA now has a professional, full-time army (despite a revolutionary heritage that considered anything other than a citizens' part-time militia a start down the road to tyranny). But in times of international stress things can and do change. Even in peacetime it is an offence not to register. It is even possible that anyone liable to the draft who came back to the UK to avoid it would be liable to be handed over to the US authorities under the appropriate Visiting Forces Act. Remember that US draft dodgers during the Vietnam War went to Canada or Sweden *not* the UK!

COMING BACK TO THE UK

Returning to the UK can be as great a decision as going away in the first place. For many it's even more difficult: new roots have been put down, it's always easier to stay put, and home starts to appear like the foreign country it has actually become.

What's changed?

- the government (or not as the case may be);
- the currency (coins for English £1 notes if you left years ago!);
- TV channels (all day TV, extra channels);
- motorway network (which can be disorienting);
- the cost of everything (£2+ a pint, payable with a single coin);
- very (too?) American?
- European Union integration (passport and courts);
- house prices (US urban costs in the UK southeast).

Some things haven't changed:

- the unpredictability of the weather (three fine days then a thunderstorm);
- London taxis;
- real ale (but at what a price!).

And so on. These are what await someone returning now after only a couple of years in the USA. What will have changed if and when you get back in five or ten years?

When you are away change will continue as ever, and you'll have to meet it all at once if you return. If you'd left in 1971 and kept in touch only by telephone, Christmas cards, a quick dash back for a funeral, plus British television programmes on the PBS network, what would Britain of 2009 look like? Answer: a foreign country.

How to make contact back home

You'll need to explore as wide a variety of approaches as possible:

- Put the word out that you are interested in returning home for the right job. Let your contacts know you are thinking of moving back if the right slot opens up. Here having kept in touch will pay off. Come back to conferences (even if at your own expense) to keep a high profile, to let colleagues in your field know that you haven't fallen off the edge of the world and, perhaps as vital, to remind prospective employers you are still interested and keeping in touch.

- Read the British newspapers (as available online) for any idea of what's coming vacant, who to contact (even if you are too late for particular jobs).

- Write to friends and contacts to widen your circle. Email is a godsend here.

- Approach UK agencies with a CV – they may be looking for someone with US experience.

- Use British search engines rather than their US version (such as *www.yahoo.co.uk, www.google.co.uk*)

US taxation

You'll need to prove to the IRS you'll be leaving with no tax debt. If you leave fully paid up you'll be due a tax refund in due course, unless you left at the very end of the tax year. Leaving at the right time can be as advantageous to your tax situation as getting married at the right point in the tax year used to be.

UK National Insurance

If you've been out for more than three years you'll need to re-establish yourself. Employers will usually do this for you.

UK Immigration

At international airports you'll get through with either a UK or US passport, though if you are obviously not returning as a tourist, UK papers, such as a birth certificate, may ease your way. An American spouse with a US passport coming in with a British spouse should get the paperwork sorted out with the UK authorities in the USA, but usually it's easier for a US passport holder to enter the UK as a six months tourist, changing status as per the procedure outlined by:

- **Home Office Immigration & Nationality Department**, Lunar House, Wellesley Road, Croydon CR0 2BY. Tel: (020) 8686 0688. Calls taken in rotation, closing at 4.00 pm. First try the Home Office Web page: (*www.homeoffice.gov/ad/hpg.htm*).

- UK government leaflets HC169 and HC503 explain the rules in detail. A fiancé(e) can enter this way, but if you apply for fiancé(e) (rather than tourist) entrance you'll need to provide written proof of a planned wedding within *three* months, and the visa will be for a maximum of three months.

UK Revenue & Customs

There's no need to provide the detailed listing necessary on entering the USA, but be honest and don't try to bring in restricted items (especially pets). Personal effects over six months old will come in duty free. If you feel someone is trying to use you to bring illegal substances into the UK there's a free UK number provided by HM Revenue & Customs (0800 59 5000) (*www.hmrc.gov.uk*).

Pets

If you need to ask how much it costs to bring a pet over and to have it go through quarantine you can't afford it (a happy, helpful hint offered by our Embassy in Washington DC). Expat Focus has a useful update plus links to its web page (*www.expat.focus.com*).

RETURNING HOME

You can move home, find a large supermarket nearby, drive on the motorway to work, and hardly notice you've changed countries. But spirits will cost about twice as much as in the USA, blue jeans a lot more, and petrol even more again. You'll miss your US friends of course, but enjoy remeeting your British ones. You'll enjoy good shoe shops, with width fittings for children, a range of beers, but the still couldn't care less attitude of so many shop assistants will be a delight you'll soon realise you hadn't missed at all. Eating out will be less frequent, though you'll probably do it more than your British friends. The weather may be a bit of surprise, especially the lack of both long-standing snow or stable hot weather.

Salaries will seem low: they generally are. People in the middle income bracket are less well off in the UK. Those lower or higher may well be better off. But holidays will probably be twice those you had in the USA. Being able to visit the continent will of course mean cheaper foreign holidays – but EU regulations have still not reduced air fares to levels comparable to those within the USA, though cut price airlines have almost got there.

Families that hated going to the USA may well hate returning. US sport, fast-food, late-night shopping and the swimming pool in the sunshine may all seem like paradise lost, especially for teenage children or a spouse whose career progress has been broken yet again. Fortunately pre-teen children adjust well given love, attention and food. Teenagers are something else. Moving away from friends, especially a first love, can be traumatic, especially if tackled heavy handedly.

Children will have to change schools so it will help to move in sync with the natural breaks in the school year, preferably between years, ideally when a change of school would be involved anyway. If your child started school in the USA they'll be behind comparable British children, if only for having started later.

Coming back to go to university might not be a good idea without considerable organisation. Scottish students starting at English or Welsh universities with a school education one year shorter can have major difficulties, especially in technical subjects. How much less prepared will students from the USA be! Better try for British A-levels via a college of further education before applying for university. Arriving at university after such a bridge can be very profitable. And older students generally get better degrees.

If you have been on a mutual academic or teachers' exchange slotting back in again may take no time at all: children return to their old friends and a new teacher, your own car may seem much smaller than you remember (and perhaps none the worse for wear) and various changes in the house, garden and neighbourhood will gradually make themselves known. But if you have been away for several years on contract or secondment you need to consider:

- US and UK tax consequences – in the year of return you may actually be eligible for tax rebates!

- UK capital gains liabilities on US investments sold off on returning home

- renewed National Insurance liability (including the implications of having missed paying in for several years)

- regaining any tax advantages on any long-held life assurance policies.

US English

The official language of the State of Illinois shall be known hereafter as the 'American' language and not as the 'English' language.

Act of Illinois Legislature 1923

American English sprang originally from British English, and in certain ways and in certain areas retains its heritage in a form far more traditional than generally found in Britain. The speech of Appalachia can be traced back to the hills of Ulster, the Scottish borders, and the West Country. And a US performance of Shakespeare's plays is likely to involve pronunciation and intonation far more familiar to the Bard himself than anything he'd hear in Stratford today. British English has moved on from its Elizabethan stage. Only in the peripheral areas of the English-speaking world can the older, most truly Anglo-Saxon forms be found.

But US English moves on too. The simplicity of Anglo-Saxon usage has been its downfall. It simply doesn't sound sophisticated enough in an increasingly cosmopolitan age. There isn't, after all, a truly Anglo-Saxon word for 'sophisticated'! So Americans have sought to improve their standing by 'improving' their English, by which they mean using long words in ever more complex patterns. It has something to do with the rise of meritocracy, the professionalism of so much of American life, but mostly the need to sound as if you are at the cutting edge of science and progress. If regional accents in the USA carry no indication of social standing then vocabulary and syntax will have to do so instead.

A little simultaneous translation from Shakespeare may show what's involved:

Original:	Modern USA:
It is a tale	It is in narrative form
told by	vocalised by
an idiot,	an individual of arrested mental development

full of	emphasising the
sound and	audio and
fury,	hyperindignant components
signifying	possessing
nothing	no meaningful insight

The impact of Latin-based words and Germanic-sounding sentences has been enormous. Today there's also computer terminology. Memories *download*, people *interface*, surely classic cases of GIGO (Garbage In, Garbage Out). School Latin will finally be of some use to help get to grips with all the prefixes: *counterurbanization*, *exurban*, and don't forget *post-industrial*, or worse *postmodern* (too often shortened to po-mo).

The American language is indeed flexible and dynamic. You can even make things seem better by your choice of terms. Don't have a family row: enjoy an aggressive interpersonal interaction. You don't like the idea of hiring a cleaner? Then hire a domestic hygiene specialist. And that wasn't a pay-cut. That was a downward income adjustment. Video clips of MTV (the music video channel) are not repeated regularly, rather they are made to withstand 'heavy rotation'! At Universal Studios Hollywood no one is sick after the T-Rex attack and 85ft waterfall plunge, they suffer 'protein spillage'. And remember: when house hunting you should be wary of living downwind of the effluent treatment plant.

A few place pronunciations:

Peru (Indiana)	PEEroo
Cairo (Illinois)	KAYroe
Versailles (Kentucky)	Ver sales
Maryland	Mairal'nd
St Louis	Synt Lewis
Michigan	Mishegan
New Orleans	New Orluns
Syracuse (New York)	Sirracuse
Des Moines	De Moyn

A common language with a different vocabulary:

British	*American*
choice	trade-off
cheap	cost-effective
new	state of the art
do	implement

Glossary

The first American had to invent Americanisms, if only to describe the unfamiliar landscape, weather, flora, and fauna confronting them.

American	British
AAA ('triple A')	American Automobile Association
antenna	aerial
apartment	flat
appraisal	valuation
area code	dialling code
asphalt	tarmac (surface of airport runways in US)
ATM	cashpoint/hole in the wall
automobile	car (automobile is rare these days)
baby carriage	pram
back pack	rucksack
back-up light	reversing light
baggage	luggage
Band-Aid	sticking plaster (US term is a brand name)
bankroll	foot the bill
barrette	hair slide
baseboard	skirting board
(bath)robe	dressing gown
bathroom	toilet (WC)
bathtub	bath
bell pepper	pepper (green, yellow or red vegetable)
beltway, loop	ring road
bill	note
billion	thousand million
biscuit	scone (but lighter in texture)
blacktop	tarmac
bobby pin	hair grip
bomb	fail ('it bombed')
broiled	grilled
broker	estate agent

brewpub	pub that brews its own beer
brownbag	working lunch (traditionally came in a brown paper bag)
bureau	chest of drawers
busy signal	engaged
BYO	bring your own (bottle)
cable	telemessage
call collect	reverse the charges
can	tin (food)
candy	sweet
Canuck	Canadian (derogatory)
carnival	travelling fair or circus
cattle guard	cattle grid
CEO	chief executive officer (managing director)
chaser	long drink (usually beer) to follow a spirit
check	restaurant bill (or a cheque).
checkers	draughts (board game)
checking account	current account with cheque book
checkroom	cloakroom (usually without a toilet)
chicory	endive
chips	crisps (though with fish can mean British-style fries)
cider	apple juice (non alcoholic)
close out	end of range sale
closet	cupboard (usually built in)
clothes pin	clothes peg
CPR	Cardiopulmonary Resuscitation
coach class	tourist class
collect call	reverse charge call
comfort station	roadside toilets
comforter	eiderdown (used with sheets unlike a duvet)
community chest	a local fund for neighbourhood charities
community college	publicly funded FE-like college
condo(minimum)	flats (usually with communal facilities like a laundry room)
conductor	train guard
cookie	biscuit
cook out	barbecue
cord	electrical lead or flex
corn	maize, sweet corn
corn starch	cornflour

cotton batting	cotton wool
cotton candy	candy floss
crackers	biscuits (with soup)
crawl space	under floor void
crazy bone	funny bone
creek	stream (fresh water brook)
crosswalk	pedestrian crossing
cuffs	trouser turn-ups
curb	kerb (edge of paved sidewalk NOT a containment verb)
custom made	bespoke, made to measure clothing
Daylight Saving Time	Summer Time
dead end	suburban cul-de-sac
deck	pack of cards or wooden patio
delivery truck	van
denatured alcohol	meths
desk clerk	receptionist
dessert	pudding
detour (on sign)	diversion
diaper	nappy
differ...than	differ...from
dime	10 cent coin
diner	café
direct drafting	direct debit
district attorney	public prosecutor
divided highway	dual carriage-way
Dixie	South (of Mason-Dixon line)
docent	guide (usually museum volunteer)
doctor's office	surgery
draft, the	conscription
drapes	net curtains
drug store	pharmacy, chemists
druggist	chemist, pharmacist
dry goods store	drapery, haberdashery
dual citizenship	having citizenship of two countries at once
dumpster	skip
duplex	semi-detached house or two-floored apartment
easy over	eggs fried both sides
eggplant	aubergine

El	elevated railway (in Chicago).
elevator	lift
emergency room (ER)	casualty department
entrée	main course
eraser	rubber
expressway	motorway
Fall	Autumn
fanny bags	bum bags
Fannie Mae	Federal National Mortgage Association
faucet	tap
FDIC	Federal Deposit Insurance Corporation
feminine napkin	sanitary towel
fender	car wing (not the bumper)
fifth	bottle of spirits (one fifth US gallon)
fire truck	fire engine
first floor	ground floor
first name	Christian name
flagpole	flag pole
flashlight	torch (in US a torch has flames)
fog lights	white lights low down on the front (not bright red ones on the back – which don't seem to exist on US cars)
food stamps	coupons bought by poor people at below face value for use in food shops at face value
football	American football
four way	cross roads
Freddie Mac	Federal Home Loan Mortgage Corporation
freeway	motorway
french fries	chips (but longer and thinner)
furnace	central heating boiler
garage sale.	car boot sale in one's own driveway
garbage	rubbish, refuse
garbage can	dustbin
garter belt	suspender
gas	petrol
gear shift	gear lever
gearshift	manual transmission
general delivery	Poste Restante
girl scouts	girl guides

GI Bill	Popular name for Serviceman's Readjustment Act (1944) entitling veterans to post-discharge benefits
go, to	take away, carry out
goaltender	goalkeeper
golden raisin	sultana
GOP	Republican Party ('Grand Old Party')
goose bumps	goose pimples
grade	gradient (slope)
grade crossing	level crossing
green card	permit to live in USA permanently (no longer green)
ground electrical	earth
gumboots	Wellingtons
gurney	wheeled stretchers
happy hour	half-price drinks in late afternoon
hard cider	cider (alcoholic)
head	toilet (originally naval expression)
help	servants (particularly a euphemism for black servants)
hideaway	bed-settee
highway	main road
hobo	tramp
hockey	ice hockey (not field hockey)
hog	pig
honorific	honorary
hood	bonnet of car
horny	randy
hose	tights
HOV	High Occupancy Vehicle (lane restriction on commuter roads)
house-trailer	caravan
icebox	refrigerator
incorporated	limited liability company
intersection	cross roads
INS	Immigration and Naturalization Service (now US Citizenship & Immigration Service)
IRA	Individual Retirement Account
IRS	Internal Revenue Service (US tax office)
janitor	caretaker
JAP	Jewish-American-Princess (or any spoilt rich girl)

jay walking	illegal crossing of street
jello	jelly
jelly	jam
jelly roll	Swiss roll
john	toilet (slang)
kerosene	paraffin
kindergarten	nursery
jump rope	skipping rope
jumper	short dress (not a sweater)
Kleenex	tissues (brand name used generically)
klutz	socially inept person
legal holiday	bank holiday
levelized billing	budget payment plan
licence plate	number plate (often called a 'tag')
Lifesavers	Polo (both are brand names)
limey	a Brit (British sailors ate limes to ward off scurvy)
line	queue
line cord	mains lead
liquor store	off licence
loaded	drunk
long distance	trunk call
lumber	timber (in US timber is still standing)
mailgram	telemessage
mail man	postman ('postal carrier' is taking over in US)
mall	shopping centre or grassy city centre (Washington DC)
Martini	3 parts vermouth, 1 part gin + olive
mean	bad tempered (rather than stingy)
median	central reservation (dividing strip between carriageways)
men working	road works
mezzanine	floor between main floors
micro breweries	real ale producers
mortician	undertaker
moving van	pantechnicon, removal van (also 'panel truck' in US)
movies	films, cinema
muffler	silencer
napkin	serviette
nickel	5 cent coin
night letter	overnight telegram

NRA	National Rifle Association (major gun lobby)
oatmeal	porridge
observatory	viewing platform
oil pan	sump
one way (ticket)	single ticket
on/off ramp	slip road onto limited access highway
outage	power loss
outhouse	privy
outlet	socket for telephone or electrical power
overalls	dungarees
overpass	flyover
pacifier	dummy
paddle	bat (for table tennis)
pants	trousers
pantyhose	tights
parka	anorak (does not imply obsessive interest in computers)
parking garage	multi-storey car park
parking lot	car park (outdoors)
pastor	minister of religion
pavement	any paved area sealed against water by asphalt or concrete (such areas can be for foot traffic or vehicular traffic)
penitentiary	prison
penny	one cent (yes the British term survived the Revolution)
penny sale	special offer where second item costs only one cent
period	full stop
person to person	personal call
phone booth	call box
pitcher	jug
poison ivy	similar to Virginia creeper (but poisonous)
popsicle	iced lolly
potato chips	crisps
pot holders	oven gloves
preppy	lifestyle associated with young people of social elite
pre-natal	ante-natal
preserves	commercially made jam or marmalade
private school	public (posh and private) school
public facilities	public toilets/conveniences
public school	publicly funded state school

pullout, pulloff	lay by
pump	low-cut slip-on woman's shoe
purse	handbag
quarter note	crotchet in music
railroad crossing	railway level crossing
rain check	promise to take up an invitation at a later date
ramp	motorway slip road
range	cooker
realtor	estate agent
redcap	porter (airport or railway station)
redneck	right-wing blue-collar worker
reforestation	reafforestation
Revolutionary War	American War of Independence
résumé	curriculum vitae (CV)
restroom	toilet
roadway	carriageway
roast	joint (an American joint is an illegal cigarette)
robe	dressing gown
roll	tube (cardboard cylinder for certain sweets)
rooming house	lodging house
rotary	roundabout
roundtrip (ticket)	return
row house	terrace house
rubber boots	Wellingtons
rubbers	condoms
rubbing alcohol	surgical spirit
run	ladder (in tights)
running shoes	trainers
rutabaga	swede (vegetable)
RV	recreational vehicle (motorised caravan)
sales clerk	shop assistant
sanitary napkin	sanitary towel
savings and loan	building society
scalper	tout
schedule	timetable
school	any institute of education (including higher education)
Scotch Tape	Sellotape (both terms are brand names)
SEC	Securities and Exchange Commission

sedan	saloon car
seeing eye dog	guide dog
server	waiter or waitress
shade	window blind
sherbet	sorbet
shoestring	bootlace, shoelace
shrimp	prawn
sidewalk	pavement
sixteenth note	musical semi-quaver
skivvies	underpants and vest
sled	sledge
smoked herring	kipper
sneakers	trainers
snow peas	mange tout
soccer	football
soda	any soft fizzy drink
special delivery	express post
spool	reel of sewing thread
squash	vegetable marrow
stand in line	queue
station wagon	estate car
stick shift	gear lever
store	shop
stove	cooker, oven (for cooking not heating)
straight	neat (liquor)
streetcar	tram
stroller	push chair (also 'baby buggy')
stub	counterfoil
subway	underground railway/tube
sunny side up	eggs fried without being turned over
suspenders	braces (for men)
sweats	tracksuit
tag	car number plate
teller	cashier
thread	cotton
3.2 beer	fairly weak beer with 3.2 per cent alcohol
thumbtack	drawing pin
tic-tac-toe	noughts and crosses

tie	sleeper on rail track
toll-free number	free number (1-800 prefix)
townhouse	terrace house (often upmarket)
tractor-trailer	articulated lorry
traffic circle	roundabout
trail	track or footpath away from roads
trailer	caravan
tramway	cable car
transit	public transport
transmission tower	electricity pylon
trash	rubbish
trash can	dustbin
truck	lorry
truck stop	transport café
trunk	boot of car
turnpike	toll road
turn signals	indicators on car
tuxedo	dinner jacket
TVA	Tennessee Valley Authority (regional development agency)
two weeks	fortnight (a term rarely used in the USA)
twofers	two for the price of one
under basement	cellar
undershirt	vest
underpass	subway (pedestrian only)
unlisted number	ex-directory
union suit	long johns
USCIS	United States Citizenship and Immigration Service
vacation	holiday
VA	Veterans' Administration (deals with benefits for discharged members of armed forces). Virginia, if final address item
valance	pelmet
van	mini van
vest	waistcoat
veteran	anyone honourably discharged from the US forces
VCR	video (cassette recorder)
wallet	purse
wash up	freshen up (hands and face, not dishes)

washroom	loo/WC
WASP	White Anglo-Saxon Protestant
welfare	dole
whole note	musical semi-breve
windshield	windscreen
wire	telegram
wrench	spanner
WPA	Work Projects Administration (a 1930s make-work agency)
yard	garden (US term doesn't imply hard surface area)
yield (on sign)	give way
yuppy	young upwardly mobile professional
zee	zed (last letter of the alphabet)
zip code	post code (5 or 10 digits)
zucchini	courgette

Spelling differences

It can be difficult to remember who uses which variant.

American	British
airplane	aeroplane
aluminum	aluminium
archeology	archaeology
anesthesia	anaesthesia
catalog	catalogue
check	cheque
center	centre
color	colour
defense	defence
draft	draught
favorite	favourite
gray	grey
gynecology	gynaecology
hauler	haulier
honor	honour
humor	humour
jewelry	jewellery
license	licence (license is a verb, licence a noun in UK)

maneuver	manoeuvre
meter	metre
mold	mould
pajamas	pyjamas
practice	practise (practise is a verb, practice a noun in UK)
program	programme (programs on PCs, programmes on TV in UK)
sulfur	sulphur (US spelling is now used by UK pharmacists)
thru	through (but only on road signs)
tire	tyre
vise	vice (tool, not a chronic bad habit)

Generally -*or* word ending is equivalent to -*our* in British English, -*er* at word ending is sometimes equivalent to British -*re*. In American English the final *e* is removed from verbs before adding -*ing*, though the American practice is becoming quite common in Britain. Americans prefer -*ize* and -*ization* whereas British prefers -*ise* and -*isation*, often to emphasise a European rather than American identity.

There are many exceptions to the above rule: 'glamour' rather than 'glamor' and 'advertising' rather than 'advertizing' in the USA. And the British 'centre' and 'theatre' are rapidly displacing the American 'center' and 'theater' (looking European they seem more suitably sophisticated for artistic matters). Of course even where words are used in common, their implications may be quite different. The American seem to believe, for instance, that the word 'death' refers to something that can be postponed indefinitely by reading the right self-help books.

For a painless catalogue of language differences see Anthea Bickerton *American English-English American* and in far greater detail Robert C. Champman *The Dictionary of American Slang*. Implications are discussed by Bill Bryson *Made in America* and Jane Walmsley *Brit-Think, Ameri-Think*.

Statutory Public Holidays

New Year's Day	1 January
Martin Luther King's Birthday	third Monday in January
Washington's Birthday	22 February
Memorial Day	Last Monday in May (46 states)
Independence Day	4 July
Labor Day	First Monday in September
Columbus Day	Second Monday of October (32 states)
Veterans' Day	11 November ('Armistice Day')
Thanksgiving	Fourth Thursday in November
Christmas Day	25 December

Beware

Public holidays are state not federally authorised. Most states give all the above holidays, which are also enjoyed by federal employees throughout the USA. Lincoln's Birthday is observed (in northern but not southern states) 12 February.

For a listing of public holidays and other observed days (from Armed Forces Day via Mother's Day to United Nations Day) see the London US Embassy website.

If you want to travel beyond the USA to its neighbours and want to know whether you'll arrive on their biggest, everything closes down, holiday take a look at *www.national-holidays.com*.

State Tourist Offices

Most of the tourist offices listed below are part of each state's own administration which is not necessarily based in the largest city. For instance, Albany is the capital for New York, Annapolis for Maryland, Harrisburg for Pennsylvania. But with modern electronic phone and computer links the actual office can be physically almost anywhere. Often the only public presence will be at freeway rest areas on entering the state where there will be a supply of maps and brochures for the visitor to take away.

State	Numbers	Web site
Alabama	(334) 242 4169	www.touralabama.org
Alaska	(907) 465 2010	www.travelalaska.com
Arizona	(602) 255 3618	www.arizonaguide.com
Arkansas	(501) 682 7777	www.arkansas.com
California	(916) 322 1396	www.gocalif.ca.gov
Colorado	(303) 892 3848	www.colorado.com
Connecticut	(860) 256 2800	www.crvisit.com
Delaware	(302) 739 4271	www.visitdelaware.com
District of Columbia	(202) 789 7000	www.washington.org
Florida	(904) 488 5607	www.flausa.com
Georgia	(404) 962 4000	www.exploregeorgia.com
Hawaii	(808) 923 1811	www.gohawaii.com
Idaho	(208) 334 2470	www.visitid.org
Illinois	(312) 793 2094	www.enjoyillinois.com
Indiana	(317) 232 8860	www.enjoyindiana.com
Iowa	(515) 242 4705	www.traveliowa.com
Kansas	(785) 296 2009	www.travelks.com
Kentucky	(502) 564 4930	www.kentuckytourism.com
Louisiana	(504) 342 8100	www.louisianatravsvel.com
Maine	(207) 287 5711	www.visitmaine.com
Maryland	(410) 757 3400	www.mdisfun.org
Massachusetts	(617) 727 3201	www.massvacation.org

Michigan	(517) 373 0670	*www.michigan.org*
Minnesota	(612) 296 5029	*www.exploreminnesota.com*
Mississippi	(601) 359 3297	*www.visitmississippi.org*
Missouri	(314) 751 4133	*www.visitmo.com*
Montana	(406) 761 6453	*www.visitmt.com*
Nebraska	(402) 471 3797	*www.visitnebraska.org*
Nevada	(775) 687 4322	*www.travelnevada.com*
New Hampshire	(603) 271 2343	*www.visitnh.gov*
New Jersey	(609) 292 2470	*www.visitnj.org*
New Mexico	(505) 827 7400	*www.newmexico.org*
New York	(212) 803 2200	*www.iloveny.com*
North Carolina	(919) 733 4171	*www.visitnc.com*
North Dakota	(701) 328 2525	*www.ndtourism.com*
Ohio	(614) 466 8844	*www.ohiotourism.com*
Oklahoma	(405) 521 2406	*www.travelok.com*
Oregon	(503) 378 3451	*www.traveloregon.com*
Pennsylvania	(717) 787 5453	*www.experiencepa.com*
Rhode Island	(401) 277 2601	*www.visitrhodeisland.com*
South Carolina	(803) 734 1700	*www.travelsc.com*
South Dakota	(605) 773 3301	*www.travelsd.com*
Tennessee	(615) 741 2159	*www.state.tn.us/tourdev*
Texas	(512) 462 9191	*www.traveltex.com*
Utah	(801) 538 1030	*www.utah.com*
Vermont	(802) 828 3236	*www.vermontvacation.com*
Virginia	(804) 786 2051	*www.virginia.org*
Washington (State)	(360) 725 5052	*www.tourism.wa.gov*
West Virginia	(304) 588 2200	*www.callwva.com*
Wisconsin	(608) 266 2161	*www.travelwisconsin.com*
Wyoming	(307) 777 7777	*www.wyomingtourism.org*

Most states also have free 800 numbers, but as these can only be accessed from within the USA or Canada I have only listed those numbers that can be used from the UK. It is probably best to use the website in the first instance. The 800 numbers are listed by the *Miami Herald* online (30 January 2007) or at *familyguides.com*, a most useful site for anyone going to the USA.

Most of the above websites are run by the state office for tourism and travel, though some states have no such office leaving such matters to the private sector. In this case the private equivalent web page has been listed. In some instances both are available.

Since the closure of the United States Travel and Tourism Administration (USTTA) there has been no central source of tourist information for the USA in Britain. The *Visit USA Association*, however, is a non-profit organisation representing US states, airlines, hotels, car-hire firms and tour operators.

Now that all states and the District of Columbia and certain regions, such as the Capital Region USA (Virginia, Washington DC and Maryland), have websites as accessible in the UK as in the US, it is no longer necessary to have access to US tourism information based in the UK where we can get at it for a local call. However, most states developed locally-based UK links when the federal agency, the USTTA (see above) was closed down. The main VisitUSA web page has both a map and a state-by-state listing of its local UK connections. Just as a sample, here is my own home-from-home state of Maryland's guide in this listing:

Maryland Tourism Marketing Partnership, Link House, 140 The Broadway, Tolworth, Surrey KT6 7JE. Tel: (020) 8339 6048. Fax: (020) 8339 6001. Email: *tmp.uk@btinternet.com*. Websites: *www.mdisfun.org* or *www.capitalregionusa.org*.

This is pretty much what you get for each and every state, though the most important link may well be what you started with – the US-based Maryland Tourism site (*www.mdisfun.org*). MD is the postal shorthand for Maryland, subliminally recognised by most Americans these days.

Most UK contacts can usually supply you with leaflets and brochures if requested.

For further links see *www.nationalgeographic.com/traveler/resources.html*. There's also lots of useful material at the Lonely Planet web page (*www.lonelyplanet.com*), the Great Outdoor Recreation pages (*www.gorp.com*) and the Rough Guides page (*www.roughguides.com*).

Further Reading

Bloom, A., *The Closing of the American Mind*, Simon & Schuster, New York, 1987.

Bond, M., *Gutsy Women: More Travel Tips and Wisdom for the Road*, Travellers' Tales, 2007.

Bradbury, M., *Stepping Westward*, Arena, London, 1984.

Brayer-Hess, M., *The Expert Expatriate: Your Guide to Successful Relocation Abroad; Moving, Living, Thriving*, Intercultural Press, New York, 2002.

Brogan, H., *The Pelican History of the United States of America*, Penguin Harmondsworth, 1986.

Burgess, A., *The Expatriate's Guide*, Neville Russell, London, 1986.

Carrion, R., *USA Immigration Guide*, Sphinx, New York, 2004.

Day, R., *Working the American Way: How to Communicate Successfully with the Americans at Work*, How To Books, Oxford, 2004.

Furnell, M., *Daily Telegraph Guide to Living & Retiring Abroad*, Kogan Page, 1990.

Gania, E.T., *US Immigration Step-by-Step*, Sourcebooks, New York, 2003.

Glozen, G., *The Daily Telegraph Guide to Working and Living Overseas*, Kogan Page, London, 1990.

Gray, W., *Travel with Kids*, Footprint Handbook, 2007.

Griffin, S., *Work Your Way Around the World*, Vacation Work, Oxford, 2007.

Hirsch, E.D., *Cultural Literacy, What Every American Needs to Know*, Vintage Books, New York, 1988.

Hobbs, G., *The Directory of Jobs & Careers Abroad*, Vacation Work, Oxford, 2004.

Hughes, R., *American Visions*, Harvill, London 1997.

Ibarra, S., Breaux, A. and Dube, V., *Let's Go: USA*, Let's Go Publications, 2007.

Jones, R., *Getting a Job in America*, How To Books, 7th edition, Oxford, 2003.

Lanier, P., *Living in the USA*, Intercultural Press, 1988.

Lechmere, A., and Pybus, V., *Live and Work in the USA and Canada*, Vacation Work, Oxford, 2007.

Liebman, H.G., *Getting into America*, How To Books, Oxford, 2004.

Lodge, D., *Changing Places*, Harmondsworth, 1975.

Mills, Stephen F., *The American Landscape*, KUP, Edinburgh, 1997.

Moss, M. and G., *Handbook for Women Travellers*, Piatkus, London, 1995.

National Geographic Society, *National Parks of the United States*, Washington DC 2006.

Owen, D., *High School: Undercover with the class of '80*, Viking, New York, 1981.

Potter, D. M., *People of Plenty: Economic Abundance and the American Character*, University of Chicago Press, Chicago, 1954.

Ryan, D. S., *America: A Guide to the Experience*, Kozmik, London, 1986.

Savageau, D., *Places Rated Almanac*, Prentice Hall, New York, 2007.

Stanford, J., *Holidays and Travel Abroad*, The Royal Association for Disability and Rehabilitation (RADAR), London (6th edition), 1991.

Tristram, C., *Have Kids Will Travel*, McMeel, London, 1997.

Trudgill, P., *Coping with America*, Blackwell, Oxford, 1982.

Wanning, E., *Culture Shock! USA*, Kuperard, London, 2003.

Wicks, R. and Schultz, F., *Long Stays in America*, David & Charles, Newton Abbot, 1986.

Wood, K., *Globetrotter's Bible*, HarperCollins, 1995.

Weights and Measures

US imperial measures of length are the same as in the UK but measures of capacity are somewhat different: the US gallon is smaller than the British equivalent (1 US gallon = 0.83 UK gallon); the US hundredweight (cwt) is smaller than the British (being 100 lb rather than 112 lb); a US ton is short (2,000 lb rather than 2,240 lb, whereas a metric tonne is 2,204 lb).

All imperial and US measures are gradually being replaced by metric (SI) measures, in theory if not in people's minds. As in the UK the change-over is long and drawn out, in comparison to Canada where it was short and sweet.

British visitors who think of themselves as firmly non-metric may find to their surprise that they are more metric than they thought when confronted with US measures. The author once mistook a 12 degrees weather report for 12 degrees Celsius rather than 12 degrees Fahrenheit, jumped out of the car and almost froze.

Index